# ZAGATSURVEY®
25TH ANNIVERSARY

# 2004

# LAS VEGAS
# RESTAURANTS

With bonus Nightlife section

**Local Restaurant Editor: James P. Reza**

**Local Nightlife Editor: Jerry Fink**

**Local Coordinator: Carol Austin-Fink**

**Editor: Betsy Andrews**

Published and distributed by
ZAGAT SURVEY, LLC
4 Columbus Circle
New York, New York 10019
Tel: 212 977 6000
E-mail: lasvegas@zagat.com
Web site: www.zagat.com

# Acknowledgments

The editors would like to thank all those without whose support this book would not have been possible, including Geoff Carter, Gregory Crosby, Norine Dworkin, Staci Reza, Muriel Stevens, KVBC-TV, the Las Vegas Convention & Visitors Authority, *Las Vegas Mercury* managing editor Geoff Schumacher, Andrew Kiraly and the rest of the editorial staff, as well as Weststar Credit Union.

This guide would not have been possible without the hard work of our staff, especially Caren Campbell, Reni Chin, Griff Foxley, Schuyler Frazier, Jeff Freier, Shelley Gallagher, Curt Gathje, Katherine Harris, Natalie Lebert, Mike Liao, Dave Makulec, Jennifer Napuli, Rob Poole, Troy Segal and Sharon Yates.

# Contents

**NIGHTLIFE**
**Most Popular** . . . . . . . . . . . . . . . . . . . . . . . . . 131
**TOP RATINGS**

# About This Survey

Here are the results of our *2004 Las Vegas Survey,* covering some 555 restaurants, bars and clubs as tested by over 3,600 avid local restaurant- and club-goers. This marks the 25th year that Zagat Survey has reported on the shared experiences of diners like you.

What started in 1979 in New York as a hobby involving 200 friends rating local restaurants has come a long way: Today we have over 250,000 surveyors and have branched out to cover entertaining, golf, hotels, movies, music, nightlife, resorts, shopping, spas and theater. Most of these guides are also available by subscription at **zagat.com,** where you can vote and shop as well.

By regularly surveying large numbers of avid customers, we hope to have achieved a uniquely current and reliable guide. A quarter-century of experience has verified this. This *Survey* is based on roughly 611,000 meals and evenings out. Of the surveyors, 40% are women, 60% men; the breakdown by age is 19% in their 20s; 30%, 30s; 21%, 40s; 19%, 50s; and 11%, 60s or above. Our editors have synopsized our surveyors' opinions, with their comments shown in quotation marks. We sincerely thank each of these surveyors; this book is really "theirs." Of course, we are especially grateful to our editors, James P. Reza, a dining and entertainment columnist for the *Las Vegas Mercury,* and Jerry Fink, an entertainment writer for the *Las Vegas Sun,* and our coordinator, Carol Austin-Fink, a freelance writer.

To help guide our readers to Las Vegas' best meals and best buys, we have prepared a number of lists. See Most Popular (page 9), Top Ratings (pages 10–14) and Best Buys (page 15). Nightlife lists begin on page 131. In addition, we have provided 72 handy indexes and have tried to be concise. Also, for the first time, we have included Web addresses.

**To join any of our upcoming *Surveys,* just register at zagat.com.** Each participant will receive a free copy of the resulting guide when it is published. Your comments and even criticisms of this guide are also solicited. There is always room for improvement with your help. You can contact us at lasvegas@zagat.com. We look forward to hearing from you.

New York, NY
December 24, 2003

Nina and Tim Zagat

# What's New

Forget buffets – only 18% of our Vegas surveyors frequent them. Steakhouses make up almost 13% of this *Survey*, but more than meat meets the stomach. Moderately priced, stylish spots are filling the gap between the low and high ends.

**Betting on the Middle:** Casual chic is on the menu in downscaled dining by Vegas vets. More than a third of reviewers favor Italian, and Piero Selvaggio of Valentino sates cravings with his Caffe Giorgio in Mandalay Place. Mon Ami Gabi alumni Ramon Triay and John Simmons light up the Convention Corridor with Firefly, Sin City's first tapas bar, and Tinoco's Bistro expands to the Arts District.

**Nickle-and-Dime Dining:** Urbane, wallet-friendly chains link up to Vegas with hip, healthy burritos at Chipotle, partywise pupus at Kona Grill and fancy fondue at The Melting Pot. LA landmark Canter's Deli piles on pastrami in Treasure Island, while Craftsteak's Tom Colicchio is due to bring budget sandwich sensation 'Wichcraft to the MGM in 2004. Locals leave the Strip for the strip mall, lured by inexpensive ethnics like the new Pakistani, Halal Restaurant Tandoor.

**Top Nosh:** Things have never been better at the top. Sophisticated seafooders flood the desert with Tom Moloney's AquaKnox at the Venetian, the An family's Crustacean at the Aladdin and Michael Mina's Seablue at the MGM. That hotel has also swapped one stylish Italian for another, as Stephen Hanson's Fiamma Trattoria replaces olio!

**Future Gambles:** In 2004, Bobby Flay is scheduled to set the tables afire at Caesars with Mesa Grill. Mandalay Bay has inked in Alain Ducasse, Hubert Keller of SF's Fleur de Lys and Rick Moonen of NYC's rm. NYC's Tao brings happy-hour harmony to the Venetian, where Thomas Keller of Napa's French Laundry also unveils a new concept.

**Sin Is Back In:** Following the family-friendly '90s, we've turned back toward sin. Nearly 60% of our night-owl surveyors say they prefer the naughty to the nice. Newcomer gentlemen's clubs Jaguar's, Sapphire and Spearmint Rhino have been erected. Ultra-lounges OPM in the Forum Shops, Risqué at the Paris and the MGM's Tabú tempt trendsters, while Mandalay Bay's Coral Reef and the Palms' ghostbar and Rain still captivate crowds. With after-hour haunts like Drai's at the Barbary Coast, night and day merge seamlessly. And though Blue Note and Kitchen Cafe have gone to bed, the House of Blues' upcoming OBA lounge arises to enrich the night.

With the average cost of a meal ($34.60) up only 3.4%, no wonder 40% of our Vegas surveyors are eating out more often than two years ago: reasonable tabs are a sure bet.

Las Vegas, NV
December 24, 2003

James Reza
Jerry Fink

# Ratings & Symbols

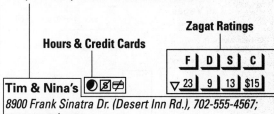

**Name, Address, Phone Number & Web Site**

**Zagat Ratings**

**Hours & Credit Cards**

| F | D | S | C |
|---|---|---|---|

**Tim & Nina's** ◑ 🄯 ⊄    ▽ 23 | 9 | 13 | $15

*8900 Frank Sinatra Dr. (Desert Inn Rd.), 702-555-4567;*
*www.zagat.com*

> ☑ "Daily guest celebrity chefs" from around the world along
> with "decor that changes according to the cuisine being
> served" is the concept at this "unique" Strip Eclectic where
> Mondays might mean Classic French dishes beside a mock
> Champs Elysées and Tuesdays, dumplings atop a faux Great
> Wall of China; naysayers find it "gimmicky" and "hit-or-miss"
> ("the Australian chef undercooked my kangaroo") but
> tout the "indoor ice skating on Norway nights."

**Review, with surveyors' comments in quotes**

Restaurants with the highest overall ratings and greatest
popularity and importance are printed in CAPITAL LETTERS.

Before reviews a symbol indicates whether responses
were uniform ■ or mixed ☑.

**Hours:** ◑ serves after 11 PM
⠀⠀⠀⠀⠀🄯 closed on Sunday

**Credit Cards:** ⊄ no credit cards accepted

**Ratings:** Food, Decor and Service are rated on a scale of
**0** to **30**. The Cost (C) column reflects our surveyors' estimate
of the price of dinner including one drink and tip.

| F Food | D Decor | S Service | C Cost |
|---|---|---|---|
| 23 | 9 | 13 | $15 |

**0–9** poor to fair ⠀⠀⠀⠀**20–25** very good to excellent
**10–15** fair to good ⠀⠀⠀⠀**26–30** extraordinary to perfection
**16–19** good to very good ⠀⠀▽ low response/less reliable

For places listed without ratings or a numerical cost estimate,
such as an important newcomer or a popular write-in, the
price range is indicated by the following symbols.

| I | $15 and below | E | $31 to $50 |
|---|---|---|---|
| M | $16 to $30 | VE | $51 or more |

# Most Popular

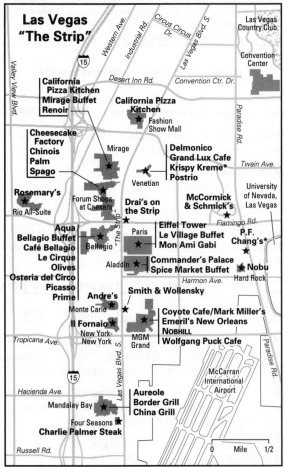

# Most Popular

| | |
|---|---|
| 1. Picasso | 21. Andre's |
| 2. Aqua | 22. Eiffel Tower |
| 3. Aureole | 23. Grand Lux Cafe |
| 4. Bellagio Buffet | 24. Charlie Palmer |
| 5. Emeril's New Orleans | 25. Krispy Kreme* |
| 6. Delmonico | 26. Rosemary's |
| 7. Prime | 27. China Grill |
| 8. Le Cirque | 28. Smith & Wollensky |
| 9. Commander's Palace | 29. Chinois |
| 10. Olives | 30. Border Grill |
| 11. Renoir | 31. Coyote Cafe/M. Miller's |
| 12. Spago | 32. NOBHILL* |
| 13. Cheesecake Factory | 33. Spice Mkt. Buffet |
| 14. Mon Ami Gabi | 34. Drai's on the Strip |
| 15. Palm | 35. California Piz. Kit. |
| 16. Nobu | 36. Café Bellagio |
| 17. Osteria del Circo | 37. Il Fornaio |
| 18. P.F. Chang's | 38. Wolfgang Puck Cafe |
| 19. Le Village Buffet | 39. Mirage Buffet |
| 20. Postrio | 40. McCorm. & Schmick's |

It's obvious that many of the restaurants on the above list are among the Las Vegas area's most expensive, but if popularity were calibrated to price, we suspect that a number of other restaurants would join the above ranks. Given the fact that both our surveyors and readers love to discover dining bargains, we have added a list of 80 Best Buys on page 15. These are restaurants that give real quality at extremely reasonable prices.

---

* Indicates a tie with restaurant above

# Top Ratings

Top lists exclude restaurants with low voting.

## Top 40 Food

| | |
|---|---|
| **28** Nobu | **25** Wild Sage Café |
| Renoir | Hyakumi |
| **27** Picasso | Commander's Palace |
| Malibu Chan's | Fleming's |
| Le Cirque | Aureole |
| Rosemary's | Alizé |
| Aqua | Osteria del Circo |
| Bradley Ogden | Pasta Shop |
| Lotus of Siam* | Hugo's Cellar |
| Prime | Lawry's Prime Rib |
| **26** Andre's | Pamplemousse |
| NOBHILL | Palm |
| Delmonico | Charlie Palmer |
| Del Frisco's | Krispy Kreme |
| Roy's | **24** Gaetano's |
| Mayflower Cuisinier | Valentino, Piero Selv. |
| Sterling Brunch | Luxor Steakhse. |
| Michael's | Lutèce |
| Steak House | Morton's |
| Shintaro | Verandah |

## By Cuisine

**American (New)**
**27** Rosemary's
Bradley Ogden
**26** Sterling Brunch
**25** Wild Sage Café
Aureole

**American (Traditional)**
**22** Egg & I
Cheesecake Fact.
**21** Buffet, The
**20** Carson St. Cafe
Tenaya Creek

**Chinese**
**26** Mayflower Cuisinier
**24** Lillie Langtry's
Shanghai Lilly
Jasmine
**23** Royal Star

**Continental**
**26** Michael's
**25** Hugo's Cellar
**23** 3950
Isis
**21** Buccaneer Bay

**Eclectic**
**24** Bellagio Buffet
Second St. Grill
**23** Spice Mkt. Buffet
**22** Zax
**20** Bay Side Buffet

**French**
**26** Andre's
**25** Pamplemousse
**24** Lutèce
**23** Isis
**22** Le Village Buffet

# Top Food

## French (New)
**28** Renoir
**27** Picasso
    Le Cirque
**25** Alizé
**23** Drai's on the Strip

## Italian
**25** Osteria del Circo
    Pasta Shop
**24** Gaetano's
    Valentino, Piero Selv.
    Onda

## Japanese
**28** Nobu
**26** Shintaro
**25** Hyakumi
**23** Mikado
    Blue Wave

## Mexican
**22** Baja Fresh
    Rubio's Baja
    Garduño's
    Border Grill
**21** Chipotle

## Pizza
**23** Metro Pizza
**21** Canaletto
    Lupo, Tratt. del
**20** Le Provençal
    Sammy's

## Seafood
**27** Aqua
**24** Emeril's
    Neros
    Buzio's
    808

## Southwestern
**23** Coyote Cafe/M. Miller's
**22** Z'Tejas Grill
    Garduño's
**17** Chili's Grill
    Roadrunner

## Steakhouses
**27** Prime
**26** Delmonico
    Del Frisco's
    Steak House
**25** Fleming's

# By Special Feature

## Breakfast
**25** Commander's Palace
**24** Verandah
**23** Coyote Cafe/M. Miller's
**22** Pinot Brasserie
    Egg & I

## Brunch
**26** Sterling Brunch
    Steak House
**25** Wild Sage Café
    Commander's Palace
**24** Verandah

## Buffet (Hotel)
**24** Bellagio Buffet
**23** Spice Mkt. Buffet
**22** Le Village
**21** Village Seafood
    Buffet, The

## Hotel Dining
**28** Nobu
    Hard Rock Hotel
    Renoir
    Mirage Hotel
**27** Picasso
    Bellagio Hotel
    Le Cirque
    Bellagio Hotel
    Aqua
    Bellagio Hotel

## "In" Places
**28** Nobu
**25** Alizé
**23** Mon Ami Gabi
    3950
    China Grill

# Top Food

## Late Dining

**27** Malibu Chan's (2 AM)
**23** Ruth's Chris (varies)
Smith & Wollensky (3 AM)
**22** Grand Lux Cafe (24 hrs.)
Café Bellagio (24 hrs.)

## Newcomers/Rated

**27** Bradley Ogden
**22** Ah Sin
**20** Tre
Gaylord's
**19** Canter's Deli

## Newcomers/Unrated

AquaKnox
Fiamma Tratt.
Firefly
Seablue
Teru Sushi

## People-Watching

**28** Nobu
Renoir
**27** Picasso
Le Cirque
Aqua

# By Location

## Downtown

**26** Andre's
**25** Hugo's Cellar
**24** Lillie Langtry's
Second St. Grill
**23** Pullman Grille

## East of Strip

**28** Nobu
**27** Lotus of Siam
**26** Del Frisco's
Roy's
**25** Lawry's Prime Rib

## East Side

**25** Pasta Shop
Krispy Kreme
**23** Capriotti's
Metro Pizza
Broiler

## Green Valley

**25** Wild Sage Café
**24** Gaetano's
**23** Blue Wave
**22** Bonjour
Rubio's Baja

## Henderson

**22** Baja Fresh
Fatburger
Viaggio
**21** Chipotle
BullShrimp

## North Las Vegas

**24** Austin's Steakhse.
**22** Baja Fresh
Memphis BBQ
Fatburger
**19** Outback Steakhse.

## Northwest/Summerlin

**23** Capriotti's
Grape Street
**22** Baja Fresh
P.F. Chang's
Rubio's Baja

## Strip

**28** Renoir
**27** Picasso
Le Cirque
Aqua
Bradley Ogden

## West of Strip

**27** Rosemary's
**26** Mayflower Cuisinier
**25** Alizé
**24** Buzio's
**23** Ruth's Chris

## West Side

**27** Malibu Chan's
Rosemary's
**26** Roy's
**25** Wild Sage Café
Fleming's

# Top 40 Decor

| | | | |
|---|---|---|---|
| **29** | Picasso | **24** | Mon Ami Gabi |
| **28** | Alizé | | China Grill |
| | Renoir | | Charlie Palmer |
| **27** | Aureole | | Antonio's |
| | Prime | | Roy's |
| | Le Cirque | | Shanghai Lilly |
| **26** | Osteria del Circo | | Onda |
| | Top of the World | | Drai's on the Strip |
| | Tre | | Terrazza |
| | Jasmine | | 3950 |
| | Little Buddha | | Delmonico |
| | Zax | | Quark's |
| | Eiffel Tower | | Verandah |
| | Moongate | **23** | Kokomo's |
| **25** | Shintaro | | Rainforest Cafe |
| | Aqua | | Fleming's |
| | Bradley Ogden | | Craftsteak |
| | NOBHILL | | Austin's Steakhse. |
| | Andre's | | Lutèce |
| | VooDoo | | Olives |

## Outdoors

| | |
|---|---|
| Ah Sin | Marche Bacchus |
| Border Grill | Mon Ami Gabi |
| Cafe Tajine | Olives |
| Japengo | Verandah |

## Romance

| | |
|---|---|
| Alizé | Michael's |
| Andre's | NOBHILL |
| Charlie Palmer | Pearl |
| Eiffel Tower | Picasso |
| Hugo's Cellar | Renoir |
| Le Cirque | Top of the World |

## Rooms

| | |
|---|---|
| AquaKnox | Eiffel Tower |
| Aureole | Lutèce |
| China Grill | Postrio |
| Commander's Palace | Simon Kitchen |
| Craftsteak | Smith & Wollensky |

## Views

| | |
|---|---|
| Alizé | Osteria del Circo |
| Eiffel Tower | Panevino Rist. |
| Japengo | Top of the World |
| Olives | VooDoo |

# Top 40 Service

| | |
|---|---|
| **28** Renoir | Aureole |
| **27** Picasso | Jasmine |
| **26** Prime | Hugo's Cellar |
| Michael's | Del Frisco's |
| Andre's | Lawry's Prime Rib |
| Le Cirque | Antonio's |
| Bradley Ogden | Onda* |
| Pamplemousse | Osteria del Circo |
| **25** Luxor Steakhse. | Nobu |
| Aqua | Morton's |
| Verandah | Isis |
| Alizé | Lutèce |
| Delmonico | Austin's Steakhse. |
| Roy's | Steakhouse, The* |
| Pasta Shop | **23** Valentino, Piero Selv. |
| NOBHILL | Piero's Italian |
| Commander's Palace | Sterling Brunch |
| Charlie Palmer | Palm |
| Rosemary's | Fleming's |
| **24** Zax | Lillie Langtry's |

# Best Buys

## Top 40 Bangs for the Buck

1. Krispy Kreme
2. Rubio's Baja
3. Baja Fresh
4. Fatburger
5. Capriotti's
6. Chipotle
7. Egg & I
8. Tintoretto Bakery
9. Firelight Buffet
10. Buffet, The
11. Crown & Anchor
12. Metro Pizza
13. Roxy's Diner
14. Feast Around the World
15. Macayo Vegas
16. Doña Maria
17. La Salsa
18. Fresh Mkt. Sq. Buffet
19. Big Dog's
20. Carson St. Cafe
21. Paradise Buffet
22. Guadalajara
23. French Mkt. Buffet
24. Roadrunner
25. Feast, The
26. Memphis BBQ
27. Mr. Lucky's 24/7
28. Chicago Brewing
29. Sammy's Pizza
30. Lotus of Siam
31. Chevys Fresh Mex
32. Chili's Grill
33. J. C. Woologhan's
34. Paradise Gdn. Buffet
35. Spice Mkt. Buffet
36. Courtyard Buffet
37. Chicago Joe's
38. Stage Deli
39. Garduño's
40. Applebee's

## Other Good Values

Bangkok Orchid
Blue Wave
Bootlegger Bistro
Broiler
Cafe Heidelberg
Caffe Giorgio
Canter's Deli
Cheesecake Fact.
Coco's
Coffee Pub
Fasolini's Pizza
Firefly
Food Express
Frank & Fina's
Garden Ct. Buffet
Grand Lux Cafe
Halal Rest.
Hill Top Hse.
Hush Puppy
Ice House
In-N-Out Burger
Joyful House
Komol Rest.
Kona Grill
La Barca
Marche Bacchus
Montesano's
Nora's Cuisine
Pasta (fa-zool)
Paymon's Med.
Pink Taco
Red, White & Blue
Sam Woo BBQ
Sedona
Tenaya Creek
Thai Room
Togoshi Ramen
Venni Mac's
Verandah
Viva Mercado's

# Restaurant Directory

### Ah Sin ◑    22  21  20  $41
*Paris Las Vegas, 3655 Las Vegas Blvd. S. (bet. Flamingo Rd. & Harmon Ave.), 702-946-7000; www.parislasvegas.com*

☑ "Experienced sushipiles" "go for the great view of the Strip from the outdoor cafe and come away with a new favorite place to dine", this "trendy" Pan-Asian companion to the Paris' Risqué nightclub; the "simple, elegant" "station-to-station setup's" "great variety" of "solid, sexy" selections, including "enormous, artfully presented" raw fish, will have you "oohing and ahing", though the staff needs a geography lesson as the Far East fare is ferried by servers "as slow as in Europe."

### AJ's Steakhouse ⊠    ▽ 25  25  25  $51
*Hard Rock Hotel & Casino, 4455 Paradise Rd. (bet. Flamingo Rd. & Harmon Ave.), 702-693-5500; www.hardrockhotel.com*

■ This "excellent retro-style steakhouse" in the Hard Rock Hotel just east of the Strip feeds nostalgists hungry for that Rat Pack vibe; "top-quality beef" and "tasty, well-prepared side dishes" are delivered by a "friendly, accommodating staff" that's "good at problem solving" in "porterhouse country" where you can "hear yourself talking", even over the singer at the piano bar – "Sinatra would have loved it."

### Alan Albert's    21  17  20  $50
*3763 Las Vegas Blvd. S. (bet. Harmon & Tropicana Aves.), 702-795-4006*

☑ "Tender" "big cuts", "excellent blue cheese dressing and a decent wine list" "match" the photos of "old-time Las Vegas" at this cow palace "for the ages"; one "big plus"? – it's on the Strip but "not in a hotel", making it "great for getting away from the casino madness"; have your "picture taken with a giant lobster", but expect to pay a pretty penny for the privilege of eating it at the "overpriced" joint.

### Al Dente    19  18  20  $39
*Bally's Las Vegas Hotel, 3645 Las Vegas Blvd. S.*
*(bet. Flamingo Rd. & Tropicana Ave.), 702-967-7999;*
*www.ballys.com*

☑ "Reliable" if "uninspired" Northern Italian served "quickly and courteously" at "fair prices" amid an "authentic family ambiance" make for a "convenient" pit stop for players at Bally's; "a little more privacy from table to table would be nice" for diners on the downlow while culinary critics crave pasta not quite as "tough" as the name of the joint implies.

### ALIZÉ    25  28  25  $64
*Palms Casino Hotel, 4321 W. Flamingo Rd. (Arville St.), 702-942-7777; www.alizelv.com*

■ Dine on a "decadent meal in the sky" at "great" chef Andre Rochat's "romantic", "fancy-schmancy" New French flaunting the city's "best view of the Strip" "through floor-to-ceiling glass on three sides" "56 stories up" and to the west atop the Palms, one of "Vegas' hippest resorts"; don't neglect the foreground, though, as when the "discreet, professional staff" sets down the flowered plates and "removes the silver lids in unison – ta-da!" – they reveal "truly superb" culinary treasures.

### All American Bar & Grille　　　17　15　17　$28

*Rio All-Suite Hotel & Casino, 3700 W. Flamingo Rd. (bet. I-15 & Valley View Blvd.), 702-252-7767; www.playrio.com*

◪ "If you're staying at" the Rio All-Suite Hotel west of the Strip and want "a comfortable place to watch" your favorite team on the telly and "enjoy" a "quick", "delicious burger" or mesquite-grilled "steaks and chops", this "sports-book" destination "right by the casino" offers a "decent deal"; plummeted ratings reveal that, otherwise, the "underwhelming" fare is "not worth the time", and "dated" "decor has got to go."

### America ◐　　　15　16　13　$23

*New York-New York Hotel & Casino, 3790 Las Vegas Blvd. S. (Tropicana Ave.), 702-740-6451; www.nynyhotelcasino.com*

◪ "Get some breakfast and some keno in on the way to bed" at this 24/7 Traditional US of A'er on the Strip, a "noisy room" "dominated by a huge map of the U.S." where the huddled masses feed on "reasonably priced" "homestyle" "specialties from every state"; "there's lots of hustle bustle" here, but little of it comes from the "unbelievably bad" service, and the food's just "not as good as the original in NYC" "yawn" gourmands who gripe "if this is America, take me to Europe!"

### Amlee Gourmet　　　▽　19　15　19　$21

*3827 E. Sunset Rd. (Sandhill Rd.), 702-898-3358*

◪ A "longtime local favorite", this "small storefront" Asian "a bit off the beaten track" on the East Side offers "attentive service" and "consistent quality" that some Sinophiles sigh "rivals Hong Kong"; malcontent mandarins mash "standard fare" that "could be more flavorful", fussing that it only appeals to those who "don't want to drive to the real Chinese food" in Chinatown.

### Andiamo　　　▽　23　23　23　$46

*Las Vegas Hilton Hotel, 3000 Paradise Rd. (bet. Desert Inn Rd. & Karen Ave.), 702-732-5664; www.lvhilton.com*

■ "We enjoyed" admit conventioneers who, after daylong panel discussions and a whole lot of hand pumping, pine for "soothing dining" at this romantic Northern Italian–Mediterranean in the Las Vegas Hilton east of the Strip where the open kitchen creates a "great atmosphere" for plying a plateful of "very good" pasta; if you and your colleagues are still debating your profession's hot-button issues, "ask for the special eight-person room" and hash it out with your peers in private.

## ANDRE'S ❶　　　　　26 | 25 | 26 | $61

*Monte Carlo Resort & Casino, 3770 Las Vegas Blvd. S. (bet. Harmon & Tropicana Aves.), 702-798-7151*
*401 S. Sixth St. (bet. Bridger & Clark Aves.), 702-385-5016* 🖾
*www.andrelv.com*

■ Francophilic followers of "hometown celebrity chef" Andre Rochat's "toooooo romantic" eateries (the "original" "cozy" "auberge in the French countryside" transported to Downtown and the "peaceful respite" "a world away", and yet within, the Monte Carlo casino) "would eat here every night"; "prepare to be pampered" with "superb" fare ferried by "attentive, well-informed, entertaining" servers at a "Vegas tradition", but expect tabs that reflect the cost of the "exquisite Versace china."

### Anna Bella　　　　　▽ 26 | 17 | 24 | $29

*Vallejo Ctr., 3310 S. Sandhill Rd. (Desert Inn Rd.), 702-434-2537*

■ "Rent a car and drive" to the East Side where everybody from big "gatherings" to "amorous couples tucked into cozy booths" is "welcome" to dig into "great osso buco" and other "excellent" "old-fashioned" dishes at this "warm, friendly" and "deservedly" "crowded" "neighborhood Italian"; where "strip" isn't capitalized and refers to a "mall" location, it's "not particularly fancy", but it's got so much "family ambiance", it's "like walking into a *Godfather* movie."

### Antonio's　　　　　23 | 24 | 24 | $48

*Rio All-Suite Hotel & Casino, 3700 W. Flamingo Rd. (bet. I-15 & Valley View Blvd.), 702-777-7777; www.playrio.com*

■ "What a surprise!" – "Harrah's hasn't managed to ruin this excellent" "NY-style traditional Italian" west of the Strip; the "attentive staff" helps, but the fare, including some "innovations", is "great" with or without the "strolling guitar" to accompany it in a "small, elegant" and "noisy" room you'll walk away from "stuffed – but not as stuffed as the waiters' shirts" snicker casual diners.

### Applebee's　　　　　14 | 14 | 16 | $17

*Best of the West, 2070 N. Rainbow Blvd. (Lake Mead Blvd.), 702-648-1065*
*820 E. Warm Springs Rd. (I-215), 702-837-8733*
*3340 S. Maryland Pkwy. (Desert Inn Rd.), 702-737-4990*
*Smith's Shopping Ctr., 500 N. Nellis Blvd. (Stewart Ave.), 702-452-7155*
*3501 S. Rainbow Blvd. (Spring Mountain Rd.), 702-220-3070*
*1501 N. Green Valley Pkwy. (Pebble Rd.), Henderson, 702-914-2691*
*699 N. Stephanie St. (Sunset Rd.), Henderson, 702-433-6339*
*1635 W. Craig Rd. (Martin L. King Blvd.), North Las Vegas, 702-657-6483*
*www.applebees.com*

◪ When foodies ask "why would you go to Vegas and eat at" a "typical chain" American with the "same food, decor and service" no matter "what state or city" you're in?, "tourists" "tired of spending money" answer, because "the riblets are excellent", the "chicken fajita roll-ups are great", the "tap beers are surprisingly fresh" and this "safe haven" for "families" is "snappy, bright and cheery"; "blah! blah! blah!" the gourmands retort, it's "a little better than McDonald's (but not much)."

## AQUA
27 25 25 $67

*Bellagio Hotel, 3600 Las Vegas Blvd. S. (Flamingo Rd.), 702-693-7111; www.bellagio.com*

■ "It's hard not to blush" at the "stunning attention to detail" in this "swimmingly wonderful" Bellagio "beauty"; Michael Mina brings "delish" fish to "the middle of the desert" for the top Seafooder in this *Survey,* offering "high rollers" "exquisite" ocean items ("especially a lobster pot pie" that's "all it's cracked up to be") and an "outstanding tasting menu"; service is "like a ballet", as waiters move "gracefully" through the "posh", "romantic" room for an "upscale experience" that is "worth the home equity loan."

## AquaKnox
– – – E

*Venetian Hotel, 3355 Las Vegas Blvd. S. (bet. Flamingo & Spring Mountain Rds.), 702-414-3772; www.venetian.com*

Chef Tom Moloney hooks the style-conscious, quenching their thirst for the new by converting the former Star Canyon in the Venetian into a Californian-influenced contemporary seafooder; the fish house grills a great lobster and flies shellfish in daily for the raw bar in a room where a waterfall cascades over the walk-in wine cellar.

## Asia
20 21 20 $35

*Harrah's Las Vegas, 3475 Las Vegas Blvd. S. (Flamingo Rd.), 702-693-6000; www.harrahs.com*

☑ "Escape from the casino noise" at this "fine" Pan-Asian in Harrah's where "attentive servers" sling "reasonably priced", "well-prepared" if "pedestrian" faves like spicy kung pao chicken or tender beef with asparagus in black pepper sauce, and sophisticated Sinophiles boo the "boring food", and if you're hiding from your loan shark, the "bright" room might make you "feel like everyone is watching you."

## AUREOLE
25 27 24 $69

*Mandalay Bay Hotel, 3950 Las Vegas Blvd. S. (Hacienda Ave.), 702-632-7401; www.charliepalmer.com*

☑ It's 'bottoms up' at Mandalay Bay's oenophilic outpost of Charlie Palmer's "happening" NYC New American where sipping at the bar is "excellent" "when sitting beneath" the cable-guided "goddesses" of the grape "flying" up the 3,000-bottle "tower of power", centerpiece of the "stunning interior"; "the best food that too much money can buy" "wows crowds" of "glitterati", but if the "sommeliers are helpful" in navigating the "cool computerized wine list", the rest of the "snotty" staff "needs to uncork its attitude."

**Austin's Steakhouse**    24  23  24  $46
*Texas Station Hotel, 2101 Texas Star Ln. (bet. Lake Mead Blvd. &*
*Rancho Dr.), North Las Vegas, 702-631-1033;*
*www.stationcasinos.com*
☑ "You wouldn't expect such a high-class steakhouse"
"out in the boonies" of North Las Vegas, but here it is;
at this "elegant" "gem", the "gracious, attentive staff"
wrangles to table "huge", "thick steaks cooked perfectly"
followed by some of the "best bread pudding" for an
"excellent locals'" meal "in a downscale location" that
some "cowboys" consider "spendy for a casino restaurant."

**Baja Fresh Mexican Grill**    22  12  18  $9
*Mission Ctr., 1380 E. Flamingo Rd. (Maryland Pkwy.),*
*702-699-8920*
*Sahara Pavilion, 4760 W. Sahara Ave. (Decatur Blvd.),*
*702-878-7772*
*Summerhill Plaza, 7501 W. Lake Mead Blvd. (Buffalo Dr.),*
*702-838-4100*
*The Lakes, 8780 W. Charleston Blvd. (bet. Durango Dr. &*
*Rampart Blvd.), 702-948-4043*
*9310 S. Eastern Ave. (Sunset Rd.), Henderson, 702-563-2800*
*Sunset Galleria Shopping Ctr., 675 Mall Ring Circle (Sunset Rd.),*
*Henderson, 702-450-6551*
*Texas Station Hotel, 2101 Texas Star Ln. (bet. Lake Mead Blvd. &*
*Rancho Dr.), North Las Vegas, 702-307-1717*
*www.bajafresh.com*
■ It's all in "the name" at the "absolutely freshest" "yuppie
burrito chain", "a healthier fast-food alternative" to "the
overblown, all-you-can-eat, mass-produced joints"; "get
your Mexicana fix" "quickly, easily and conveniently" with
"large portions" of *muy delicioso* "super grilled mahi mahi
tacos" "drenched in the delightful choices at the salsa
bar" – they're "the bomb!"

**Bally's Steakhouse**    23  18  21  $48
*Bally's Las Vegas Hotel, 3645 Las Vegas Blvd. S.*
*(bet. Flamingo Rd. & Tropicana Ave.), 702-739-4111;*
*www.ballys.com*
☑ 'Well-aged' describes both the "succulent steaks" and
Bally's "old-school" thirtysomething cow palace itself
where a "menu of standards", including "the best Caesar
salad" and "fantastic surf 'n' turf", is "predictable, in a good
way"; with a "way-too-dark", "clubby" decor that "needs
updating", it's "nothing fancy" – just a joint for "hearty food
at hearty prices."

**Bamboleo**    ∇  18  18  16  $31
*Rio All-Suite Hotel & Casino, 3700 W. Flamingo Rd. (bet. I-15 &*
*Valley View Blvd.), 702-247-7983; www.playrio.com*
☑ The Rio just west of the Strip was one of the first resorts
to boast culinary variety, and this "easygoing Mexican"
fills the south-of-the-border bill with "authentic", "huge

portions" at "reasonable prices" in a margarita-fueled, "hectic atmosphere" with "very nice seating", "either by the bar" for "a look out to the casino" or "toward the back"; it's a good thing the vibe is so "entertaining" as jaded *gente* dis fare that "needs a little imagination."

### Bangkok Orchid    ▽ 19 | 14 | 17 | $17 |
*Smith's Shopping Ctr., 4662 E. Sunset Rd.*
*(bet. Mountain Vista St. & Sunset Rd.), Henderson,*
*702-458-4945*
■ "There's a reason" this low-cost Thai "hidden" in a Henderson "shopping center" is "a favorite with the locals", and it's not just the fact that there are "no traffic hassles" in these parts; after more than a decade, the "good soups", "wonderful" pad Thai and other "food is still great", even if "the portions are smaller", and the service remains "on the slow side."

### Battista's Hole in the Wall    15 | 16 | 18 | $25 |
*4041 Audrie St. (bet. Flamingo Rd. & Las Vegas Blvd.),*
*702-732-1424*
◪ "If you like red sauce, checkered tablecloths, old wine bottles used for candles" and a "strange little creature with an accordion" "exclaiming 'I'm hot tonight!'", then this "funky" "monument to old Vegas" east of the Strip is your kind of "fun"; "pictures of celebs, politicos and wise guys" stare down upon you and the rest of the "tourists" gobbling "large portions" of "hearty, cheap Italian"; "why would you want to", ask "foodies", when it's all so "bad" that even the "free wine is overpriced"?

### Bay Side Buffet    20 | 19 | 17 | $24 |
*Mandalay Bay Hotel, 3950 Las Vegas Blvd. S. (Hacienda Ave.),*
*702-632-7402; www.mandalaybay.com*
◪ A "pretty good buffet in a land of buffets", Mandalay Bay's "wonderful" Eclectic all-you-can-net "array" features an "abundance of fresh seafood", "various nationalities' dishes prepared well", an "outrageous dessert bar" and all the other fresser's "favorites"; it's sure "not chintzy", but it can be "a zoo", which the "mediocre service" does nothing to manage, so "go just before the dinnertime onslaught" and enjoy a "tummy bulging" binge in a "calming", "cool" spot overlooking the pools.

### BELLAGIO BUFFET    24 | 19 | 19 | $29 |
*Bellagio Hotel, 3600 Las Vegas Blvd. S. (Flamingo Rd.),*
*702-693-7111; www.bellagio.com*
■ Next to a royal flush, the best spread at the Bellagio is this Eclectic "buffet for people who would otherwise not be caught dead at one"; an "embarrassment of riches" including "orgasmic" Kobe beef, "mountains of excellent king crab legs" and Sunday brunch's "bottomless" bubbly, this "opulent" "feast" might be "higher priced" than other

"smorgasbords", but "never has quality matched quantity like this" belch "oversized stomachs", particularly if they're cruising past the "long wait" with a "comp for the pass line."

### Benihana Hibachi    20 | 21 | 22 | $39 |

*Las Vegas Hilton Hotel, 3000 Paradise Rd. (bet. Desert Inn Rd. & Karen Ave.), 702-732-5334; www.lvhilton.com*

▨ With all that "chop, chop, sizzle, sizzle, voila!", it's "a little loud", but there's "no better show" than at the "original themed Japanese" "retro-kitsch Vegas dining experience" on the Strip: "the chefs are very skilled and entertaining" as they "make your dinner in front of you" in a space "complete with sound effects, fog machines", "straw huts and a fish pond"; sedate diners sample Robata, the adjacent Asian where the cooks are safely ensconced in the kitchen, while snobs skip this "McDonald's for hibachi" altogether.

### Bertolini's    19 | 20 | 18 | $31 |

*Forum Shops at Caesars Palace, 3500 Las Vegas Blvd. S. (Flamingo Rd.), 702-735-4663*
*Village Sq., 9500 W. Sahara Ave. (west of Fort Apache Rd.), 702-869-1540*
*www.mortons.com*

■ "It helps to have delicious risotto and a glass of wine to do your ogling by" when you're patio dining "outside without being outside" at the "ultimate people-watching vantage point within the Forum Shops" at Caesars; "because of the fountains and mall", it's "fairly noisy" and "chaotic", but in a town with only a "few sure things to bet on, this is one of them": a "convenient", "moderately priced Italian" that can be "surprisingly good"; the West Side location is sans the shopaholic "celeb sightings."

### Big Al's Oyster Bar ◑    ▽ 18 | 13 | 15 | $24 |

*Orleans Hotel & Casino, 4500 W. Tropicana Ave. (Arville St.), 702-967-4930; www.orleanscasino.com*

▨ "Very fresh oysters" come raw on the half-shell or cooked into "decent" pan fries and stews at this Orleans Cajun-Creole just west of the Strip where the dive in ratings could be attributed to this year's low votes; beyond the "good seafood", the "casual" "atmosphere leaves much to be desired", and "service is slow", so "grab a seat at the counter to watch" the "open kitchen" "for entertainment – and to make sure you're not forgotten."

### Big Dog's ◑    18 | 13 | 17 | $16 |

*1511 N. Nellis Blvd. (bet. Monroe & Owens Aves.), 702-459-1099*
*6395 W. Sahara Ave. (Torrey Pines Dr.), 702-876-3647*

▨ Wolf down a "burger, Coke and fries", a "good brat", "stand-out BBQ pork", or "if you're from Wisconsin and lonely for walleye", an order of that Cheesehead fish at this "cute" set of "neighborhood places" "with a doggie motif" on the East and West Sides; they're "crowded, smoky and noisy", but when you're "not looking for anything fancy" and you wanna bark at the "ball game", they offer "a real enjoyable experience – for a bar!"

### Big Kitchen Buffet   17  13  16  $19

*Bally's Las Vegas Hotel, 3645 Las Vegas Blvd. S.*
*(bet. Flamingo Rd. & Tropicana Ave.), 702-967-4930;*
*www.ballys.com*

◪ What "used to be the king of Strip buffets" still stacks up "affordable", "decent food" in "a wide variety of choices" (including Traditional American faves and "superb Chinese") "if you don't need a super high-end meal", but despite a recent touch-up, the "old Vegas decor" that is "more big sink than Big Kitchen" still "needs a face-lift", and the joint itself is "just another cattle call."

### Billy Bob's   22  17  19  $32

*Sam's Town Hotel, 5111 Boulder Hwy. (Flamingo Rd.),*
*702-454-8031; www.samstownlv.com*

◪ Rustle up your appetite for "big food in a fun western atmosphere" at this cow palace in Sam's Town on the East Side where "mostly locals" chow down on "huge steaks" and new menu items like Maine lobster at "more reasonable prices than the fancier places on the Strip", even though critics beef it's still "too expensive for quality" that's simply "not bad"; escape the "distracting '60s music" in the "typical cowboy digs" by grabbing a seat on the new outdoor patio.

### Binion's Ranch Steakhouse   22  19  20  $41

*Binion's Horseshoe Hotel, 128 E. Fremont St., 24th fl. (Main St.),*
*702-382-1600; www.binions.com*

◪ "You can almost feel" patriarch Benny "looking down on you from that big casino in the sky" at this "traditional" steakhouse with "superb views" on top of the Horseshoe Hotel Downtown where the meat comes from "stock raised by the Binions themselves"; make "like Dan Tana" dining on a slab "at a fair price, served up with a big slice of old Vegas style" by a "discreet" staff in a "mellow" setting where you can ignore the old hands who say it should be "put out to pasture."

### Black Mountain Grill ◕   21  18  17  $25

*11021 S. Eastern Ave. (Green Valley Pkwy.), Henderson,*
*702-990-0990; www.blackmountaingrill.com*

■ "One of the finest neighborhood restaurants you could imagine" in a tourist town is this "nice, upscale sports bar with surprisingly" "varied and appealing" New American cuisine, from breakfast's "huge ham steak" to a "small but excellent beef Wellington" at dinnertime; "part of the Tommy Rocker chain" of local joints throughout Vegas, the Green Valley grill has a "mountain lodge supper club" ambiance that is "inviting" enough to make even out-of-towners "feel at home."

### Blackstone's Steak House  23 | 21 | 22 | $52

*Monte Carlo Resort & Casino, 3770 Las Vegas Blvd. S.*
*(bet. Harmon & Tropicana Aves.), 702-730-7777;*
*www.monte-carlo.com*

☑ "Shari Lewis wouldn't enjoy eating here – the lamb chops are incredible", and the "NY strips and filets" and "massive roast beef" are "excellent" too; "lots of heavy wood and glass and mirrors make up" the "quiet, clubby" environs of "a true steakhouse", "a great place to meet with business people" inside the Monte Carlo; female puppeteers might feel it "could lose its men-only look" as well as a few bucks off its "pricey" tarrifs, while a "cold" staff lends "no magic" to a spot "named after a magician."

### Blue Wave  23 | 16 | 16 | $24

*4300 E. Sunset Rd. (Green Valley Pkwy.), Henderson, 702-947-2583*

■ "Bring an appetite" to this "all-you-can-eat" "Japanese seafood buffet" and swallow a whaleful of "probably the best value for sushi" in Green Valley, plus a "spectacular" "variety" of "fresh", "hot" dishes; the decor isn't much to look at, but the "great presentation" of oceanic eats fulfills all the senses, and best of all, you "won't have to take out a second mortgage" to feed here.

### Bob Taylor's Ranch House  19 | 18 | 16 | $35

*6250 Rio Vista St. (Ann Rd.), 702-645-1399;*
*www.bobtaylorsranchhouse.com*

☑ Once "on the outskirts of the city", this "1950s dude ranch" is now "in the middle of subdivisions", but the "long drive" through the tangle of Northwest "road construction" is "worth it for the decor"; sporting "great old entertainment pictures" and all "a little too Western", the "quaint" setting is home to an "institution" that has been mesquite-grilling "great steaks" for almost 50 years; still, modernist "meat lovers" mumble that this beef barn is "past its prime."

### Bonjour Casual French  ∇ 22 | 18 | 22 | $37

*Colonnade Sq., 8878 S. Eastern Ave. (bet. I-215 & Pebble Rd.),*
*702-270-2102; www.bonjourvegas.com*

☑ "Yum, yum, oui, oui" fawn Francophiles flocking to Green Valley's "great little neighborhood" bistro, where "unsnotty" Cannes natives Marie and Bernard Calatayund break the French service mold with "charming waiters" who present "food that's simple yet elegant" and a "short but good" selection of California and French wines; nevertheless, at these prices, it's "not much of a value", particularly for stylists who tut at the "trite decor."

### Bootlegger Bistro ☽  19 | 18 | 18 | $27

*7700 Las Vegas Blvd. S. (Robindale Rd., opp. Belz Factory Outlet*
*World), 702-736-4939; www.bootleggerlasvegas.com*

☑ "An aging celebrity who's been out of the limelight might show up, sing a few bars" and "shuffle, turn, step, step" for a little "impromptu entertainment" "during your dinner" south of the Strip at this "good and garlicky" Southern Italian "taste of old Las Vegas" "owned by Nevada's lieutenant governor"/songstress Lorraine Hunt; the "food is nothing special", but for "a nightclub atmosphere 24 hours a day", locals say, "hey, I like the joint, ok?"

## BORDER GRILL                22 | 18 | 19 | $32

*Mandalay Bay Hotel, 3950 Las Vegas Blvd. S. (Hacienda Ave.), 702-632-7403; www.mandalaybay.com*

◪ Created by *Too Hot Tamales'* celeb chefs Susan Feniger and Mary Sue Milliken, this "colorful, upbeat" Mandalay Bay Mexican divides surveyors like the Rio Grande: amigos applaud "light but complex taste treats" such as "plantain empanadas to die for", "awesome" seviche and "snappy" salsas, while naysayers nix "inflated prices" and "spotty" service ("the help must be sipping the margaritas") and charge the place "relies too much on its owners' rep."

## BRADLEY OGDEN              27 | 25 | 26 | $72

*Caesars Palace, 3570 Las Vegas Blvd. S. (Flamingo Rd.), 702-731-7110; www.caesars.com*

■ Connoisseurs come to Caesars Palace not to bury Ogden but to praise him for his "extravagant, outstanding" New American, with "superb" organic dishes, like a "foodie-heaven" "Maytag blue cheese soufflé", presented with "serious china and linens" by a "warm", "engaging" staff; "farm-fresh doesn't come cheap" though, so you'd "better win big or you'll leave hungry" – or go for lunch, "the same sublime experience for one-third the cost."

## Broiler                    23 | 16 | 20 | $26

*Boulder Station Hotel, 4111 Boulder Hwy. (Lamb Blvd.), 702-432-7777*
*Palace Station Hotel, 2411 W. Sahara Ave. (Rancho Dr.), 702-367-2408*
*www.stationcasinos.com*

■ This set of Station surf 'n' turfers on the East Side and west of the Strip serves "consistently good food" "at a bargain price", according to loyal locals; there's a "live lobster tank" and "great filet mignon", but the "best part" is the "excellent salad bar", a "wonderful array" from "granola to hearts of palm"; come with "modest expectations" (read: ignore the "old garage-sale-reject" decor) and you might just be "pleasantly surprised."

## Buccaneer Bay              21 | 22 | 22 | $45

*Treasure Island Hotel, 3300 Las Vegas Blvd. S. (Spring Mountain Rd.), 702-894-7223; www.treasureisland.com*

■ Swashbucklers who set sail to this "hidden gem" on the Strip say its "jolly good" Continental menu is a treasure chest of "delicious steaks" and "best-ever crème brûlée";

the "accommodating" crew "caters to your every need", whether you stow away in "cozy" "dining alcoves" or sit by the window to "watch the pirates sink the British frigate"; meanwhile, a few "disappointed" landlubbers lament it's "cheesy" and "underwhelming."

### Buffet    ▽ 15 | 13 | 14 | $15

*Las Vegas Hilton Hotel, 3000 Paradise Rd. (bet. Desert Inn Rd. & Karen Ave.), 702-732-5111; www.lvhilton.com*

◪ Conventioneers who congregate east of the Strip contend the Hilton's Traditional American gorgefest is "like your high school cafeteria, Vegas-style", i.e. "good for lunch", "neither remarkable nor bad" with a price that's "lower than most"; in short, "you'll be filled but not fulfilled."

### Buffet, The    21 | 17 | 19 | $16

*Golden Nugget Hotel, 129 E. Fremont St. (Main St.), 702-385-7111; www.goldennugget.com*

■ This Traditional American self-serve at the Golden Nugget is the "best buffet Downtown", say smorgasbord savants; it's "a great value" for "high-quality", "well-presented" fare (including the signature "don't-miss" bread pudding) in a "tastefully restrained" "old-school Vegas" room; still, those accustomed to Strip-style sprawl say the "small" space is "crowded" with "very long lines."

### BullShrimp    21 | 21 | 20 | $38

*Green Valley Ranch Station Hotel, 2300 Paseo Verde Pkwy. (Green Valley Pkwy.), Henderson, 702-942-4110; www.bullshrimp.com*

◪ Beefeaters are bullish on local chef Gustav Mauler's "modern, sleek" surf 'n' turfer at Henderson's "always hip Green Valley Ranch", bellowing for its "unique and funky presentation" of chops and crustaceans and the "don't-miss" house-specialty chopped salad; disenchanted diners deem the decor "cavernous", the prices "inflated" and the meal "nice but not spectacular": "the owner's name alone will not carry this place."

### Burgundy Room    ▽ 23 | 17 | 21 | $37

*Lady Luck Casino Hotel, 206 N. Third St. (Ogden Ave.), 702-477-3000; www.ladylucklv.com*

■ "Recall the city's Rat Pack heyday" at this tiny "'50s-style" steakhouse/seafooder "hidden" Downtown in the Lady Luck, the "unlikeliest" spot for "to-die-for" Châteaubriand, "tableside Caesar salad" and "fantastic cherries jubilee", all proffered by a "doting" staff; vintage vibe notwithstanding, surveyors say the "room needs some sprucing up."

### Buzio's    24 | 20 | 20 | $44

*Rio All-Suite Hotel & Casino, 3700 W. Flamingo Rd. (bet. I-15 & Valley View Blvd.), 702-252-7697; www.playrio.com*

■ "Bouillabaisse and cioppino snobs rejoice" at "one of the best seafood restaurants in Vegas" located just west of the Strip "overlooking the pool" at the Rio, where some of "the desert's best" ocean eats are "pricey but always fresh" and the servers are "knowledgeable and friendly"; "tourists like it" but the "natives are still fishing", arguing that the place "needs a face-lift."

**Café Bellagio** ◑    20 | 21 | 20 | $27

*Bellagio Hotel, 3600 Las Vegas Blvd. S. (Flamingo Rd.), 702-693-7356; www.bellagio.com*

☑ "Think of it this way – you're likely to lose money at Bellagio" anyway, so go ahead and get the "$25 breakfast" at this "airy" 24/7 Contemporary American coffee shop abutting the "spectacular" conservatory where eagle-eyed eaters may even "glimpse some glitterati" going for the "two-cuts-above" "late-night munchies" and a little "drunken keno"; "huge lines" can make "proficient" service "glacially slow", though, and elevated expectations leave put-out people pouting that the place is "pedestrian."

**Cafe Heidelberg**    ▽ 22 | 15 | 16 | $24

*610 E. Sahara Ave. (bet. Maryland Pkwy. & Paradise Rd.), 702-731-5310*

■ "Dieters beware" – Deutsch treats like "flavorful" Wiener schnitzel, "deliciously authentic warm potato salad" and "sinful" apple strudel tempt Teutonic taste buds at this "old-school" 1958 storefront location just east of the Strip; it "feels like home" to German gourmands, what with the "wide selection of imported" native lagers and ales, in-house delicatessen and occasional accordion music; be prepared, however, for "brash" servers who may have a tendency to be "surly."

**Cafe Lago** ◑    17 | 18 | 16 | $25

*Caesars Palace, 3570 Las Vegas Blvd. S. (Flamingo Rd.), 702-731-7110; www.caesars.com*

☑ Caesars Palace's requisite round-the-clocker renders "dependable and consistent" Traditional American à la carte cuisine supplemented on weekends by a "varied but not lavish" buffet spread; the "bright, new" lake-themed setting includes a "patio overlooking" the "spectacular" pool as well as performances by a "really good piano player", but surveyors shrug it's just a "greasy spoon dolled up in high drag."

**Cafe Nicolle** ☒    19 | 19 | 20 | $29

*Sahara Pavilion, 4760 W. Sahara Ave. (Decatur Blvd.), 702-870-7675; www.cafenicolle.com*

☑ High-profilers hanker for this "classy" west-of-Strip Continental's "super seafood", "friendly service", "lovely outdoor dining" and a lounge enhanced by a jazzy ivory tickler, but now that the aging decor is "beginning to look a little rundown", many maintain that "even the see-and-be-seen crowd is in need of a change."

### Cafe Tajine ◐　　　▽ 19 | 21 | 21 | $31

*Hyatt Regency Lake Las Vegas Resort, 101 Montelago Blvd.*
*(Lake Las Vegas Pkwy., off Boulder Hwy.), Henderson,*
*702-567-1234; www.hyatt.com*

■ There is "not a camel in sight" at this Casablancan
casbah at Henderson's Hyatt Regency on Lake Las Vegas,
a "beautiful" "Moroccan-themed" poolside oasis where
the "emphasis is on service and ambiance"; the menu of
Mediterranean meals is "unremarkable" by comparison,
perhaps a boon to bashful biters who believe the fare's
exotic "influences" are too subtle to "intimidate those of
us who have never traveled to Africa."

### Caffe Giorgio ⊠　　　– | – | – | M

*Mandalay Place, 3950 Las Vegas Blvd. S. (Tropicana Ave.),*
*702-920-2700*

Restaurateur Piero Selvaggio now has two eateries
on the Las Vegas Strip with the opening of this casually
elegant delicatessen and full-service cafe in the new
Mandalay Place shopping mall; featuring pasta and Italian
surf 'n' turf, a gelato counter and a stylish bar at which
diners can sip from the notable wine cellar, the eatery
allows patrons to pick at Valentino-style specialties in a
more relaxed environment.

### California Pizza Kitchen ◐　　　19 | 14 | 17 | $20

*Fashion Show Mall, 3200 Las Vegas Blvd. S. (Fashion Show Ln.),*
*702-893-1370*
*Mirage Hotel, 3400 Las Vegas Blvd. S. (Spring Mountain Rd.),*
*702-791-7357*
*www.cpk.com*

☑ "Catch your horse coming down the stretch on the big
screens while munching" at this sprightly "boutique pizza"
chainster set above the "bustling" Mirage sportsbook; you
"get exactly what you expect": "great salads", "reliable,
fresh pasta" and that "tremendously creative" wood-fired
specialty "with every topping imaginable"; disenchanted
diners drawl, "there's no such thing as a leisurely meal" amid
the "din", though the same can't be said of the "long wait";
N.B. the Fashion Show Mall location opened in late 2002.

### Canaletto　　　21 | 23 | 20 | $41

*Venetian Hotel, 3355 Las Vegas Blvd. S. (bet. Flamingo &*
*Spring Mountain Rds.), 702-733-0070; www.ilfornaio.com*

☑ "It's easy to get lost in the romance" of this Northern
Italian inside the Venetian – "with a little imagination", it's
"as close as Las Vegas can get to Venice dining, faux
alfresco" "without the pigeons"; "very attentive" servers
deliver "innovative but authentic" pizza, pasta and fish,
and the "live opera" and "great people-watching" on the
"ersatz" Piazza di San Marco pump up "*la dolce vita*"; still,
"disappointed" diners would rather throw Il Fornaio's "hit-
or-miss" *cugino* in the mock Grand Canal.

---

**Canal Street Grille**    23 | 19 | 22 | $33

*Orleans Hotel & Casino, 4500 W. Tropicana Ave. (Arville St.),
702-365-7111; www.orleanscasino.com*

■ Enjoy "high-quality" surf 'n' turf at this "dressy" "oasis" in the Orleans west of the Strip, where "excellent" Alaskan king crab legs are one of the "good value" faves on a "fine menu"; sporting a cozy fireplace, "wonderful, big booths" and "terrific service", it's a "nice place to impress a lady if you're on a budget" – just 'cause it's in Vegas, "who says it has to be noisy, flashy and pricey?"

**Canter's Deli ❶**    19 | – | 13 | $16

*Treasure Island Hotel, 3300 Las Vegas Blvd. S.
(Spring Mountain Rd.), 702-894-7111;
www.cantersdeli.com*

■ "For those who miss Fairfax Avenue", this sibling of LA's Jewish deli "institution" is a "welcome arrival", particularly now that it's moved into its permanent spot at Treasure Island where "on-the-go gamblers" dig into a "quick" but belly-busting "bite" of pastrami or corned beef, along with "great shoe string fries"; the folks here pickle their own cukes and bake their own pastries, but "how will they get the characters who are the [City of Angels] staff to move out" to the desert?

**Canyon Ranch Cafe**    21 | 17 | 19 | $28

*Venetian Hotel, 3355 Las Vegas Blvd. S. (bet. Flamingo &
Spring Mountain Rds.), 702-414-3633; www.venetian.com*

■ "For an escape from gorging" on all that pasta elsewhere in the Venetian, savor a "delicious, light" breakfast or lunch at this "tranquil", "spa-adjacent" New American, where a whisked-up "excellent egg-white omelet" "tastes as good as healthy food possibly can"; it's "handy if you're spending the day getting pampered" or "the afternoon in a bathing suit", and if the setting is "sterile", all those "half-naked people" help warm the place up.

**Capri Italian Ristorante**    ▽ 21 | 16 | 20 | $26

*Sunset Station Hotel, 1301 W. Sunset Rd. (Stephanie St.),
Henderson, 702-547-7828; www.stationcasinos.com*

◪ Take a break from the one-armed bandit in Henderson where this "better than average" Northern Italian that's "open to the slots" is "noisy" but "priced fairly", so you can afford to lose coins before your carbo load; obsessives "considering flying out to satisfy longings for the linguine pomodoro" should tote extra luggage for portions for which you "always need a doggie bag", though they might regret the airfare if the "inconsistent" kitchen is having a bad night.

**Capriotti's Sandwich Shop**    23 | 7 | 17 | $9

*7440 Cheyenne Ave. (Buffalo Dr.), 702-656-7779
3981 E. Sunset Rd. (Sandhill Rd.), 702-898-4904 ⊞*

(continued)

(continued)
## Capriotti's Sandwich Shop
*Paradise Mktpl., 3830 E. Flamingo Rd. (Sandhill Rd.), 702-454-2430*
*450 S. Buffalo Dr. (bet. Alta Dr. & Ducharme Ave.), 702-838-8659*
*Warm Springs Mktpl., 7291 S. Eastern Ave. (Warm Springs Rd.),*
*702-260-4334*
*4983 W. Flamingo Rd. (bet. Decatur Blvd. & Edmond St.),*
*702-222-3331*
*322 W. Sahara Ave. (bet. Industrial Rd. & Las Vegas Blvd.),*
*702-474-0229* 🛇 ⊅
*8450 W. Sahara Ave. (Durango Dr.), 702-562-0440*
*www.capriottis.com*

☑ "Yee haw" howl local chowhounds – "it's great to find East Coast sandwiches in the desert" at these shops sprouting up like so many cacti; from the "phenomenal" "Thanksgiving-on-a-roll" to the "awesome Capastrami" and the Vege/Burger, these are the subs "of the gods", i.e. "authentic" "with lots of variety" and "oils aplenty"; "a serious lack of decor" means you should "eat it at home", though tightwads "pass" right by altogether, whining it's "not worth the small fortune they charge for it."

## Caribe Café ⦿
17 | – | 17 | $20

*Mirage Hotel, 3400 Las Vegas Blvd. S. (Spring Mountain Rd.),*
*702-791-7356; www.themirage.com*

☑ "A real boon for those late-night, post-casino munchies", the Mirage's 'round-the-clock coffee shop offers "excellent variety at all hours"; "enormous portions" of "standard" American fare is "nothing exciting", but "if you've been up too late", at least it's "easily digested"; a "recent renovation" has rendered the "campy" Caribbean-tinged digs "less Mel's diner, more Trader Vic's", though the service remains "s-l-o-w" as ever.

## Carluccio's Tivoli Gardens
▽ 23 | 21 | 23 | $24

*Liberace Plaza, 1775 E. Tropicana Ave. (Spencer St.), 702-795-3236*

■ Once "owned by Liberace himself", this "family-friendly" East Side Italian is "surprisingly good" "at a fraction of the price" of more recent joints; rumor has it the "piano room/bar is haunted" by Mr. Showmanship, but even if it's not, its flashy, "heavy decor" embodies the spirit of the campy maestro, and its location "right next door to his museum" makes it a "great place for tourists."

## Carnival World Buffet
17 | 13 | 15 | $19

*Rio All-Suite Hotel & Casino, 3700 W. Flamingo Rd. (bet. I-15 & Valley View Blvd.), 702-252-7757; www.playrio.com*

☑ "Hoo, boy!" – "if you're on the Atkins diet", this Eclectic "buffet the size of a football field" west of the Strip "is the place for you" to gnash your way through "disgusting amounts of meat, all prepared very well"; "visit Mexico, Morocco and Japan all on one dinner plate" as you "eat your way around the world", and walk it too, i.e. "wear your traveling shoes" to traverse the "cavernous room"; unhappy trekkers tut it's "no longer as good as the hype", wondering, "will they ever redecorate this place?"

### Carson Street Cafe ●            20 | 17 | 18 | $18 |
*Golden Nugget Hotel, 129 E. Fremont St. (Main St.), 702-385-7111; www.goldennugget.com*
■ Mine the "gigantic menu" for "big, big portions" of "quality food at a good price" at this "all-hours" American diner Downtown; "lunchtime can be busy" thanks to the "county courthouse next door", making it "the best place in town to try to meet an attorney" – and you'll have the time to chat up your esquire, since the service can be "slow, slow, slow."

### Cathay House            20 | 16 | 18 | $23 |
*5300 Spring Mountain Rd. (bet. Decatur Blvd. & Lindell Rd.), 702-876-3838; www.cathayhouse.com*
■ "Get window seating" for a "great view of the Strip", but keep one eye out for the "carts full of delicious goodies" piloted by the "nicest people imaginable" at this "classic" West Side Chinese that some Sinophiles say serves the "best dim sum in town", even "at night"; though it offers "no exciting surprises", "the regular menu is very good too."

### Center Stage            ▽ 17 | 21 | 18 | $26 |
*Plaza Hotel & Casino, 1 S. Main St. (Fremont St.), 702-386-2110; www.plazahotelcasino.com*
◪ For three decades, the Plaza Hotel's glass-domed Downtown American has provided "excellent value in an old Vegas setting", pairing moderately priced "good" grub with "prime seats for" "the Fremont Street Experience"; most diners agree "the view is worth more than the food", though some bargain hunters hail it for having at least the "appearance of an expensive restaurant."

### Chang of Las Vegas            22 | 19 | 21 | $27 |
*Bally's Las Vegas Hotel, 3645 Las Vegas Blvd. S. (bet. Flamingo Rd. & Tropicana Ave.), 702-967-7999; www.ballys.com*
*Gold Key Shopping Ctr., 3055 Las Vegas Blvd. S. (bet. Cathedral Way & Convention Center Dr.), 702-731-3388*
■ Enjoy "San Francisco quality" (or better) "at Vegas prices" at the Strip's set of separately owned Sino pseudo-siblings; both feature "servers who go out of their way" to help navigate the "good variety" of dishes, but "adventurists" acclaim the Gold Key site, which dishes up "amazing dim sum", "the closest thing to real Hong Kong Chinese" in town.

### Chapala's ●            ▽ 14 | 11 | 13 | $15 |
*3335 E. Tropicana Ave. (Pecos Rd.), 702-451-8141*
*2101 S. Decatur Blvd. (Sahara Ave.), 702-871-7805*
◪ Amigos low on *dinero* value these "family-friendly" East Side and West Side "classics" for being "a little more

authentic" than some of the other Mexicans around; sure it's "too dark inside" and the "Southern California–style" menu can be a bit "boring", but they've "been around forever" (or at least since 1965), so "they must be doing something right."

### CHARLIE PALMER STEAK    25  24  25  $67
*Four Seasons Hotel, 3960 Las Vegas Blvd. S. (Four Seasons Dr.), 702-632-5120; www.charliepalmersteak.com*

■ "Slip away to the Four Seasons" and chef Charlie Palmer's "pricey" "plush" "place for beef" where, amid a "setting of palms, wood trim and some Spanish Mission touches", diners succumb to "expertly prepared" steaks that are "always tender, moist and delicious" and to staffers "falling over themselves to please you"; a "welcome" "bastion of quiet and class", "this non-gambling venue" is far "away from the noise of losers' groans" – but "you better hope lady luck's with *you* afterwards to pay off" the bill.

### CHEESECAKE FACTORY, THE    22  18  19  $25
*Forum Shops at Caesars Palace, 3500 Las Vegas Blvd. S. (Flamingo Rd.), 702-792-6888*
*750 S. Rampart Blvd. (Alta Dr.), 702-951-3800*
*www.thecheesecakefactory.com*

◪ Faced with a menu that "reads like a novel", "even finicky eaters" "can pick something and be happy" at these Strip and Summerlin "upscale chain" links; factory strikers decry the "herd mentality" that makes them "insanely, inexplicably busy" and so "noisy" that "conversation is impossible"; but who needs to talk when you're gorging on "surprisingly good" American "comfort food" served "for small prices" in portions "geared toward dinosaurs", while "saving room" for some "truly decadent cheesecake?"

### Chevys Fresh Mex    16  14  16  $17
*4090 S. Eastern Ave. (Flamingo Rd.), 702-731-6969*
*6800 W. Sahara Ave. (Rainbow Blvd.), 702-220-4507*
*Galleria Mall, 1300 W. Sunset Rd. (Stephanie St.), Henderson, 702-434-8323*
*www.chevys.com*

◪ Though it's "probably not the most authentic" Mexican around, this "good-value" Valley-wide "California chain" serves "consistent", "freshly made" fare ("my taco was still mooing at me"), with "above-average" chips and "tasty" "roasted tomato salsa" revving the engines of happy-hour munchers; others, however are stalled by what they deem "bland Americanized" eats and "typical" "franchise" decor.

### Chicago Brewing Company ◑    18  16  19  $19
*2201 S. Fort Apache Rd. (bet. Charleston & Sahara Aves.), 702-254-3333*

■ "The microbrewery is the draw" at this "fun", "crowded" neighborhood West Sider "with a Chicago feel" that offers a half-dozen "good homemade beers" (and root beer too) on tap; they also cook up a "nice selection" of American pub grub, including their signature deep dish pizza; the "good service" – which has improved since our last *Survey* – ensures you'll get to the nearby multiplex on time.

### Chicago Joe's ⌧     21 | 15 | 22 | $22
*820 S. Fourth St. (bet. Gass & Hoover Aves.), 702-382-5637; www.chicagojoesrestaurant.com*

■ It's "worth the trouble to find" this "quaint", "tiny brick" Downtown "landmark for old-time locals" and lunching lawyers that "feels like a speakeasy", though the "excellent" staff serves "mouthwatering" "Italian specialties" rather than bathtub gin; "generous portions" make it one of "the best values in Vegas", even if some cautious citizens express concern over "the quality of the neighborhood."

### Chili's Grill & Bar     17 | 16 | 15 | $17
*2011 N. Rainbow Blvd. (Lake Mead Blvd.), 702-638-1482*
*2520 S. Decatur Blvd. (Sahara Ave.), 702-871-0500*
*10080 S. Eastern Ave. (bet. Ribbon Rd. & Rte. 146), 702-407-6924*
*9051 W. Charleston Blvd. (west of Rte. 159), 702-228-0479*
*2751 N. Green Valley Pkwy. (Sunset Rd.), Henderson, 702-433-3333*
*www.chilis.com*

■ This "consistent" (some say "predictable") diner chain makes its mark across the city with "quick service" and "reasonable prices" on those Southwestern and Traditional American comfort-food favorites, "good fajitas or a nice burger"; though it's often filled with "many kids", the full bar and hearty appetizers, like the signature Awesome Blossom fried onion, means it could work "for a cheap date" – assuming "you've tried everything else in Vegas."

### CHINA GRILL     23 | 24 | 21 | $47
*Mandalay Bay Hotel, 3950 Las Vegas Blvd. S. (Hacienda Ave.), 702-632-7404; www.mandalaybay.com*

■ The "young, vibrant crowd" "can't get enough" of the "cool" vibe at this "dark, mysterious" Mandalay Bay Asian, a "trendy outpost of the longtime NY fave"; though "pricey", it's "great for a group" to share "elegant and creative" dishes, like the "must-try lobster pancakes" or "to-die-for calamari salad", "piled high in colorful arrangements"; P.S. "check out" "the Brave New World bathrooms" – "all with individual TVs" – and the "awesome bar scene", packed with lovelies "starving for attention."

### Chin Chin     18 | 15 | 17 | $26
*New York-New York Hotel & Casino, 3790 Las Vegas Blvd. S. (Tropicana Ave.), 702-740-6300; www.chinchin.com*

◩ "For those trips when you're not winning enough" to blow a wad on chow, this chain link addresses the need for sustenance with a "huge menu" of "low-cost (for the Strip)" eats; but while some chins wag favorably over the "healthy", "creative "Californian-Chinese cuisine" (especially the "excellent chicken salad"), others are more chin-tzy with praise, pouting over "food without any flair."

### CHINOIS
23 | 19 | 20 | $40

*Forum Shops at Caesars Palace, 3500 Las Vegas Blvd. S. (Flamingo Rd.), 702-737-9700; www.wolfgangpuck.com*
Surveyors are split over "Wolfgang Puck's take on Asian-French cuisine"; while it attracts "beautiful people eating beautiful food" that bears the master's "unique", "stylin'" signature, many maintain it's "not up to the standards of the Santa Monica original"; a drooping Decor score also reinforces reservations about "gaudy" digs and "high noise level" – though if the "bright, lively atmosphere" is not "to your liking", you can always "sit outside and watch the show of shoppers at the Caesars Forum" stores.

### Chipotle
21 | 14 | 14 | $11

*3475 Las Vegas Blvd. S. (Flamingo Rd.), 702-836-0804*
*4530 S. Maryland Pkwy. (Harmon Ave.), 702-436-9177*
*10251 S. Eastern Ave. (Sahara Ave.), Henderson, 702-361-6438*
*1311 W. Sunset Rd. (Stephanie St.), Henderson, 702-436-7740*
*www.chipotle.com*
"Healthy" edibles "need not always be expensive", as proven by this popular Mexican chain, whose "fresh", "high-quality" ingredients provide "fast food that's well above the norm" – specifically, "great big burritos" and tacos, weighing in at 20 oz; a "casual" but "chic", raw, urban room where "they always have music playing" complements the "made-to-order" munchies at the Strip site; N.B. the other locations opened post-*Survey.*

### Coachman's Inn ◐
– | – | – | M

*3240 S. Eastern Ave. (Desert Inn Rd.), 702-731-4202*
The coach never turns into a pumpkin at this "old-style Vegas" Traditional American on the East Side serving "sublime" standards – both on the menu and Friday nights at the mike – to nightcrawling Cinderellas 24/7 in a portrait-filled, exposed-brick setting; "sometimes the service can be a little slow when they're very busy", so you might have to wait awhile for that prime rib and that peanut butter pie.

### Coco's
▽ 13 | 11 | 15 | $15

*9210 S. Eastern Ave. (Serene Ave.), Henderson, 702-614-2772;*
*www.cocosbakery.com*
"Fairly new to Henderson", this "chain coffee shop" from California cooks up three squares of Traditional American "comfort food" each day; though it's "not a bad place to have a sandwich or salad", an in-house bakery where "the pies are delicious" is the highlight, making desserts "the best part of a meal" that gourmands say "resembles airplane food" – maybe the impending "liquor license" will help?

## Coffee Pub
— — — I

*2800 W. Sahara Blvd. (Paseo Del Prado), 702-367-1913*
For nearly two decades, this comfortable cafe west of the Strip has dished up "more food than you need" during "great breakfasts", followed by freshly made salads and sandwiches for lunch, plus "good specialty coffees" that overflow "a very large mug" all day long to keep politicos, journalists and business owners pumped for action; the laid-back vibe, indoor-outdoor seating and friendly staff lure locals to a place everyone simply knows as The Pub.

## COMMANDER'S PALACE
25 23 25 $55

*Desert Passage at Aladdin, 3663 Las Vegas Blvd. S. (Harmon Ave.), 702-892-8272; www.commanderspalace.com*
■ The Aladdin's "worthy offspring of the great New Orleans" Brennan family Cajun-Creole institution is "a bastion of civilization in a sea of sweatpants and spandex"; amid "gorgeous" "reminders of the Vieux Carre", "out-of-this-world" pecan-encrusted fish and "bread pudding made to order" "from heaven" are ferried by a "knowledgeable staff" with "graciousness and charm"; "while it ain't the original – what in Vegas is?" – it's still "tons" of "top-drawer" "fun", especially during the "transporting jazz brunch."

## Como's Steakhouse
— — — VE

*Lake Las Vegas Resort MonteLago Village, 10 Via Brianza (Lake Mead Dr.), Henderson, 702-567-9950; www.lakelasvegas.com*
Chef "Joseph Keller's style permeates fresh menu items" at his new, relatively undiscovered sib to Napa Valley's Bouchon; beneath a "hand-painted ceiling", the upscale-casual surf 'n' turf "oasis" at the MonteLago Village in the gorgeous Lake Las Vegas Resort serves a "great" slab of beef and "out-of-this-world fries", but "the staff needs to work together a little longer to make it all happen."

## Conrad's
∇ 22 19 20 $51

*Flamingo Las Vegas, 3555 Las Vegas Blvd. S. (Flamingo Rd.), 702-733-3502; www.flamingolasvegas.com*
◪ "The perfect place" "to cheat on your loved one" might be this "little-known quality steakhouse" on the Strip where the "comfy, wraparound booths, although well-worn, pleasantly keep your party" "private", and a staff that "treats you like royalty" stokes the "romantic" vibe; the meat is "delicious", the "desserts are fabulous", but spendthrifts say "for the prices, they could throw in the spinach."

## Costa del Sol
19 18 18 $28

*Sunset Station Hotel, 1301 W. Sunset Rd. (Stephanie St.), Henderson, 702-547-7814; www.stationcasinos.com*
■ Meek mates order from the 'mild side' while captains courageous go for the ever-changing 'wild side' of the

menu at this "surprisingly delightful" Green Valley fish house and adjacent oyster bar where "fanny pack–wearing tourists" dive into the "oustanding salad [and soup] bar" for "an enormous amount of food" at "a fair price"; amid Sunset Station's clanging, it's "noisy", but the "cold, fresh raw offerings" and "simmering seafood concoctions" are "a step above standard mid-level casino fare."

### Country Inn     _ _ _ _ 1

*1401 S. Rainbow Blvd. (Charleston Blvd.), 702-254-0520*
The East Side location's gone out to pasture, but at the West Side site of this Traditional American "senior and family" favorite, "a hearty, comfortable breakfast" still "goes perfect with a Sunday paper", "priming the body and spirit for a day of gambling" in a town that knows no blue laws; "don't look for lots of imagination", just "piping hot rolls with honey" and "the best complete turkey dinner" for a "satisfying", "old-fashioned" "good value" at the end of your winning or losing streak.

### Courtyard Buffet     14 12 16 $16

*Stratosphere Hotel & Tower, 2000 Las Vegas Blvd. S. (north of Sahara Ave.), 702-380-7777; www.stratlv.com*
◪ "Kick off your trip to Vegas" "eating around the world" on the "cheap" at this "decent" Eclectic spread at the north end of the Strip; if you "don't expect Emeril's", the "fresh eats" might "exceed your expectations"; but if you're looking for more than the "standard buffet fare", it's "too much of too little", so "flat out don't bother."

### Coyote Cafe/     23 19 20 $39
### Mark Miller's Grill Room

*MGM Grand Hotel, 3799 Las Vegas Blvd. S. (Tropicana Ave.), 702-891-7349; www.coyote-cafe.com*
◪ "Zingy Southwestern flavors" "get taste buds flowing" like the Rio Grande at the "festive" MGM outpost of chef Mark Miller's "New Mexico mother restaurant"; after a decade, "this place can still crank out a wicked sauce" for "gorgeous plate presentation" of "interesting choices" (including "unique breakfasts") to "chaotic", "casual" packs in the cafe; some who've ponied up for the fancy Grill Room find it "disappointing", and sensitive bottoms say seating feels like the "chairs were rode hard and put away wet."

### Craftsteak     24 23 23 $68

*MGM Grand Hotel, 3799 Las Vegas Blvd. S. (Tropicana Ave.), 702-891-7318; www.mgmgrand.com*
■ "One from Column A, two from Column B, a sauce from C – and you're not in a Chinese restaurant!"; for a "primer on artisanal and organic foods" featuring "grass-fed beef", "craft your own meal" at Manhattan chef Tom Colicchio's surf 'n' turfer in the MGM; this "gorgeous" "high roller" "gets better the larger your group", as "family-style" feasting

makes "grazing on so many" "pure", "unique flavors" "the most fun"; spoilsports who "don't like to serve themselves" miss out on "incredible vegetables" and "moo-velous" meat.

**Crown & Anchor** ◑                    17  17  16  $14
*1350 E. Tropicana Ave. (bet. Eastern Ave. & Maryland Pkwy.), 702-739-8676; www.crownandanchorlv.com*

☑ "A great after-work drinks place" no matter what time you get off shift, this 24/7 "pub brings true English tradition" to the East Side, with some of "the best fish 'n' chips", a "huge" "European beer selection", "soccer matches" on the telly and live tunes; the staff is "slow" at this "college kid hangout", but you're here to "unwind", so "grab some bangers 'n' mash and a few pints and forget you're in LV."

**Crustacean Las Vegas**              ▽ 19  27  20  $63
(aka Prana)
*Desert Passage at Aladdin, 3663 Las Vegas Blvd. S. (Harmon Ave.), 702-650-0507; www.pranalasvegas.com*

☑ Given a name change and a "bad location" in the Desert Passage, few have ferreted out LA's noted An family in their "over-the-top Asian" serving "divine" French-Vietnamese dishes like "heavenly garlic noodles" with giant tiger prawns; the "exotic" duplex is dressed in booths fashioned from antique opium beds, from which "the most beautiful people" emerge to hoof it on the dance floor on "weekends" when the attached Prana nightclub gets cooking.

**DEL FRISCO'S DOUBLE**              26  23  24  $63
**EAGLE STEAK HOUSE**
*3925 Paradise Rd. (Corporate Dr.), 702-796-0063; www.delfriscos.com*

■ "Attentive servers treat everyone like a whale" – not the marine mammal but, in Vegas parlance, a high roller; and what does a big spender eat for an "elegant break from the tables"? – "nothing but savory steak", "juicy, delicious" and "perfectly done" with "fabulous" sides, "fantastic" wines and "hot, messy bread brought right away" at this "excellent", "high-end" beef palace east of the Strip where a Wednesday–Saturday pianist adds "polish" to the "white lines, heavy wood and cigar bar" of the "clubby" environs.

**DELMONICO**                         26  24  25  $63
*Venetian Hotel, 3355 Las Vegas Blvd. S. (bet. Flamingo & Spring Mountain Rds.), 702-414-3737; www.emerils.com*

■ "Emeril knows how to keep it real" at his "modern and uncluttered" Venetian "meat lover's dream", where Food Network chef Lagasse "kicks steaks up a notch" so "you don't need a knife"; an "(almost overly) attentive wait staff" ensures a "special experience", delivering "spicy, juicy", "decadent comfort foods" via "signature synchronized service"; "your wallet and cardiologist will be mad, but your stomach will thank you."

### Doña Maria
20 | 12 | 20 | $16

*3205 N. Tenaya Way (Cheyenne Ave.), 702-656-1600*
*910 S. Las Vegas Blvd. (Charleston Blvd.), 702-382-6538*
*www.donamariatamales.com*

■ "*Arriba, arriba* to Doña Maria" for "authentic", "hard-to-find" "handmade tamales" ("in three varieties: pork, chicken and cheese") and "excellent margaritas" "with plenty of tequila" to wash down "the best" *muy caliente* chipotle salsa; "if you can get past the fluorescent lights" and the "tacky, tacky decor" at these "relaxed" "old favorite" Mexicans in Central Vegas and the Northwest, the "warm, familial staff" is "friendly, even to gringos."

### Don Miguel's
▽ 22 | 17 | 22 | $21

*Orleans Hotel & Casino, 4500 W. Tropicana Ave. (Arville St.), 702-365-7111; www.orleanscasino.com*

■ "*Que bueno!!!!*" – "get off the Strip and eat with the locals" at this Tex-Mex "find" in the Orleans Hotel just west of the madness, a "pleasant surprise" for "good lunch specials", "wonderful fajitas" and "great margaritas", all at a "modest price for what you get"; there's "no long wait" here, but even if there were, the tortilla making display would keep you entertained while you cool your jets.

### Draft House Barn & Casino ●
▽ 17 | 14 | 16 | $14

*4543 N. Rancho Dr. (Craig Rd.), 702-645-1404*

■ "If you're from Wisconsin, you'll feel right at home" "slopping it down" with the rest of the Cheeseheads at this 24/7 Northwest "shrine" to the Green Bay Packers where ya gotta "try the fried pickles", "the delicious brat sandwich with sauerkraut" and other "good, hearty" Midwestern specialties at "reasonable prices"; wash it all down with one of four homemade beers, the list of which will expand when the microbrewery opens next door late in 2003.

### Dragon Noodle Co.
– | – | – | M

*Monte Carlo Resort & Casino, 3770 Las Vegas Blvd. S. (bet. Harmon & Tropicana Aves.), 702-730-7965; www.dragonnoodleco.com*

Dining dragons will dig this upmarket casual Pan-Asian in the Strip's Monte Carlo run by the folks at Market City Caffe; the extensive lunch and dinner menus are heavy with the namesake comfort food, plus rice, dim sum and other savories complemented by a dozen well selected wines by the glass, a variety of sakes and an extensive list of brews from a tea bar that makes for an inviting late-night stop.

### Dragon Sushi
– | – | – | M

*Chinatown Plaza, 4115 Spring Mountain Rd. (bet. Arville St. & Valley View Blvd.), 702-368-4336*

"Quietly flying under the radar of the local sushi scene", this tiny, "creative" spot west of the Strip in the Chinatown Mall slices "very fresh" fish in "generous" portions; fanatics "flock" here, maintaining "it's worth the drive" off the Strip to "save" on "unusual items" like "the shooter, a jalapeño/spicy tuna creation", which might have you breathing fire like the joint's namesake.

### Drai's on the Strip
23 | 24 | 22 | $53

*Barbary Coast Hotel & Casino, 3595 Las Vegas Blvd. S. (Flamingo Rd.), 702-737-0555; www.draislasvegas.com*
When you're dining in "luxury" on "fab" New French fare, it "boggles the mind to know that in a few hours the tables will be pushed aside and the party of the year will go on Wednesday–Saturday", but that's how restaurateur Victor Drai wrings the most out of his "sexy "gem hidden" in the "improbable basement" of that "dump", the Barbary Coast; "good-looking", "cool travelers" go for "candlelit" "tête-à-têtes" amid "over-the-top" "big cat decor", though foodie fogies fuss about "noise" and "just ok meals."

### Egg & I, The
22 | 11 | 19 | $14

*West Lake Plaza, 4533 W. Sahara Ave. (bet. Arville St. & Decatur Blvd.), 702-364-9686; www.eggandi.com*
"Locals" preen over this "always crowded", "friendly, efficient" Traditional American west of the Strip where the "inexpensive", "voluminous and tasty egg plates" get an ova-tion from a "Vegas that still loves" the "great breakfasts and brunch", despite "cheap country decor"; egg-ceptional for omelettes "the morning after", it "may not be the best place for the pancake people, but that's why it's not called Pancake & I"; N.B. a family-friendly murder mystery dinner show plays Wednesday–Saturday.

### EIFFEL TOWER
22 | 26 | 22 | $69

*Paris Las Vegas, 3655 Las Vegas Blvd. S. (bet. Flamingo Rd. & Harmon Ave.), 702-948-6937; www.parislasvegas.com*
"Look down your nose at the people on the Strip" from atop the "half-size re-creation" of the Parisian landmark; the "fabulous view of the Bellagio fountains" complements a "marvelous" French menu and "reserve wines" "similar" to those found "in Toulouse and Cannes"; beyond the "panorama", coin-counting connoisseurs crack "the bill is as high as the elevator will take you" for "food as phony as the tower", with all-too-authentic servers who "treat you like you just parked your mobile home" outside.

### 808
24 | 23 | 21 | $52

*Caesars Palace, 3570 Las Vegas Blvd. S. (Flamingo Rd.), 702-731-7731; www.caesars.com*
Maui "meets Paris", Florence, Canton and other spots at Jean-Marie Josselin's "innovative" Hawaiian "hidden in a corner of Caesars Palace" where the "very ono" (native for 'delicious') seafood is whipped up with an "interesting mix of many ethnic" influences; the "chic", "minimalist" decor matches the fare's "fantastic presentation", but

though the "excellent appetizers" and "creative" fish dishes are "interesting" enough, combined with "underwhelming" service, they're "not quite worth the clams."

### Elements                    ▽ 25 | 22 | 26 | $56

*Aladdin Resort & Casino, 3667 Las Vegas Blvd. S. (Harmon Ave.), 702-785-9003; www.aladdincasino.com*

■ "The four elements" are the basis of the "snappy menu" at the Aladdin's "sophisticated" "jewel", where "attractively plated" "steaks so tender you don't need a knife" and "delicious" seafood are supplemented by a 600-bottle wine list overseen by "gracious servers"; the "theme plays into" a "savvy decor" featuring a "waterfall", a fire wall, earthy "plants" and the wind? – perhaps that's represented by the "noise" in the air from "the band in the casino."

### EMERIL'S NEW ORLEANS FISH HOUSE          24 | 19 | 22 | $51

*MGM Grand Hotel, 3799 Las Vegas Blvd. S. (Tropicana Ave.), 702-891-7374; www.emerils.com*

◪ Bam-fans swear "you can almost smell the Mississippi" at the MGM's "fantastic fish house", a "charming N'Awlins bistro" where "ragin' Cajun" and Creole are presented by Lagasse's "smart" synchronized servers; the joint's "packed to the gills" with "tourists" so "you gotta like noise", while noise from the "underenthused" implies "Emeril needs to go back in the kitchen and out of the limelight"; to avoid the hype, "grab a bowl of gumbo and a drink at the bar."

### Empress Court               23 | 22 | 21 | $45

*Caesars Palace, 3570 Las Vegas Blvd. S. (Flamingo Rd.), 702-731-7731; www.caesars.com*

■ "Great Cantonese" is "elegantly presented" to the few "wealthy" imperials who have discovered this "stunning" Strip court "overlooking the fabulous Caesars pool"; desert dwellers marvel at seafood that is "unbelievably fresh" in a "quiet" escape with "impeccable" service, but commoners cry over "astronomical" prices.

### Fasolini's Pizza Cafe ⊠         ▽ 25 | 18 | 23 | $19

*Decatur Crossings, 222 S. Decatur Blvd. (Meadows Ln.), 702-877-0071*

■ "Outstanding food at a wonderful price" is the draw at this "excellent" "family-owned" "Italian diner", a "great little find" in a West Side shopping center where some of the "best pizza west of Chicago" and "wonderful meatball sandwiches" come by way of "friendly service"; though it "can be a bit slow at times", "the food is worth the wait."

### Fatburger ◑                 22 | 9 | 14 | $9

*3763 Las Vegas Blvd. S. (bet. Harmon & Tropicana Aves.), 702-736-4733*
*Lucky's Shopping Ctr., 2845 S. Nellis Blvd. (Vegas Valley Dr.), 702-457-1727 ⊟*

(continued)
**Fatburger**
*4525 N. Rancho Dr. (Craig Rd.), 702-658-4604* 🖰
*Santa Fe Station Hotel, 4949 N. Rancho Dr. (bet. Lone Mountain Rd. & Rainbow Blvd.), 702-839-9610* 🖰
*4851 W. Charleston Blvd. (Decatur Blvd.), 702-870-4933* 🖰
*6775 W. Flamingo Rd. (Rainbow Blvd.), 702-889-9009* 🖰
*4663 E. Sunset Rd. (bet. Green Valley Pkwy. & Mountain Vista Rd.), Henderson, 702-898-7200*
*Green Valley Ranch Station Hotel, 2300 Paseo Verde Pkwy. (Green Valley Pkwy.), Henderson, 702-617-2209*
*Sunset Station Hotel, 1301 W. Sunset Rd. (Stephanie St.), Henderson, 702-450-7820*
*Texas Station Hotel, 2101 Texas Star Ln. (bet. Lake Mead Blvd. & Rancho Dr.), North Las Vegas, 702-638-4175*
*www.fatburger.net*
◪ Some space cowboys say "the best burgers in the galaxy" can be had at these "great American fast-food" "joints" "for sloppy eating" citywide 24/7; "fat, hot, juicy", "tender" "old-school patties at their most decadent" are "cooked up fresh" "with just the right hint of grease" to be devoured alongside thick or thin "tasty" "fries" and bona fide "ice cream milkshakes"; skinflint feeders find it "a little pricey" and the "decor and service are what you would expect, but who cares?" – this "scuzzy place" "rocks."

**Feast, The** 15 11 15 $14
*Boulder Station Hotel, 4111 Boulder Hwy. (Lamb Blvd.), 702-432-7777*
*Palace Station Hotel, 2411 W. Sahara Ave. (Rancho Dr.), 702-367-2411*
*www.stationcasinos.com*
◪ Like their sister Stations, these "locals" casinos on the East Side and west of the Strip offer a "great bargain" in "very fresh-tasting" American action-station smorgasbords and "nice salad bars"; of course they're "not fancy" and suffer the common complaint that "quantity wins over quality", but there's "always a good selection and decent pricing", so if you're losing at the gambling tables, these groaning tables will "do in a pinch."

**Feast Around the World Buffet** 17 13 15 $14
*Sunset Station Hotel, 1301 W. Sunset Rd. (Stephanie St.), Henderson, 702-547-7814*
*Texas Station Hotel, 2101 Texas Star Ln. (bet. Lake Mead Blvd. & Rancho Dr.), North Las Vegas, 702-631-1000*
*www.stationcasinos.com*
◪ "Local" dining room chair travelers seeking "value" find a "typical" Eclectic buffet at these "very pleasant" North Las Vegas and Henderson casino chain all-you-can-eats, where a "great" global variety suggests they are "good places to go when you don't know what you want"; those

accustomed to Strip spreads say "there are better in Vegas", citing a "long wait" for merely the "same old, same old."

### Fellini's
22 | 18 | 21 | $39

*Stratosphere Hotel & Tower, 2000 Las Vegas Blvd. S. (north of Sahara Ave.), 702-380-7777*
*5555 W. Charleston Blvd. (bet. Decatur & Jones Blvds.), 702-870-9999* ⊠
*www.fellinislv.com*

■ Only six years young but considered "a touch of the old" "*Goodfellas*" Sin City, these "cozy" Northern Italian joints "rival Little Italy" for "excellent" fare and "wonderful" service; "the decor could use a face-lift", but menu additions from further down The Boot keep your attention on your plate at the Stratosphere, while "live piano" and a fireplace lend "romance" to the West Side where, if the setting doesn't interest you, the clientele might: "it's not unusual to dine next to the mayor" and other "local bigwigs."

### Ferraro's
24 | 18 | 23 | $40

*5900 W. Flamingo Rd. (bet. Decatur & Jones Blvds.), 702-364-5300; www.ferraroslasvegas.com*

■ "It's the Rat Pack all over again" so "dress up and enjoy yourself" at this "intimate", "romantic" West Side Italian boasting a back-when "Vegas look and feel"; the Ferraro family "treats its regulars well" with "quite attentive service" (Gino "visits every table and talks with patrons") and "huge portions" of "rich, meaty" signature osso buco and "gnocchi that melts in your mouth", and though longtimers note "the decor seems to be getting a little tired", it remains "a must when wanting to get away from the Strip."

### Festival Buffet
▽ 19 | 14 | 15 | $14

*Fiesta Rancho, 2400 N. Rancho Dr. (Lake Mead Blvd.), 702-631-7000; www.fiestacasino.com*

■ Serve yourself all you can stand from a "wonderful selection" that includes "ribs, sushi, fish 'n' chips, enchiladas and milkshakes" at this "good" Eclectic Northwest buffet "frequented by locals" for weekend prime rib nights and the addition of crabs on Friday, even though fussy fressers feel this foodfest "used to be better."

### Fiamma Trattoria
– | – | – | E

*MGM Grand Hotel, 3799 Las Vegas Blvd. S. (Tropicana Ave.), 702-891-7600; www.brguestrestaurants.com*

Pitching in with the MGM's ongoing effort to upscale its restaurants, Manhattan's Stephen Hanson splashes down in Vegas with an outpost of his upscale Italian in a modestly remodeled spot formerly occupied by über-hip olio!; stylish turns on traditional offerings spice up a menu heavy with comfort foods, and a chic bar attracts a trendy crowd to curl up near a modern masterpiece of a fireplace while sipping cocktails like the Twice Tempted, a spiced Sidecar.

## Fiore Steakhouse　23 | 23 | 23 | $53

*Rio All-Suite Hotel & Casino, 3700 W. Flamingo Rd. (bet. I-15 &*
*Valley View Blvd.), 702-777-7702; www.playrio.com*

■ "Personalized service" complements "very special
preparation of Northern Italian specialties" and "excellent
steaks" at this "soothing" Rio restaurant west of the Strip;
don't let your handbag get in the way of a "romantic" meal –
just put it down on the "side bench they provide", start your
meal with "delicious" "fresh baked breads in every flavor",
and top it off with "out-of-this-world desserts" and a smoke
on the "great cigar terrace"; an "escape from the lights
and sounds of the casino", "it's expensive, but worth it."

## Firefly ●　– | – | – | M

*3900 Paradise Rd. (bet. Flamingo Rd. & Twain Ave.), 702-369-3971*

Tapas-style dining finally takes flight in this buffet-heavy
town with this bright, new Spaniard, a late-night, indoor-
outdoor nosh spot by two Mon Ami Gabi alumni, Ramon
Triay and chef John Simmons, just east of the Strip near
Restaurant Row; flit through tastes from artichoke toasts and
mango babyback ribs to tuna sashimi and Parmesan frites
while getting lit on a pitcher of the housemade sangria.

## Firelight Buffet　15 | 16 | 17 | $13

*Sam's Town Hotel, 5111 Boulder Hwy. (Flamingo Rd.),*
*702-454-8044; www.samstownlv.com*

◪ "For a mid-level casino", this "easy-on-the-budget" East
Side buffet "exceeds expectations" with an Eclectic slew
of live-cooking stations turning out "better-than-average"
eats; still, it's not lighting any fires with foodies who label it
a "so-so" "trough filled with starches and moist meat", and
clean-air proponents pout that it "so reeks of cigarette
smoke, it's hard to evaluate the food."

## Fleming's　25 | 23 | 23 | $50

*8721 W. Charleston Blvd. (bet. Durango Dr. & Rampart Blvd.),*
*702-838-4774; www.flemingssteakhouse.com*

■ "Who needs the Strip?" wonder "suburban" "locals"
when the West Side has this "incredible" "place to go" for
"huge" "steaks done just right", wonderful side dishes that
are large enough to share", plus "some exceptional meals
for non–meat eaters"; an "upscale and expensive" arm of
the Outback chain, it's "clubby but not exclusive", boasting
a "busy bar" and an "awesome wine list" including 100 by
the glass preferred by a "flawless" staff that "knows the
difference between a Chardonnay and a Viognier."

## Florida Cafe　▽ 24 | 8 | 18 | $15

*Howard Johnson Hotel, 1401 Las Vegas Blvd. S.*
*(bet. Charleston & Oakley Blvds.), 702-385-3013;*
*www.floridacafecuban.com*

■ A "nice change of pace that you'll never find", this "Cuban
treat" is "the best place to eat if you are tired of acting like

a high roller"; "don't be put off by its location in a Howard Johnson near the hostels" in Central Vegas, or by the bare-bones digs, as the "inexpensive" "locals' secret" serves up "ropa vieja, Cubano sandwiches and *moros y cristianos* [white rice with black beans] that are not to be missed."

### Food Express ◑
| – | – | – | I |

*2003 S. Decatur Blvd. (Sahara Ave.), 702-870-1595*
Few respondents have discovered this "awesome hole-in-the-wall" Chinese in a strip mall west of the Strip, where busloads of Asian tourists arrive to order from the hand-written erasable menu supplementing the extensive printed English version; a live tank adds swimming selections to the Cantonese menu and late-night dining attracts the locals, but at any hour, "don't expect much from the service."

### Francesco's
| 23 | 19 | 22 | $46 |

*Treasure Island Hotel, 3300 Las Vegas Blvd. S. (Spring Mountain Rd.), 702-894-7223; www.treasureisland.com*
■ "A nice, quiet place to dine in a very noisy city" and a very noisy casino, this "elegant" "gem" in Treasure Island "serves food that tastes like what one finds in Italy", i.e. "the real thing, not the new stuff", in a space adorned with artwork by Vegas headliners; the crew in the open kitchen plates "wonderful sauces and flavors", but they could use a heavier hand – "the portions are very small for the price."

### Frank & Fina's Cocina
| – | – | – | I |

*5550 W. Charleston Blvd. (Jones Blvd.), 702-878-8669*
An A-frame "hidden treasure" in the Northwest is the site for this unassuming but "authentic" Mexican tended by the Pacheco clan; hearty combos (try your burrito chimichanga-style), a brief but tasty all-day breakfast menu, plenty of vegetarian options and passable wine margaritas make it "worth the experience" for everyone from students to hikers returning hungry from a day in Red Rock Canyon.

### French Market Buffet
| 19 | 15 | 17 | $17 |

*Orleans Hotel & Casino, 4500 W. Tropicana Ave. (Arville St.), 702-365-7111; www.orleanscasino.com*
◪ "The crawfish are excellent if you are up for shelling them yourself", and why wouldn't you be when you're dishing up most of your own Eclectic chow anyway at this "value buffet" west of the Strip?; "Cajun-Creole favorites", Chinese, Mexican, Mongolian and other treats "add imagination" "compared with the run of casino" gut busters, though all-you-can-eaters attest that the spread is still "middling."

### Fresh Market Square Buffet
| 17 | 14 | 18 | $16 |

*Harrah's Las Vegas, 3475 Las Vegas Blvd. S. (Flamingo Rd.), 702-369-5000; www.harrahs.com*
◪ A "great place for breakfast", a "reasonable lunch" or an "ok" dinner, particularly if you're with "kids", is Harrah's

"typical quick and cheap" Continental "buffet with all the fixings" "from all nations and lots of 'em"; ignore decor that "needs a tasteful update", "go for the bananas Foster" and sample the rest of the "good selection", courtesy of a staff that is "always making sure you have enough of everything", "keeping you satisfied . . . and very bloated."

### Full Ho Chinese Cuisine    − − − 1

*240 N. Jones Blvd. (I-95), 702-878-2378*
Locals love the Northwest's "best" panfried won tons and chow mein at this "great" if "greasy" "Chinese joint" that "has withstood the test of time" since way back in 1991 with "tasty" dishes such as grandfather chicken; a staff that's "very friendly in that gruff way" might leave you wondering "if you're being catered to or bossed around", but it's "authentic, that's for sure."

### Gaetano's    24  22  22  $35

*10271 S. Eastern Ave. (Siena Heights Dr.), Henderson, 702-361-1661*
■ Rory and Gaetano Palmeri are "owners who care about their customers", keeping their "personal attention" "on premises" "to ensure your dining experience" at their "warm", "wonderful" Northern Italian newcomer in Green Valley; with "delicious" menu items like "incredible gnocchi and butternut squash ravioli", 10 to 15 "tempting specials" per night and those "pleasant" proprietors prompting you to eat, "no one goes hungry here."

### Gallaghers Steakhouse    23  18  20  $51

*New York-New York Hotel & Casino, 3790 Las Vegas Blvd. S. (Tropicana Ave.), 702-740-6450; www.nynyhotelcasino.com*
◪ "What a piece of meat" "moo" "boisterous" munchers at New York-New York's "manly" "reproduction" of a "venerable" Manhattan "original" where "excellent" "dry-aged steaks" come to table "still sizzling from the grill" along with "showstopping" sides; Gotham "natives" beef that the "inconsistent entrees" are "nothing like the namesake's", but the "noise" and the "overpricing" are pure Big Apple.

### Gandhi India Cuisine    ▽ 23  14  16  $22

*4080 Paradise Rd. (Flamingo Rd.), 702-734-0094; www.gandhicuisine.com*
◪ "Authentic Indian cuisine" lures locals to this area favorite east of the Strip where the sprawling "lunch buffet is good if you're not sure what to get" from a menu as wide as the Ganges; if "some food is excellent and some is not", carb cravers can't go wrong with the 10 varieties of clay oven bread, which should hold 'em over when the "service isn't so quick"; N.B. Las Vegas Boulevardiers won't have to travel for their curry when a second location opens in the Polo Plaza at year's end.

### Garden Court Buffet
– | – | – | I

*Main Street Station Hotel, 200 N. Main St. (Ogden Ave.), 702-387-1896; www.mainstreetcasino.com*

"The best buffet Downtown", according to some, is "the best buffet in Las Vegas when you combine price, quality and variety" at this undiscovered, "gorgeous" garden-themed gorgefest at the Main Street Station; "above-average" Eclectic selections from nine cooking stations include the standards, plus Pacific Rim specialties, wood-fired pizza and pasta and a seafood extravaganza on Friday nights.

### Garden of the Dragon
– | – | – | M

*Las Vegas Hilton Hotel, 3000 Paradise Rd. (bet. Desert Inn Rd. & Karen Ave.), 702-732-5111; www.lvhilton.com*

"Good", "moderately priced" Szechuan, Peking-style, Mongolian and Cantonese, including signature salt-and-pepper shrimp, remains a bit of a secret at this Chinese overlooking the gardens of Benihana Village east of the Strip; however, the "nice people" on staff can't cool down firebreathing foodies who feel it's "not too original."

### Garduño's
22 | 19 | 17 | $23

*Fiesta Rancho, 2400 N. Rancho Dr. (Lake Mead Blvd.), 702-631-7000; www.fiestacasino.com*
*Palms Casino Hotel, 4321 W. Flamingo Rd. (Arville St.), 702-942-7777; www.palms.com*

◪ Amigos "love the guacamole prepared tableside", "great fajitas" and "many choices at the salsa bar", particularly those that "make them sweat", at these "reliable" Mexican/Southwesterners; the Northwest is "quite a ways from the Strip, but for locals, that's a good thing", while the west-of-Stripper "can get raucous on weekends"; the "staggering variety of margaritas" will lift you into "tequila heaven", if you can get the "slow" staff to bring your drinks.

### Gaylord's
20 | 19 | 19 | $37

*Rio All-Suite Hotel & Casino, 3700 W. Flamingo Rd. (bet. I-15 & Valley View Blvd.), 702-777-2277; www.gaylords.com*

◪ "Goodness gracious me!" – in a city not exactly known for its South Asian cuisine, this "new arrival" from Northern California west of the Strip is "verrrry interrrresting"; "solid" mesquite-fired Tandoori kebabs, "delicious lamb curry" and other "excellent, authentic Indian" dishes, including a "great weekend brunch", are delivered "in a very attractive setting" overlooking the Rio pool by servers who waiver wildly from "amazing" to "confused."

### Geisha Steakhouse
– | – | – | E

*Townhouse Shopping Ctr., 3751 E. Desert Inn Rd. (Sandhill Rd.), 702-451-9814*

No, they're not geishas doing the slicing and dicing here, but this East Side "hibachi experience", "a Vegas institution" since 1972, is still "great" for Japanese tabletop cooking and "plenty of it"; the "sauces are actually better than those at the big chains", and if the decor is "bare-bones", who needs all that flash when it's otherwise "like Benihana's, only friendlier and cheaper"?

### Golden Steer Steakhouse          ▽ 22 | 20 | 22 | $47 |

*308 W. Sahara Ave. (bet. Fairfield Ave. & Tam Dr.), 702-384-4470; www.goldensteerlv.com*

◪ "The Fred Flintstone cut of prime rib will tip the table" and "the twice-baked potatoes are about half the size of a regulation NFL football" at this fortysomething "throwback to the Rat Pack days" west of the Strip where "good ol' boys" get their "thick, juicy steak" fix; as for the beef bonanza's "bordello atmosphere", "you can almost picture the old Mob making deals" amid all that "red velvet and leather" left over from when the "excellent servers who've been there forever" were still wet behind the ears.

### GRAND LUX CAFE ●          22 | 20 | 19 | $25 |

*Venetian Hotel, 3355 Las Vegas Blvd. S. (bet. Flamingo & Spring Mountain Rds.), 702-414-3888; www.venetian.com*

■ "Great food in epic proportions" is "perfect for the 4 AM feeding when you get in from a night of partying" at the Venetian's "always-busy" 24/7 "coffee shop on steroids"; sure, it's just a "jazzed-up", "noisy" "next-generation Cheesecake Factory", but it's "pretty darn impressive" and "works for all the same reasons" as its parent chain: it ain't luxe, but fans grandly "rave" about "unbelievable variety" at a "reliable, informal dining spot" where "everything is great" and "everyone is happy."

### Grape Street          23 | 19 | 19 | $27 |

*Summerhill Plaza, 7501 W. Lake Mead Blvd. (Buffalo Dr.), 702-228-9463*

■ "From the vine came the Grape"; a "wonderful wine list" with 75 by the glass poured in flights by a "knowledgeable staff" at "not a high markup" leads oenophiles to "crowd" this "fabulous" Mediterranean "escape" in the Northwest; it's a "nice little place" for dining as well on signature chicken Gorgonzola pasta, "must-have" baked Brie and a "chocolate fondue [that] rocks"; "a seat outside" away from the "loud" dining room "makes the experience."

### Guadalajara          18 | 17 | 17 | $17 |

*Boulder Station Hotel, 4111 Boulder Hwy. (Lamb Blvd.), 702-432-7777*
*Palace Station Hotel, 2411 W. Sahara Ave. (Rancho Dr.), 702-367-2411*
*Sunset Station Hotel, 1301 W. Sunset Rd. (Stephanie St.), Henderson, 702-547-7777*
*www.stationcasinos.com*

■ "Good, reliable Mexican" is on the platter at these Station Casino cost-conscious mini-chain cantinas, where "the price is great for the amount of food you get"; the "great salsa bar" that's 18 varieties strong and "excellent", cheap margaritas keep thrifty caballeros "coming back for more."

### Habib's Persian Cuisine ☒   ∇ | 17 | 14 | 15 | $27 |
*Sahara Pavilion, 4750 W. Sahara Ave. (Decatur Blvd.),*
*702-870-0860; www.habibspersiancuisine.com*
■ "The best dolmas in the world", say stuffed grape leaf lovers, just might be "hidden in the back corner of a strip mall" west of the Strip, at Habib Asad's "excellent Persian" "treasure"; a menu featuring beef kebabs and ice cream with rosewater is "limited" but "unique" for these parts, though the gyrations of the weekend belly dancer are not so far removed from the work of local showgirls; N.B. take home a treat from the adjacent Middle Eastern market.

### Halal Restaurant Tandoor   – | – | – | M |
*730 E. Flamingo Rd. (bet. Paradise Rd. & Swenson St.),*
*702-894-9334*
Its new owner has changed its name, but this cramped storefront east of the Strip still serves Pakistani and Indian signatures; it's just about the only joint in Vegas without a liquor license, so you'll have to settle for a mango lassi with your vegetable samosas and tandoori chicken in the casual room frequented by UNLV academics, conventioneers and members of the local South Asian community.

### Hamada ●   21 | 19 | 20 | $36 |
*Flamingo Las Vegas, 3555 Las Vegas Blvd. S. (Flamingo Rd.),*
*702-733-3455*
*365 Hughes Center Dr. (Paradise Rd.), 702-733-3005*
*J.W. Marriott, 221 N. Rampart Blvd. (Summerlin Pkwy.),*
*702-869-7710*
*Luxor Hotel, 3900 Las Vegas Blvd. S. (Tropicana Ave.),*
*702-262-4548*
*MGM Grand Hotel, 3799 Las Vegas Blvd. S. (Tropicana Ave.),*
*702-891-3016*
*Polo Towers Plaza, 3743 Las Vegas Blvd. S. (Harmon Ave.),*
*702-736-1984*
*Rio All-Suite Hotel & Casino, 3700 W. Flamingo Rd. (bet. I-15 &*
*Valley View Blvd.), 702-777-2770*
*Stratosphere Hotel & Tower, 2000 Las Vegas Blvd. S.*
*(north of Sahara Ave.), 702-380-7777*
*www.hamadaofjapan.com*
▣ It's "awesome" to "eat sushi into the early morning" amid "celebs", "bartenders, cocktail waitresses and showgirls" in the relocated East Side flagship of this "institution" offering "different styles of Japanese cooking including teppan" to enjoy with your "raucous" group in the new tatami room; at the other branches, hungry gamblers score "nice", "easy" bites "right off the casino floor"; "this ain't Tokyo, Toto", and it's also "not Nobu, but for half the price and a lot less attitude", it "does a noble job."

### Happy Days Diner
　　　　　　　　　–　–　–　I

*512 Nevada Hwy. (Ave. B), Boulder City, 702-294-2653*
Rock backwards around the clock to the "1950s" at this
"authentic", "old-fashioned" "diner with a small-town feel"
"in the heart" of clean, green Boulder City; relax in the
preconceived ambiance of one of the nation's first planned
communities (and the only Nevada town without gambling)
while munching three squares a day that include the
expected burgers, fries and milkshakes, as well as the
unexpected veggie burger.

### Hard Rock Cafe ●
　　　　　　　　　16　21　16　$24

*4475 Paradise Rd. (Harmon Ave.), 702-733-7625;*
*www.hardrock.com*
☑ "Sit, eat and shout at your neighbor" at this "celebration
of rock" east of the Strip, "another in a chain" "crowded"
with parents popping "Advil" and "kids" chair "dancing to
'YMCA'", "buying T-shirts" and downing "classic" American
grub plunked down by waiters who "think they're music
stars"; this "party" is "way too loud", but "when you want a
burger, it might as well be a really good one" – otherwise,
it's "a wasted trip", "unless you're young, cheap and don't
appreciate good service."

### Harley-Davidson Cafe
　　　　　　　　　13　20　15　$24

*3725 Las Vegas Blvd. S. (Harmon Ave.), 702-740-4555;*
*www.harley-davidsoncafe.com*
☑ "Get your motor running, head [out] on the Strip", looking
for adventure and some of "the best mac 'n' cheese in town"
at this "hog" "shrine" with "hangin' Harleys cruising around
the ceiling" beneath "biker buddies" and "moto mamas"
"chowing down" on Traditional US of A grub; the "food is
tolerable", the service is "spotty", but the "memorabilia"
is "to die for."

### Harrie's Bagelmania ∅
　　　　　　　　　–　–　–　I

*Twain Ctr., 855 E. Twain Ave. (Swenson St.), 702-369-3322;*
*harries.tripod.com*
"Boxers, referees and has-been headliners" get theirs
with a schmear at this "funky" "hangout" east of the Strip,
a "friendly", "old-fashioned deli" with "quality" bagels,
"good eggs", "nice sandwiches" and "no atmosphere" to
speak of; that's as it should be, say "famous old-timers" –
this "change from a hotel coffee shop" feels "just like
you want" it to.

### Hawaiian Plantation House
　　　　　　　　　19　20　20　$32

*10940 S. Eastern Ave. (Horizon Ridge Pkwy.), Henderson,*
*702-990-6341*
☑ It's hard to imagine "Hawaiian-infused culinary creations"
in the middle of the Mojave, but former Kapalua chef Craig
Connole manages to "bring all the memories" of the islands
to Green Valley's "find off the Strip", with "a great selection

of seafood and sauces", plus "refreshing and flavorful" salads at "moderate cost"; however, the "fun, tropical atmosphere" threatens to "outshine cuisine" that "may be a bit extreme for some" desert diners who find "nothing good enough to contemplate a repeat visit."

### Hill Top House Supper Club　　　　–　–　–　M
*3500 N. Rancho Dr. (Jay Ave.), 702-645-9904*
It's "like going to your uncle's for dinner" (if the guy were an "old Las Vegas" cook, that is), at this Traditional American eatery in a converted "1950s-era" home in the Northwest; it has not changed much since its opening in 1972, so the "succulent" "fried lobster", "great steaks and chops", panfried chicken, "small and tasty salad bar", "hot, fresh baked bread" and retro frogs' legs, all prepared "fresh to order", are just as "fun" to eat as when the Wojtowicz family first started cooking.

### Hilton Steakhouse　　　　　　　　–　–　–　E
*Las Vegas Hilton Hotel, 3000 Paradise Rd. (bet. Desert Inn Rd. & Karen Ave.), 702-732-5111; www.lvhilton.com*
Dating from the year James Bond swaggered about the hotel in *Diamonds Are Forever,* this "terrific", "old-time" surf 'n' turfer east of the Strip remains a "solid performer in a town full of performers"; when the "friendly staff" brings you your martini – shaken, not stirred, of course – the "filet to die for" will have you raising your glass and cheering, "very good, Mr. Hilton."

### Hugo's Cellar　　　　　　　　25　21　24　$49
*Four Queens Casino Hotel, 202 Fremont St. (Casino Center Blvd.), 702-385-4011; www.fourqueens.com*
◼ "When you want to impress someone", step "down the stairs to the class [act] of Downtown", a "delightfully retro" Continental "Rat Pack"-er with "romantic ambiance"; "the staff will pamper you from start to finish" with "tableside salad tossed" "to your specifications", "plentiful" steak and lobster, a "top-shelf wine list" and "a long-stemmed rose" for female guests; and if modernists mutter the act seems "tired", faithful "cellar dwellers" counter it's "dated, but aging gracefully."

### Hush Puppy　　　　　　　▽　20　13　18　$20
*1820 N. Nellis Blvd. (Lake Mead Blvd.), 702-438-0005*
*7185 W. Charleston Blvd. (bet. Buffalo Dr. & Rainbow Blvd.), 702-363-5988*
◼ "If you like it fried, this is the place to go" exclaim expat Southerners who periodically "stop by to eat all of the catfish in the house" at these West and East Side Dixie specialists; although "good, basic, down-home" seafood is the main catch, there are other "hard-to-find" selections such as "the best green tomato relish" and the namesake dish "served hot with real butter" in a "friendly", "laid-back atmosphere."

### Hyakumi
25 | 20 | 22 | $44

*Caesars Palace, 3570 Las Vegas Blvd. S. (Flamingo Rd.),*
*702-731-7110; www.caesars.com*

■ "Within the tumult of a large casino, this lovely oasis", with "nice lighting and bamboo", is "one of the best places" on the Strip for "gorgeous appetizers" followed by "deftly prepared" sushi and "delicious" teppanyaki "cooked at the table" "with flair" by "charming chefs"; watching the guys with ginsus "flipping shrimp tails into diners' shirt pockets is as entertaining as the Nemo exhibit down the hall."

### Ice House Lounge ◑
– | – | – | M

*650 S. Main St. (Bonneville Ave.), 702-315-2570;*
*www.icehouselasvegas.com*

"So far, the decor outshines" the New American menu at this "sleek Downtown tavern" sporting a "modern" Miami look; "office workers and urban hipsters" slink beyond the waterfall on the pink-and-blue-lit stucco exterior to a Dino-esque duplex outfitted in stainless steel, old Vegas pics, two patios and bars made out of – you guessed it – real frozen stuff, during happy hour and when Saturday's DJ spins; the kitchen's door has been spinning too since the summer 2003 opening, as chefs have come and gone.

### Il Fornaio ◑
20 | 19 | 18 | $32

*New York-New York Hotel & Casino, 3790 Las Vegas Blvd. S.*
*(Tropicana Ave.), 702-650-6500*
*Green Valley Ranch Station Hotel, 2300 Paseo Verde Pkwy.*
*(Green Valley Pkwy.), Henderson, 702-492-0054*
*www.ilfornaio.com*

■ "You could make a meal" just out of the "superb bread" from the attached bakeries of these "pleasant" Strip and Green Valley Northern Italians; but "if you're craving" "big portions" of "simple pasta and a nice glass of wine" that are "darn good for a chain", these ovens will stoke your fires for full meals too; at the New York-New York locale, the pseudo-"outdoor" dining offers a "people-watching" "view of Central Park", or at least a reasonable facsimile thereof.

### India Palace
– | – | – | M

*505 E. Twain Ave. (bet. Paradise Rd. & Swenson St.),*
*702-796-4177; www.indiapalacelasvegas.com*

"Gandhi himself would be impressed" with the "authentic Indian food" found east of the Strip at this "comfortable" "treasure" featuring "gorgeous garlic naan and aromatic curries"; you can "park right in front", so "don't get scared away" by the "dingy location."

### Inka Si Señor
▽ 25 | 19 | 24 | $18

*2797 S. Maryland Pkwy. (Sahara Ave.), 702-731-0826;*
*www.sisenor.org*

■ Though not many respondents have discovered this young east-of-Strip Peruvian imported directly from Lima, those who have say *si* to the "variety" on a Spanish-influenced menu that showcases *crema de frijol* (creamy bean soup), plus seviches and other "excellent fresh seafood"; an "enjoyable and relaxed atmosphere" and "handsome, flirtatious waiters" don't hurt either.

### In-N-Out Burger ●⌿⊟    ▽ 28 | 12 | 17 | $6 |
*Charleston Commons Shopping Ctr., 51 N. Nellis Blvd. (bet. Charleston Blvd. & Sir George Dr.)*
*9230 E. Eastern Ave. (Serene Ave.)*
*4888 Industrial Rd. (Tropicana Ave.)*
*1960 Rock Springs Dr. (Lake Mead Blvd.)*
*2900 W. Sahara Ave. (bet. Paseo del Prado & Richfield Blvd.)*
*4705 S. Maryland Pkwy. (bet. Flamingo Rd. & Tropicana Ave.)*
*1051 W. Sunset Rd. (Marks St.), Henderson*
*800-786-1000*
*www.in-n-out.com*
■ They'd "walk a mile each way from the Strip in a gambling-induced stupor", they'd "take a cab through the drive-in", they'd even "wait 15 minutes" for "burgers made to order on fabulous buns" with "fresh-cut fries" and "thick, creamy shakes" at just about "the best" quick patty stop "in the U.S."; or at least that's what hyperbolic fans "drooling just thinking about" this "friendly" "chain" claim; it might be more like "in-n-wait", but "you will never eat" "at any other fast food place again."

### Isis    23 | 23 | 24 | $54 |
*Luxor Hotel, 3900 Las Vegas Blvd. S. (Tropicana Ave.), 702-262-4773; www.luxor.com*
■ "Dine like a pharaoh" at this mighty Luxor French-Continental sporting a "serene", "romantic" "Egyptian setting" on the Strip; recline into the "plush banquettes" beneath "gold stars in a fabric ceiling" and let the harpist and the pianist serenade you through an "extravagant, excellent" meal of "fine-dining classics" such as "beef Wellington to die for", presented with "superb" "old-style European service"; all in all, it's "an elegant place", so make sure to "dress appropriately."

### Japengo ⊠    ▽ 24 | 24 | 22 | $42 |
*Hyatt Regency Lake Las Vegas Resort, 101 Montelago Blvd. (Lake Las Vegas Pkwy., off Boulder Hwy.), Henderson, 702-567-1234; www.hyatt.com*
■ "A sushi lover's best-kept secret", the Hyatt Regency's "exotic" and "lovely" Pacific Rim room is to some sleuths of the savory "the only reason to take the long trip to the Lake Las Vegas Resort"; slices "so soft" they "literally melt in your mouth" and cooked entrees that "come out with creative flair" are served in a "colorful" setting with a "great view" of the water; "wow!" – it's "amazing that the doors aren't bursting at the seams" with customers clamoring to dine here.

## JASMINE    24 | 26 | 24 | $57
*Bellagio Hotel, 3600 Las Vegas Blvd. S. (Flamingo Rd.),
702-693-7111; www.bellagio.com*
☑ Enveloped by gardens, the lake and a "view of the
Bellagio fountains that can't be beat", this "stunning"
"jewel" is all about "beautiful people eating beautiful food
in a beautiful setting"; most find the "fine Chinese" cuisine
is dished up by "eloquent, gracious" servers, even if it
sometimes seems like "they went to Beijing and back for
the food"; however, a few profess they "don't know what
all the fuss" is about and, given the "exorbitant prices",
recommend "yoga breathing before you look at the bill."

## Jazzed Cafe & Vinoteca ●    ▽ 21 | 24 | 21 | $48
*8615 W. Sahara Ave. (Durango Dr.), 702-233-2859;
www.jazzedcafe.com*
☑ "Funky atmosphere" and "live jazz make something
special" out of this "quaint, quirky, little" West Side Northern
Italian; although the food plays backup to the music, hepcats
hail the "delicious" "made-to-order risotto", accompanied
by a "deep wine list" "priced for drinking"; all in all, a rather
"refreshing" "change from the casino restaurants."

## J. C. Wooloughan's ●    19 | 22 | 18 | $22
*J.W. Marriott, 221 N. Rampart Blvd. (Summerlin Pkwy.),
702-869-7725; www.marriott.com*
■ Summerlin Seans and Sineads seeking sustenance "west
of the River Shannon" settle in at this "fun pub" that was
built in Ireland and shipped to Las Vegas for reconstruction;
not only is it a "nice place to hang for a drink" (11 "great
ales and beers on tap"), but there's "plenty of food" –
"typical favorites" like beef-and-Guinness pie, fish 'n' chips
and berry trifle – "at good prices", plus "excellent" Gaelic
music Wednesday–Saturday.

## Joyful House Chinese Cuisine ●    ▽ 23 | 11 | 17 | $26
*4601 Spring Mountain Rd. (bet. Arville St. & Decatur Blvd.),
702-889-8881*
■ From lunch to late (3 AM), this Asian west of the Strip in
a "converted pancake house" is favored by a "Chinese
clientele" who joyfully munch their way through a "varied,
unusual menu" of "fresh seafood", including "authentic"
Hong Kong stalwarts like a "walnut shrimp that's the best
around"; all "orders are quickly served", but "night-owls"
can opt to cook it themselves at the "plentiful" shabu-
shabu buffet after 10:30 PM.

## Kathy's Southern Cooking    ▽ 23 | 7 | 17 | $18
*6407 Mountain Vista St. (Sunset Rd.), Henderson, 702-433-1005*
■ Serving Southern vittles "so authentic you swear you're
in Georgia", Mississippi or anywhere but "an unassuming
strip mall" in Green Valley, chef-owner Kathy Cook cooks
"tasty" fried chicken, "sure-to-please smothered pork

chops" and "chicken-fried steak so good, it makes you want to slap yo' mama"; it's the "homestyle" antithesis of the "foo-foo food on the Strip", "but be prepared to wait" "as they make [dishes] to order", on country time.

### Kokomo's 21 23 21 $53

*Mirage Hotel, 3400 Las Vegas Blvd. S. (Spring Mountain Rd.), 702-791-7111; www.themirage.com*

◪ Admiring adventurers of this "gorgeous", "lush tropical" "escape" "hidden" "in the middle of a rain forest" at the Mirage say "exquisite fish, seafood and steaks" – including an "outstanding lobster bisque" and a "superb" iced oceanic appetizer spread – make "reservations a must"; restless natives beg to differ: it's "not cheap", "tables fairly close together" adjacent to "waterfalls" mean "you have to raise your voice to converse" over "not impressive" meals and the "rude" staff "just doesn't care."

### Komol Restaurant – – – M

*Commercial Ctr., 953 E. Sahara Ave. (west of Maryland Pkwy.), 702-731-6542; www.komolrestaurant.com*

On the downlow east of the Strip, this Thai diner has a hole-in-the-wall feel and an "excellent", lengthy menu of recognizeable favorites including "extraordinary soup", "moist, flavorful, lean duck", "reliable pad Thai" and lots of vegetarian options, which appeal to its healthy hipster following; it's one of several ethnic joints worth the trip to the slightly worn Commercial Center.

### Kona Grill – – – M

*Fashion Village at Boca Park, 750 S. Rampart Blvd. (Charleston Blvd.), 702-547-5552; www.konagrill.com*

A hot new spot in a city rife with them, this stylish Scottsdale star comes to the Northwest just in time to enliven the burgeoning Summerlin-driven dining scene; from its indoor-outdoor bar crowded with fashion plates to its dimly lit, quiet and comfortable dining room accented by thousand-gallon aquariums, it accommodates all types to taste Pacific Rim—inspired New American fare ranging from sweet Maui onion rings to avocado egg rolls to sushi, noodles, surf 'n' turf and, yes, even pizza.

### KRISPY KREME DOUGHNUTS ◐ 25 10 17 $6

*Excalibur Hotel, 3850 Las Vegas Blvd. S. (Tropicana Ave.), 702-736-5235*
*Palace Station Hotel, 2411 W. Sahara Ave. (Rancho Dr.), 702-368-1998 ⊟*
*Rainbow Springs Shopping Ctr., 7015 W. Spring Mountain Rd. (west of Rainbow Blvd.), 702-222-2320*
*9791 S. Eastern Ave. (Silverado Ranch Blvd.), 702-617-9160*
*Venetian Hotel, 3355 Las Vegas Blvd. S. (bet. Flamingo & Spring Mountain Rds.), 702-414-3408*
*1331 W. Craig Rd. (Martin L. King Blvd.), 702-657-9575*

(continued)
**KRISPY KREME DOUGHNUTS**
*Sunset Station Hotel, 1301 W. Sunset Rd. (Stephanie St.), Henderson, 702-450-8700* ⇗
*Texas Station Hotel, 2101 Texas Star Ln. (bet. Lake Mead Blvd. & Rancho Dr.), North Las Vegas, 702-638-8200* ⇗
*www.krispykreme.com*
■ "Addicts" "made of flesh, bone and Krispy Kremes" "look for the sign" announcing a batch of the Southern-fried "warm, soft, sweet little O's of pleasure" "fresh" from the oven 'cause they "love 'em while they're hot" at these citywide links in a chain of "fattening" "meccas"; "the most orgasmic indulgences on Earth" are "like licking a wet sugar waterfall", so a few O-no's can't help but label them "over-sweet."

**La Barca Seafood**　　　　　　　–　–　–　M
*Commercial Ctr., 953 E. Sahara Ave. (west of Maryland Pkwy.), 702-792-9700*
The dish called *la ballena* at this seaside-style eatery east of the Strip puts most of the big-money Vegas shrimp cocktails to shame "at an outstanding price"; amigos of the "great seafood" shack wash down some of "the most authentic Mexican food in town" with one of 20 south-of-the-border beers in a family-friendly atmosphere where the party gets started weekends "when the mariachis play."

**Lake Mead Cruises**　　　　　　–　–　–　M
*480 Lakeshore Dr. (I-93 S.), Boulder City, 702-293-6180; www.lakemeadcruises.com*
A small crew of surveyors has shipped out on these paddlewheel "tour boats" for a "comfortable" cruise on "spectacular" Lake Mead; as it's a good idea to sail on a full stomach, the Traditional American "buffet is kept hot and available" for a "great experience" on the breakfast boat; while the "interesting" environs of the world's largest man-made reservoir are "worth more than" the "lackluster" dinner and "expensive drinks" later in the day, the "friendly staff" "tries to entertain" you when you're not on deck.

**La Salsa Fresh**　　　　　19　12　15　$14
**Mexican Grill & Cantina** ●
*Aladdin Resort & Casino, 3663 Las Vegas Blvd. S. (Harmon Ave.), 702-892-0645*
*Boulevard Mall, 3480 Maryland Pkwy. (Twain Ave.), 702-369-1234*
*Forum Shops at Caesars Palace, 3500 Las Vegas Blvd. S. (Flamingo Rd.), 702-735-8226*
*450 Fremont St. (Las Vegas Blvd.), 702-384-1720*
*Luxor Hotel, 3900 Las Vegas Blvd. S. (Tropicana Ave.), 702-739-1776*
*Riviera Hotel & Casino, 9000 Las Vegas Blvd. S. (Pebble Rd.), 702-697-4401*

(continued)

(continued)
**La Salsa Fresh Mexican Grill & Cantina**
*Showcase Mall, 3785 Las Vegas Blvd. S. (Tropicana Ave.),*
*702-240-6944*
*www.lasalsa.com*
■ "Grilled meats", "healthy" ingredients and the "salsa bar
make it different" enough to draw diners in "for a quick,
cheap meal" at this "pretty darn good Mexican" chain; as
"you might expect" for a "low-cost alternative", they're "not
the places to be seen, and all the better for it" when you're
laboring under the effects of a "margarita as big as your
leg"; N.B. Boulevard Mall is sans booze.

**Lawry's The Prime Rib**　　25 | 22 | 24 | $45 |
*Hughes Ctr., 4043 Howard Hughes Pkwy. (Flamingo Rd.),*
*702-893-2223; www.lawrysonline.com*
■ "Vegetarians need not apply" at this "spendy" "art deco"–
styled steakhouse chainster  east of the Strip where
"carnivores" "count on" "melt-in-your-mouth" namesake
"slabs" carved by "waitresses in old-fashioned uniforms"
alongside the "superb spinning salad" "prepared tableside";
given the "predictably" simple fare, the "clubby" vibe, the
"gimmicky costumes" and "show", "you couldn't get more
retro with a time machine", "but, boy, is it good."

**LE CIRQUE**　　27 | 27 | 26 | $78 |
*Bellagio Hotel, 3600 Las Vegas Blvd. S. (Flamingo Rd.),*
*702-693-8100; www.bellagio.com*
☒ Move over Cirque du Soleil – "the best circus in town" is
this "powerhouse of elegance and gastronomic pleasure"
by "real pros" Sirio Maccioni and family; "it's like you're
eating under the big top", with "flamboyant" "fabric" tenting
highlighting "decor as rich as" the "luxurious" New French
dishes "from heaven" coupled with "first-class" wines; "you
don't have much privacy" at the "crowded" tables, and the
staff is "about as uptight as it gets", but this jacket-and-tie
"spectacular" is still "worth the splurge."

**Le Provençal**　　20 | 19 | 19 | $35 |
*Paris Las Vegas, 3655 Las Vegas Blvd. S. (bet. Flamingo Rd. &*
*Harmon Ave.), 702-946-4656; www.parislasvegas.com*
☒ It may have the "nearly authentic" "sidewalk cafe feel of
France", but this "casual" Strip "bistro" serves fare from
Italy too, including some of the "best pizza in Vegas"; "well-
prepared sandwiches" make it a "better spot for lunch than
dinner", but at all hours the debate rages as to whether the
"dancing and singing waiters" are "fun" or a "drag."

**Les Artistes**　　22 | 21 | 19 | $44 |
*Paris Las Vegas, 3655 Las Vegas Blvd. S. (bet. Flamingo Rd. &*
*Harmon Ave.), 702-967-7999; www.parislasvegas.com*
☒ "You can't go wrong with a bone-in filet" following "onion
soup done the right way", and the shared porterhouse is

"amazing" at the Paris' New French *palais du boeuf*; the rest of the fare is "enjoyable", but given this "beautiful", "high-ceilinged room's" Impressionistic touches, you'd "think it would be more creative", while the servers do their "American" best to conjure "surly" Gallic "attitude."

**LE VILLAGE BUFFET** 22 22 19 $25
*Paris Las Vegas, 3655 Las Vegas Blvd. S. (bet. Flamingo Rd. & Harmon Ave.), 702-946-4966; www.parislasvegas.com*
■ "*Sacre bleu!*" – "you'll be crying" "*merci,* or more appropriately, mercy" "if you try to partake in all the awesome food" at the Paris resort's "gastronomic gem", "a cook's tour of France" with "rich", "sophisticated" servings from "various regions" that give "gluttony a good name"; savor "spectacular" "crêpes made to order", "large shrimp and meaty crab legs", "rich sauces" and "fabulous" "fresh French bread" "in a rabbit warren of connecting", "intimate" rooms, "if you can stand the wait."

**Lillie Langtry's** ⊠ 24 22 23 $34
*Golden Nugget Hotel, 129 E. Fremont St. (Main St.), 702-385-7111; www.goldennugget.com*
■ It's hard to "imagine with this name", but "hidden" inside the Golden Nugget for more than a quarter-century has been this "great combo steakhouse/Chinese"; a "relaxed", "intimate" "surprise" where "first-rate servers" present "fabulous" Cantonese and Szechuan and "perfect" filet mignon, it's "one of the best" spots for a Downtown dinner date tucked "away from the bright lights of the city."

**Lindy's** ◑ 14 11 13 $17
*Flamingo Las Vegas, 3555 Las Vegas Blvd. S. (Flamingo Rd.), 702-733-3111; www.flamingolasvegas.com*
◪ "Good if you want the stereotypical Vegas steak-and-eggs at 1 AM" in the morning, this "hospitable" 24-hour diner is the "place to grab a quick, cheap meal" "when you're drunk, staying at the Flamingo hotel" on the Strip and need "a reasonable breakfast", "reliable, hearty sandwich" or other "typical coffee shop fare"; sure, "it's nothing to brag about" but "they do the basics right."

**Little Buddha** 20 26 18 $40
*Palms Casino Hotel, 4321 W. Flamingo Rd. (Arville St.), 702-942-7778; www.littlebuddhalasvegas.com*
■ "A huge plus" for "singles fueling up for a night" at "ghostbar or Rain" is a "pre-clubbing meal" at this west-of-Strip "ultrahip" sib to the City of Lights' Buddha Bar, "where the beautiful people go for sushi" and a "scene"; the "awe-inspiring room blends the modern and the traditional" into a "funky atmosphere" stoked by "groovy music that encourages you to eat to the beat" while all around you, "barely dressed hotties" and "handsome guys" pick at "tasty", "creative Asian fusion" and sip "great cocktails."

### Lombardi's
▽ 20 | 14 | 18 | $37

*Desert Passage at Aladdin, 3663 Las Vegas Blvd. S.*
*(Harmon Ave.), 702-731-1755; www.lombardisrestaurants.com*
■ Few shoppers have uncovered this "reliable", "laid-back" Northern Italian trattoria, a "pleasant surprise" with an indoor patio near a fountain in the Strip's Desert Passage mall, where a wood-burning oven turns out a focaccia "treat" priming you for "big portions" that step "a bit above average", "provided you like lots of garlic."

### LOTUS OF SIAM
27 | 10 | 21 | $21

*Commercial Ctr., 953 E. Sahara Ave. (west of Maryland Pkwy.),*
*702-735-3033*
■ "As soon as the first bite enters your mouth", you'll sigh "wonderful, wonderful, wonderful" over "plentiful", "flavorful" Southern and "ethereal" Northern Siamese, "jewels" in the loam of a "hole-in-the-wall" east of the Strip; "put decor and location aside" and savor "addictive, delicious" "whole sizzling catfish" and "fabulous mango and sticky rice" complemented by an "excellent list of German wines"; you'll pay "ridiculously low prices for what might be the best Thai in the country."

### Lupo, Trattoria del
21 | 19 | 20 | $40

*Mandalay Bay Hotel, 3950 Las Vegas Blvd. S. (Hacienda Ave.),*
*702-632-7410; www.wolfgangpuck.com*
☑ "Puck does Italian" at Wolfgang's "better-than-expected" Mandalay Bay trattoria, baking some of the "best-ever wood-fired pizzas" and sizzling a "signature rib-eye" "so delicious" you'll want to "gnaw the bone while nobody is looking"; those "unimpressed" with the fare can feast with the eyes: the "biggest thrill" in the "noisy", "open" space is the "view of rumjungle and Red Square" to "people-watch all the scantily clad babes waiting in line to bar hop."

### Lutèce
24 | 23 | 24 | $77

*Venetian Hotel, 3355 Las Vegas Blvd. S. (bet. Flamingo &*
*Spring Mountain Rds.), 702-414-2220; www.lutece.com*
☑ "Food fit for a king" can be a "life-changing experience" for commoners who've "hit it big in the casino" and can afford this "outpost of a NY favorite"; though it's "bizarre eating fantastic French fare overlooking a fake-believe Venetian canal", the setting's "subtle elegance" and the "simple, classic" cuisine "ironically make it stand out"; baroque palates tsk that a "limited menu" and portions made for a "magnifying glass" don't merit "exhorbitant prices."

### Luxor Steakhouse
24 | 23 | 25 | $50

*Luxor Hotel, 3900 Las Vegas Blvd. S. (Tropicana Ave.),*
*702-262-4778; www.luxor.com*
■ "Step through [to] another dimension" at this "treasure in the pyramid" of the Luxor where an "outstanding stuffed portobello appetizer", "very good lobster" and "better-

than-expected steaks and chops" are ferried to table by "accommodating" servers in a "nicely decorated" room with an "old-fashioned" chophouse feel; other cow palaces in town might be "better", but this is a "nice try" only a coin's toss "away from the casino."

### Macayo Vegas 19 15 17 $16
*1741 E. Charleston Blvd. (Bruce St.), 702-382-5605*
*1375 E. Tropicana Ave. (Maryland Pkwy.), 702-736-1898*
*4457 W. Charleston Blvd. (Decatur Blvd.), 702-878-7347*
*8245 W. Sahara Ave. (Cimarron Rd.), 702-360-8210*
◪ Maybe the "oldest Mexican chain in LV" has survived since 1959 because it puts out south-of-the-border bites "that gringos can understand" at prices "decent" enough for cheapskates to chew on with "quick service" that even the busiest bellies can stomach; less "Americanized" palates should "try mixing the hot and the chunky salsa" to spark up tacos and carnitas that might seem "ordinary."

### Makino Restaurant ▽ 22 11 17 $25
*3965 S. Decatur Blvd. (Flamingo Rd.), 702-889-4477*
◪ When fin fans "on a low budget" "want to fill up with sushi", this "fabulous" "good-value" Japanese "seafood buffet" on the West Side has an "amazing" "plethora" from which to choose, with "plentiful" cooked options alongside some "excellent" raw stuff; afishionados fuss that, like any all-you-can-eat, "some dishes are good and some are not", so navigate the waters carefully.

### MALIBU CHAN'S ● 27 21 23 $31
*W. Sahara Promenade, 8125 W. Sahara Ave. (bet. Buffalo Dr. & Cimarron Rd.), 702-312-4267; www.malibuchans.com*
■ For an "innovative" "menu of Pacific Rim"–"Asian fusion", including the "best squid appetizer in Las Vegas" and the "delicious banana Chan dessert" complemented by "mouthwatering" sushi, visit this "great local joint" on the West Side; with "early-birds" landing for "excellent", "special-value" entrees and the "beautiful people" sighing "it's all about the tapas, baby" at 10 PM–2 AM "reverse happy hour", this "absolutely fabulous" "joint" is "worth the drive" anytime.

### Mama Jo's Italian Bistro 20 15 18 $22
*3655 S. Durango Dr. (bet. Spring Mountain Rd. & Twain Ave.), 702-869-8099*
*8427 W. Lake Mead Blvd. (bet. Harbor Island Dr. & Rampart Blvd.), 702-215-6262*
*1000 N. Green Valley Pkwy. (bet. I-215 & Pebble Rd.), Henderson, 702-719-6262*
◪ If this "casual" Southern Italian chain link is your "husband's favorite", make sure your mister works it off on the treadmill 'cause these "nice, little" spots serve "huge", "family-style" portions of "great gnocchi" and other staples,

"salad included", for a belt-easing meal in a "relaxed" setting; they're "not much in the decor department", but the chow "tastes great, and you can have leftovers the next day" – if your hubby doesn't get to 'em first.

### Marche Bacchus ⌧
_2620 Regatta Dr. (Breakwater Dr.), 702-804-8008_                    – | – | – | M

When the Strip's big-name Gallic chefs yearn to enjoy their native cuisine away from the pressures of their own kitchens, they venture to this "great" "French-owned" cafe for "casual lakefront patio dining" in the West Side; the Verge family introduced a full bistro menu in 2003, featuring moule frites, escargot and grilled salmon, all of which can be complemented with a retail-priced bottle from their adjacent wine store for a $10 corkage fee.

### Marc's
_7290 W. Lake Mead Blvd. (Tenaya Way), 702-562-1921_                – | – | – | M

With a casually elegant dining room and relaxing wine lounge, Marcus Ritz reels in Summerlin and Sun City citizens to sup on innovative New American fare with an "Italian steakhouse" punch; using "only the finest ingredients", the chef-owner crafts specialties such as lobster martini, "amazing steak el chico" from a family recipe, wild king salmon and bananas Foster flambéed tableside.

### MargaritaGrille
▽ 17 | 13 | 15 | $27

_Las Vegas Hilton Hotel, 3000 Paradise Rd. (bet. Desert Inn Rd. & Karen Ave.), 702-732-5111; www.lvhilton.com_

☑ When you find yourself near the Convention Center, try this east-of-Strip cantina for "tasty" "Mexican favorites" morning to night concocted with the "quality ingredients one would expect from the Hilton"; post-work partiers pour in for the "great happy-hour margarita specials", but spice lovers suspect a kitchen that "needs to kick up the flavor" is still searching for that lost shaker of salt.

### Market City Caffe
17 | 14 | 18 | $24

_Monte Carlo Resort & Casino, 3770 Las Vegas Blvd. S. (bet. Harmon & Tropicana Aves.), 702-730-7966; www.marketcitycaffe.com_

■ A "nice place to sit" and "enjoy" is this "value for a Strip Italian", the Monte Carlo's link in a SoCal chainlet where "great service" makes for a "very good", "easy dinner" and lunch; most _mangia_ the massive, "excellent antipasto buffet" and "great breadsticks", complemented by "an incredible wine list" "for this level of casual dining."

### Marrakech
▽ 16 | 24 | 21 | $31

_3900 Paradise Rd. (bet. Flamingo Rd. & Twain Ave.), 702-737-5611; www.marrakech-lv.com_

☑ "Get on board" this "fun", "fast-moving party train" with "authentic belly dancing" and a prix fixe Moroccan "meal included" that's "best enjoyed in a group" as everything, from "shrimp in lemon sauce" to "hummus with pickled veggies", is served family-style to patrons lolling on pillows in the stylish room; locals conduct "out-of-town guests" east of the Strip for an "unusual" "experience" here, even though the unimpressed express it's "not worth the trip."

### MAYFLOWER CUISINIER ☒   26 | 20 | 23 | $34 |
*Sahara Pavilion, 4750 W. Sahara Ave. (Decatur Blvd.),*
*702-870-8432; www.mayflowercuisinier.com*
■ Set sail for a west-of-Strip shopping center, and "you won't feel your time was wasted" when you land at this "delightful", "high-class", "creative Chinese-French fusion" "gem", a "longtime favorite of locals" that's "not your run-of-the-mill" Asian; you'll get "hooked on" the "beautiful presentation" and "great flavors" of "interesting dishes" including "wonderful appetizers", "Hong Kong chow mein filled with scallops, chicken, etc." and "Mongolian beef that can be cut with a fork"; it's a "great place to discover."

### McCormick & Schmick's   22 | 19 | 20 | $43 |
*335 Hughes Center Dr. (Paradise Rd.), 702-836-9000;*
*www.mccormickandschmicks.com*
◪ Some seafood slingers say "the freshest fish in the West" is found at this "fancy" franchise east of the Strip, netting a "great variety" of "scrumptious" ocean offerings "for those not wanting to deal with the casino scene"; the "reigning king of the $1.95 happy hour" packs a "great bang for the buck" for the after-work posse in a "clubby", "pleasant" atmosphere that "does not seem like a chain"; nevertheless, a few renegades "don't get what the hype's all about."

### Medici Cafe   ▽ 23 | 25 | 24 | $34 |
*Ritz-Carlton, Lake Las Vegas, 1610 Lake Las Vegas Pkwy.*
*(Grand Mediterra Blvd.), Henderson, 702-567-4700;*
*www.ritz-carlton.com*
■ Only a few have managed the "getaway" to Henderson where a "relaxing", "outstanding" Mediterranean offers "creative", "well-presented" dishes in an "impressive" setting overlooking serene Lake Las Vegas; "friendly" service is as "graceful" and "attentive" as "you would expect from the Ritz", while those in-the-know say hold back for "phenomenal desserts", like a "wonderful" apple torte.

### Melting Pot, The   – | – | – | M |
*8704 W. Charleston Blvd. (bet. Durango Dr. & Rampart Blvd.),*
*702-384-6358; www.themeltingpot.com*
Gather your friends for a communal dip in the fondue pot at the new West Side location of a chain bubbling up all over the nation; the ritual of selecting, prepping and dunking your nibbles is almost as important as the gooey grub, the wine list is user-friendly, and where 'cheesy' refers to the fare and not the vibe, the modern digs encourage casually stylish group encounters.

**Memphis Championship Barbecue**     22  18  20  $20
*2250 E. Warm Springs Rd. (Eastern Ave.), Henderson,*
*702-260-6909*
*4379 Las Vegas Blvd. N. (Craig Rd.), North Las Vegas, 702-644-0000*
*Santa Fe Station Hotel, 4949 N. Rancho Dr. (bet. Lone*
*Mountain Rd. & Rainbow Blvd.), 702-396-6223*
*www.memphis-bbq.com*

◪ Tourists aren't the only Illinois import "amid the glitter";
the state's apple wood is hauled in for "Memphis-style
barbecue" "fantastic" enough to "raise Elvis from the grave"
at this blue-ribbon chainlet smoking "lean, flavorful"
"down-home" "dry rub", including a "best-deal" sampler
of "chicken, pulled pork, ribs, beef and hot sausages";
"regulars" swear "my car automatically turns in anytime I
drive by", though surveyors "sour" on the joint's "sauce"
say it's "not as good as it's hyped up to be."

**Metro Pizza** ◗     23  13  18  $16
*Ellis Island Casino & Brewery, 4178 E. Koval Ln. (Flamingo Rd.),*
*702-312-5888* ⌐
*1395 E. Tropicana Ave. (Maryland Pkwy.), 702-736-1955*
*Renaissance Ctr. W., 4001 S. Decatur Blvd. (Flamingo Rd.),*
*702-362-7896*
*www.metropizza.com*

■ "In a town where good pizza is hard to come by", satisfy
your urge for a "real" "New York" "pie" at this "awesome"
Italian mini-chain baking "fresh and flavorful" crusts loaded
with "interesting toppings"; "the beer is cold", "the kids
will love this place" and, "most importantly, it's one of the
cleanest parlors" in town – no, it's "not the cheapest", but
it is the "best."

**MGM Grand Buffet**     16  13  15  $20
*MGM Grand Hotel, 3799 Las Vegas Blvd. S. (Tropicana Ave.),*
*702-891-7314; www.mgmgrand.com*

◪ "If you don't mind waiting in line" the MGM's Traditional
American "bargain" "belly buster" is "a good, basic buffet"
boasting "lots and lots of choices" for "lots and lots of food"
at every meal, though "it's best for breakfast" when "all the
essentials" "do the job if you're trying to fill up" before a
long bout of blackjack; but it sure is "no hall of famer": an
"invisible" staff and "boring" decor leave the "disappointed"
demanding it "be placed on the overhaul list."

**MICHAEL'S**     26  22  26  $76
*Barbary Coast Hotel & Casino, 3595 Las Vegas Blvd. S.*
*(Flamingo Rd.), 702-737-7111; www.barbarycoastcasino.com*

■ It might be "hard to believe that this long-running gourmet
room is still better than most of the new designer" haunts,
but the Barbary Coast's "venerable institution" "is out of
this world" for "classy" Continental cuisine; slip into an
"old-time red booth" amid "romantic" decor "right out of
Bugsy's days", nibble at the "special pre-meal crudité" and

don't mind the "throwback" "ladies menu" sans those "silly prices" as your "high-rolling" date treats you to signature Dover sole served by a staff that "treats you like royalty."

### Mikado
23 | 23 | 22 | $43

*Mirage Hotel, 3400 Las Vegas Blvd. S. (Spring Mountain Rd.), 702-791-7111; www.themirage.com*

■ "Eat with your eyes first" at the Mirage's "beautiful and relaxed" Japanese where a "nice selection" of "amazingly fresh sushi" and "tasty" "teppanyaki-style dinners" are served "with a smile" in "simple yet elegant" presentations amid "peaceful" streams and gardens for "a welcome respite" from the clang of "slot machines."

### Mirage Buffet
19 | 15 | 17 | $20

*Mirage Hotel, 3400 Las Vegas Blvd. S. (Spring Mountain Rd.), 702-791-7111; www.themirage.com*

◪ "For those scared off by the Bellagio's high prices", its "sister" Mirage serves "one of the better buffets for less money", an "appealingly presented" "no-surprises" Continental smorgasbord that's "a great value for a one-meal-a-day gambler"; savvy spread-goers are "not that impressed", claiming the English garden decor "needs a sprucing", but wallet-watchers point out "why spend five bucks for a glass of juice when you can have the whole nine yards for about double the price?"

### MiraLago
– | – | – | E

*Reflection Bay Golf Club, 75 Montelago Blvd. (Monte Vista Blvd.), Henderson, 702-568-7383; www.lakelasvegas.com*

Despite a midyear name change and a fresh Mediterranean menu with "definitely lowered" tariffs, this Reflection Bay Golf Club dining room remains a "best-kept secret" for "elegant" lunch and dinner and "terrific" Sunday brunch in a "fine" atmosphere; chef Roland August oversees "wonderful" signatures like pork osso buco and an ever-changing dessert menu, which can be enjoyed "outside on the patio" where the "great" view of Lake Las Vegas helps you while away the wait for "slow" service.

### MON AMI GABI
23 | 24 | 22 | $40

*Paris Las Vegas, 3655 Las Vegas Blvd. S. (bet. Flamingo Rd. & Harmon Ave.), 702-944-4224;*
*www.monamigabilasvegas.com*

■ So "remarkably authentic", it's almost "surreal", this "Parisian bistro" is "as close to the Rive Gauche as you can get"; the "casual" "steakhouse with a Gallic accent" fires up "*fantastique* French fare" and pours 14 "divine" "wines by the glass", but "go early for dinner" to "be sure" to get "an outdoor table" "on the Strip sidewalk" "terrace" "to people-watch and take in the water show" at the Bellagio; "in a town full of overpriced, overcool eateries", it's "*très bon, très chic, magnifique!*"

## Monte Carlo Pub & Brewery ◕　17　17　16　$23

*Monte Carlo Resort & Casino, 3770 Las Vegas Blvd. S.*
*(bet. Harmon & Tropicana Aves.), 702-730-7777;*
*www.monte-carlo.com*

◪ "If you're in town with your cheap friends", the Monte Carlo's "modern" microbrewery is "very good for what it is": a "really fun place" to "have a burger" or some other "cheerful pub nosh" and "to hang out and drink" "beer, beer, beer" at a "good price"; you can drown in your mug at this "informal spot" till 3 AM, though the "live dance bands" will probably "drown out your very thoughts."

## Montesano's ⊠　　▽ 20　9　18　$21

*4835 W. Craig Rd. (Decatur Blvd.), 702-656-3708*
*3441 W. Sahara Ave. (Valley View Blvd.), 702-876-0348*
*www.montesanos.com*

■ West of the Strip and in the Northwest, these locally owned "NY Italian deli"/diners pile it on "hot and plentiful" for "perfect sandwiches", "great" pizza and other "good, old-fashioned" specialties that "taste like mama just made" 'em – if the old gal is from Sicily, that is; "take home a loaf of bread", some cheese or sausages from the "attached" counter and pretend that mom is still in your kitchen.

## Moongate　　　　　22　26　22　$39

*Mirage Hotel, 3400 Las Vegas Blvd. S. (Spring Mountain Rd.), 702-791-7223; www.themirage.com*

■ When you want to moon over your meal, "a nice way to spend part of the evening" is to "relax and enjoy" the Mirage's "corner of no-rush tranquility"; "not your average" Asian eatery, this "beautiful" replica of a classical Chinese courtyard dressed in faux cherry blossoms specializes in "outstanding" Cantonese and "spicy Szechuan" seafood (from jellyfish to abalone to shark's fin), beef and pork dishes.

## Morton's, The Steakhouse　　24　22　24　$59

*400 E. Flamingo Rd. (Paradise Rd.), 702-893-0703;*
*www.mortons.com*

◪ "Watch out for bachelor parties" stampeding through "superb" filets complemented by "decent seafood", "the best molten chocolate cake" and a "great wine list" at this "manly man's steakhouse", the east-of-Strip outpost of Chicago's "formula high-end" chain; the "reliable" fare is "à la carte, so it does get pricey", and diners who "don't like to meet their meat before it's cooked" call the "verbal menu" "silly", but "if you're looking for" "a place to hold a business meeting", the "classy, not sassy", "institution" "is it."

## Mr. Lucky's 24/7 ◕　　　　18　16　18　$18

*Hard Rock Hotel & Casino, 4455 Paradise Rd. (bet. Flamingo Rd. & Harmon Ave.), 702-693-5592; www.hardrockhotel.com*

■ With "stunning servers" and "stargazing galore" on the menu, this "hip" east-of-Strip "coffee shop" "in the heart of rock 'n' roll heaven" is "always open" to "hotties" "in a drunken haze", "raucous students" and "gamblers" who've "lost their shirts" gobbling "grub" "ranging from fresh fruits" to "good, old heart-stopping" breakfasts; "basically, it's a real nice Jersey diner with some Hard Rock flare" and "a little [too] much noise", but it's "fast" and "cheap" for your fill of "eye candy" and "solid hangover food."

### Nectar
22 | 22 | 22 | $45

*Bellagio Hotel, 3600 Las Vegas Blvd. S. (Flamingo Rd.), 702-693-7223; www.bellagio.com*
■ Strip gods and goddesses gush over this "funky-good" New American featuring "food with flair" from chef John Schenk, ferried by "attentive servers" in a free-form space spilling to the "cool" "people-watching" spot at the all-white bar; a "chichi crowd" sips "fantastic" nectar, savors chile-rubbed free-range pork and makes it nearly "impossible to get a table" later in the evening – try the "early-bird" pre-theater prix fixe for one of "the biggest bargains in town."

### Neros
24 | 21 | 22 | $51

*Caesars Palace, 3570 Las Vegas Blvd. S. (Flamingo Rd.), 702-731-7731; www.caesars.com*
☑ If "a really good steak" "puts a smile on your face", wipe your chin and show your pearlies for Caesars' "unrushed" surf 'n' turfer – though the fare at this "piece of old Vegas charm" is "not necessarily groundbreaking", it is "perfectly prepared"; still, "slow" "service more comparable to that at a good Shoney's" has culinary historians speculating that "the emperor would have dined elsewhere."

### N9ne Steakhouse ◗
▽ 27 | 24 | 22 | $67

*Palms Casino Hotel, 4321 W. Flamingo Rd. (Arville St.), 702-933-9900; www.n9negroup.com*
■ "Superb" "steaks that melt in your mouth" coupled with "bold", "beautiful" sides are only half the attraction of this "chic" "meat market" "perfect for meeting gorgeous girls and handsome hunks" west of the Strip; from the "center champagne and caviar bar" to the "sterno" where you "cook your own marshmallows before you put them on chocolate-covered graham crackers", "celebs" are toasting all over the "ultrahip", "high-end" "lounge setting."

### NOBHILL
26 | 25 | 25 | $63

*MGM Grand Hotel, 3799 Las Vegas Blvd. S. (Tropicana Ave.), 702-891-1111; www.mgmgrand.com*
■ Good thing the atmosphere is so "serene" because you're in for vertigo over Aqua chef Michael Mina's "knock-your-socks-off", "roll-your-eyes-to-the-back-of-your-head good" San Francisco cuisine; organic ingredients come in "exquisite variety" for "addictive" dishes, including the "sublime lobster pot pie"; service is "professional and polished" amid a "stylin'" "California" "minimalist decor"

featuring "glass-enclosed" booths where you can cry "wow!" without bothering your neighbors.

### NOBU
28 | 23 | 24 | $69

*Hard Rock Hotel & Casino, 4455 Paradise Rd. (bet. Flamingo Rd. & Harmon Ave.), 702-693-5090; www.nobumatsuhisa.com*

■ "Whether hot or cold", Nobu Matsuhisa's "excellent" offerings are "so beautiful you hate to eat them", but do because the "master chef/showman's" "trendy" east-of-Strip Japanese serves this *Survey*'s Top Food; "crowded" with the "young and hip" having "noisy" "fun" over "exotic", "magnificent" raw fish and other "mind-blowingly" "artful" creations, it's "not a great place for the rookie", and you need to "bring your yen for incredible yang", but "its reputation precedes it", and it does "live up to the hype."

### Noodles ◐
21 | 18 | 18 | $29

*Bellagio Hotel, 3600 Las Vegas Blvd. S. (Flamingo Rd.), 702-693-7111; www.bellagio.com*

◪ Displayed in giant apothecary jars, the namesake fare is a "popular" late-night balm at this "visually interesting" Strip joint; the "comfortable", "Asian minimalist triumph" serves "very, very good noodles" and "wonderful dim sum" for an "interesting" "change of pace" that's "casual" and "cheap (for the Bellagio)"; still, a few noodlers needle it as "pricey for what you get", which is "nothing extraordinary."

### Noodle Shop, The ◐
18 | 13 | 15 | $22

*Mandalay Bay Hotel, 3950 Las Vegas Blvd. S. (Hacienda Ave.), 702-632-7777; www.mandalaybay.com*

◪ "Good for a late-night fix", this "convenient", "authentic" Mandalay Bay Mandarin serves "quick bites" of the eponymous stuff dry and in "hearty" slurpable soups, plus "great congee"; located "right on the casino floor", the ambiance won't win any awards and service sometimes seems "irritated", but at 3 AM, the otherwise "bland" "noodles taste like food from the gods."

### Nora's Cuisine
▽ 24 | 16 | 22 | $23

*6020 W. Flamingo Rd. (Jones Blvd.), 702-365-6713; www.norascuisine.com*

■ "Family-owned by real Italians" Gino and Nora Mauro, this storefront "favorite of locals" is jammed with West Siders scarfing down "plain and simple but *delicioso*" "old standards", like the signature Crazy Alfredo (loaded with chicken, sausage, shrimp and more), pork tenderloin and pizza in "ample quantities" chased by beer and wine only and accompanied by live music on weekends after 10 PM.

### OLIVES
23 | 23 | 21 | $45

*Bellagio Hotel, 3600 Las Vegas Blvd. S. (Flamingo Rd.), 702-693-7223; www.toddenglish.com*

◪ "Try not to fill up on the delicious spreads" made with a certain pitted fruit at the "happening" Strip outpost of Todd

English's "inventive" Mediterranean chain because "mega-portions" of "flavorful dishes", including "art-on-a-plate beef carpaccio" and "fabulous flatbreads" (in "creative" combinations like fig, Gorgonzola and prosciutto), follow; in an "Italian Riviera"-esque setting "on the lake at the Bellagio", it's "ideal" "for an expensive lunch" – if, dis the "disappointed", "you want to be ignored by the staff."

**Onda** 24 24 24 $50
*Mirage Hotel, 3400 Las Vegas Blvd. S. (Spring Mountain Rd.), 702-791-7223; www.themirage.com*
■ "You feel a world apart from the Strip's hustle-bustle" partaking of the "surprisingly" "fabulous Italian" fare in the Mirage's "nicely decorated" "treasure", replete with imported tile and marble for a "soft, lovely" feel made all the more "peaceful" by nightly piano; the "varied menu" runs from the "best fresh seafood platter" and "superb" "lobster ravioli" to "top-notch" osso buco; the kitchen is no longer overseen by Todd English, but the "friendly, competent" staff keeps up the standards.

**Osaka Japanese** ◑ – – – E
*4205 W. Sahara Ave. (Valley View Blvd.), 702-876-4988*
*10920 S. Eastern Ave. (Horizon Ridge Pkwy.), Henderson, 702-616-3788*
*www.lasvegas-sushi.com*
"A Las Vegas tradition" since 1967, this Japanese "original" west of the Strip and its recent Green Valley outpost offer a casual but "very traditional" environment, including a "tatami room for small, intimate gatherings", a "loud and boisterous" teppan grill and a bar turning out "great deals" on sushi that "tastes like it was just caught"; N.B. it's not affiliated with Osaka Japanese Cuisine.

**Osaka Japanese Cuisine** ◑ – – – E
*7511 W. Lake Mead Blvd. (bet. Buffalo Dr. & Tenaya Way), 702-869-9494; www.lasvegas-sushi.com*
It's "worth the trip just to hear" the piano player at the bar of this upscale-casual dinner spot, just about the "best Japanese in the Northwest", but the cuisine is set to be the new draw as former Malibu's Chan's chef, the celebrated Terence Fong, takes over the burners to improve offerings that include teppanyaki, raising the bar for Asian food in and near Summerlin; N.B. it is no cousin to Osaka Japanese.

**OSTERIA DEL CIRCO** 25 26 24 $59
*Bellagio Hotel, 3600 Las Vegas Blvd. S. (Flamingo Rd.), 702-693-8150; www.bellagio.com*
☑ Le Cirque "ringmasters", the Maccionis, move down the midway for this "epicurean" sideshow of Tuscan "delights"; "formal service" "elegantly" juggles "exquisitely prepared" plates and "fantastic wines" in a "chic, playful" "fantasy room" at the Bellagio; the "noisy", "non-stuffy" place has

barkers bellowing "run, don't walk, in your Manolo Blahniks" to this "memorable experience", while others opine that the "ridiculously priced", "overhyped" fare takes "second" billing to the "awesome view of the water show."

## Outback Steakhouse ●　　19 | 16 | 19 | $25

*Casino Royal Hotel, 3419 Las Vegas Blvd. S. (Flamingo Rd.), 702-251-7770*
*1950 N. Rainbow Blvd. (Lake Mead Blvd.), 702-647-1035*
*4141 S. Pecos Rd. (Flamingo Rd.), 702-898-3801*
*3685 W. Flamingo Rd. (Valley View Blvd.), 702-253-1020*
*8671 W. Sahara Ave. (Durango Dr.), 702-228-1088*
*4423 E. Sunset Rd. (Arville St.), Henderson, 702-451-7808*
*2625 W. Craig Rd. (Fuselier Dr.), North Las Vegas, 702-647-4152*
*www.outbacksteakhouse.com*

◪ "When you just gotta have a steak but don't want to dress up" visit this "tried-and-true" Down Under–themed chophouse chain "for a fast in and out" with the "family"; on a walkabout of Vegas, "casual" clans can sample seven locations where they grill up "huge portions" that mates swear are "the best" "for the price"; agoraphobes warn the "pleasant" "staff can be too chummy", and all those g'day's make for "noise level not good for socializing."

## Pahrump Valley Winery　　▽ 24 | 25 | 27 | $32

*3810 Winery Rd. (east of Hwy. 160), Pahrump, 775-727-6900; www.pahrumpwinery.com*

■ Hop a "helicopter", or drive over the mountains and "far from town" to mine this "diamond" tucked amid grapevines in Pahrump; "tour the winery, buy a bottle or two and enjoy yourself" over a "pleasant" Continental in a "beautiful, beautiful, beautiful" setting; foodies who've flown here chirp it's "very nice" considering it's "near the Chicken Ranch", which, this being Nevada, is not a place that raises poultry.

## Palace Cafe ●　　– | – | – | I

*Palace Station Hotel, 2411 W. Sahara Ave. (Rancho Dr.), 702-367-2411; www.stationcasinos.com*

It doesn't aspire to its name, but this "plain" "coffee shop" west of the Strip does the trick with "very good Chinese and graveyard specials" of the "down-home" American type "served all day"; your standard steak-and-eggs at $2.99 and a 99-cent breakfast are "nothing special", but if you're down on your luck, they deliver "good bang for your buck."

## Palazzo ▧　　– | – | – | M

*Tuscany Hotel & Casino, 255 E. Flamingo Rd. (Koval Ln.), 702-947-5910; www.tuscanylasvegas.com*

"Hidden" east of the Strip in the Tuscany resort lies this "pretty, little restaurant", a rustic room with a "very good" menu of "unique" Italian steakhouse specialties; relax to the music floating in from the nearby piano bar in a seat overlooking the pool while a "friendly staff" attends to you.

## PALM　　　　　　　25　19　23　$55
*Forum Shops at Caesars Palace, 3500 Las Vegas Blvd. S.*
*(Flamingo Rd.), 702-732-7256; www.thepalm.com*
■ For "the ideal NY steakhouse experience", "you can't go
wrong" with the Forum Shops' chain link of this "boys' club"
"for the expense-account crowd" where "genuinely helpful"
servers "with personalities" of a "hilariously Brooklyn"
(read: "sarcastic") bent deliver "excellent surf 'n' turf" in
"portions to make Caesar feel overstuffed" ("you could walk
the lobster on a leash"); "possibly the loudest restaurant in
town" is nevertheless "always fabulous."

## Pamplemousse　　　　　25　21　26　$50
*400 E. Sahara Ave. (bet. Joe W. Brown Dr. & Paradise Rd.),*
*702-733-2066; www.pamplemousserestaurant.com*
■ "Old-time Vegas is brought to life" at chef Georges
LaForge's east-of-Strip "quaint" thirtysomething French that
has "never lost its magic", in part due to the incantatory
powers of "impeccable" servers who "recite the menu every
night", describing the "excellent, garlicky escargot" and
rack of lamb with pistachio crust while you "pick at" "the
huge basket of crudite" brought gratis to table; "romantics"
rate it "perfect" for "a great meal with someone you love."

## Panevino　　　　　　　▽ 21　25　17　$46
## Ristorante & Gourmet Deli
*246 Via Antonio (Sunset Rd.), 702-222-2400;*
*www.panevinolasvegas.com*
☑ Development firm Marnell Corrao built and operates
this "gorgeous contemporary" Italian newcomer in their
headquarters south of the Strip, where nighttime's "stunning
view" (beyond a curving wall of glass) is matched by a
"wonderful menu" for a meal that's "quite nice" while the
"trendy" crowd bellies up to the bar or gets "comfortable"
by the fireplace in the "relaxed" piano lounge; it can get
"noisy" with "iffy" service, but "locals love" it anyway.

## Paradise Buffet　　　　17　14　15　$15
*Fremont Hotel & Casino, 200 E. Fremont St. (Casino Center Blvd.),*
*702-385-3232; www.boydgaming.com*
☑ "The cold cracked lobster claws are worth" coming out
of your shell for say fans who make "the trip" Downtown
on "seafood nights" for this Eclectic foodfest set in a
rainforest at the Fremont; "pretty good" "as buffets go", it
"has not changed much over the years", which means,
depending on who you speak to, it's been either "enjoyable",
"nothing special" or "just plain awful" for over a decade.

## Paradise Cafe ◗　　　　▽ 15　13　14　$18
*Las Vegas Hilton Hotel, 3000 Paradise Rd. (bet. Desert Inn Rd. &*
*Karen Ave.), 702-732-5111; www.lvhilton.com*
☑ "When you're really hungry" at a rarified hour, the
"wide variety" of "basic" American eats at this "casual"

"'round-the-clock" "coffee shop" east of the Strip can be the cure to a "desperate situation"; "good burgers", "great" steak-and-eggs and "graveyard specials" are served in "large portions" and aren't "too expensive", but diners who feel paradise was lost still say "blah."

### Paradise Garden Buffet   15   17   16   $18

*Flamingo Las Vegas, 3555 Las Vegas Blvd. S. (Flamingo Rd.), 702-733-3282; www.flamingolasvegas.com*

◪ If you "like to have an array at an affordable price", feast with your eyes and appetite at "a table near a window" by the "beautiful garden area with ponds, penguins, flamingos, etc." while you eat in a manner quite unlike the birds at this Eclectic Strip smorgasbord that's "a little better than your run-of-the-mill buffet"; the view "makes for a relaxing atmosphere", but ornery ornithologists opine it's punctuated by bouts of "queuing up with heavy grazers" to feed at the "trough" of "blandness."

### Pasta (fa-zool)   –   –   –   M

*Athenian Town Ctr., 4350 E. Sunset Rd. (bet. Athenian Ctr. & Green Valley Pkwy.), Henderson, 702-435-0036; www.pastafa-zool.com*

Green Valley's Tuscany Grill has given way to this casual, comfortable white-linen storefront serving traditional Italian specialties like fettuccine Alfredo and shrimp scampi, plus New York strip steaks and filet mignon, none of which runs more than $22 – a bargain in a city dining scene fashioned for high-rolling appetites.

### Pasta Mia   ∇ 21   12   18   $23

*Flamingo & Arville Plaza, 4455 W. Flamingo Rd. (Arville St.), 702-251-8871; www.pastamiawest1.com*
*Piazza Mia, 2585 E. Flamingo Rd. (bet. Eastern Ave. & Pecos Rd.), 702-733-0091*

■ You can "smell the Italian food from anywhere in a one-block radius" of these unassuming, independently owned East Side and west-of-Strip pasta shops where the stinking rose is the favorite flavor; "huge portions" of primo plates "without the frills", including "great" orange roughy, "melt-in-your-mouth lasagna" and, of course, a "fantastic garlicky salad", make them "much better than most."

### Pasta Palace   ∇ 20   17   20   $24

*Palace Station Hotel, 2411 W. Sahara Ave. (Rancho Dr.), 702-367-2411; www.stationcasinos.com*

■ For "very nice Italian" just west of the Las Vegas Strip, this pasta emporium in the Palace Station Hotel delivers "consistently good" dinners at a consistently "good price" in a "dark", "quiet" atmosphere reminiscent of a Roman villa; enjoy the namesake noodle as well as fresh seafood, pizza and some of the "best chicken Marsala ever" made all brought to your table by "great" servers.

## Pasta Shop & Ristorante  25 | 15 | 25 | $27 |
*Ocotilla Plaza, 2495 E. Tropicana Ave. (Eastern Ave.),*
*702-451-1893; www.pastashop.com*
■ "Bravo!" – "true fresh pasta" "made on-premises" is tossed with sauce for "outstanding" dishes at this "homey" "family-owned" "hole-in-the-wall" on the East Side; the "casual" joint is a "great place for a romantic date", if you and your honey are done up "in shorts and sneakers."

## Paymon's Mediterranean Cafe ● ▽ 25 | 14 | 20 | $19 |
*Tiffany Square Shopping Plaza, 4147 S. Maryland Pkwy.*
*(Flamingo Rd.), 702-731-6030; www.paymons.com*
■ "Delicious" Mediterranean and Middle Eastern meals – "outstanding gyros" and *"fesenjan* [chicken breast with walnuts and pomegranate sauce] to dream about" – are on the bill "at a price you cannot beat" at this "casual" University District stalwart, "a rare find in the chain mecca of Vegas"; with a market, a "separate hookah lounge" and a new branch opening on the West Side in December, it "continues to grow and to turn out excellent food."

## Pearl  ▽ 23 | 22 | 22 | $52 |
*MGM Grand Hotel, 3799 Las Vegas Blvd. S. (Tropicana Ave.),*
*702-891-7380; www.mgmgrand.com*
☑ Designer Tony Chi's modern "romantic" decor beckons diners to dive into this "great" Chinese in the MGM for chef Kai-Yai Yau's "pricey-but-delicious" dishes wheeled about via "impeccable", individualized "trolley service"; still, "uncomfortable seating" for "overpriced Asian froufrou" has treasure hunters huffing that it's "not yet a gem."

## P.F. CHANG'S CHINA BISTRO ● 22 | 21 | 20 | $27 |
*Aladdin Resort & Casino, 3667 Las Vegas Blvd. S. (Harmon Ave.),*
*702-836-0955*
*4165 S. Paradise Rd. (Flamingo Rd.), 702-792-2207*
*1095 S. Rampart Blvd. (Charleston Blvd.), 702-968-8885*
*www.pfchangs.com*
■ "Even if you don't like Chinese you'll like" the "interesting twist" on Mandarin at this "trendy" trio of "left coast" "noveau" "Asian hot spots", an "urban chic" "change from the usual hole-in-the-wall"; the joints are "noisy" and "always mobbed", and fans of the "unpretentious, tasty, inexpensive" "fusion" fare (including the "famous" lettuce wraps) admit it's "not authentic", but "P.F. may as well stand for 'perfectly fine.'"

## PICASSO  27 | 29 | 27 | $91 |
*Bellagio Hotel, 3600 Las Vegas Blvd. S. (Flamingo Rd.),*
*702-693-7223; www.bellagio.com*
■ "If you had a choice for your last meal on earth", the Bellagio's "fancy" New French–Mediterranean offers just the "sensual experience to savor" in your final moments; garnering Most Popular and Top Decor rankings, this "rich"

prix fixe "theater" is where "genius" Julian Serrano "artfully crafts dishes" that match the mastery of the "walls of Picassos"; "pampered by exquisite service", "open your mind" and treat the "ridiculously expensive, ridiculously good, ridiculously over-the-top" dinner as your "ultimate."

### Piero's Italian Cuisine　　23 │ 21 │ 23 │ $53 │
*355 Convention Center Dr. (bet. Las Vegas Blvd. & Paradise Rd.), 702-369-2305; www.pieroscuisine.com*
■ Like something "out of *Casino*" (a scene was filmed here), this "longtime" "local hangout" east of the Strip is as "famous" for its "people-watching" as for the kitchen's "outstanding" Northern Italian specialties and "excellent" seafood, including "stone crab from Florida" in season; it can be "expensive just to see and be seen", but "dress in black and fit right in" with the town's "old guard", who know that "gracious owner/host" Fred Glusman will "treat you right" in a setting that's "truly old Vegas", "baby."

### Piero's Trattoria　　∇ 20 │ 19 │ 21 │ $36 │
*Hughes Ctr., 325 Hughes Center Dr. (Flamingo Rd.), 702-892-9955*
◪ Evan Glusman has followed in the legendary footsteps of his father, restaurateur Freddy Glusman, with this casual sister spot serving some "excellent" Northern Italian dishes east of the Strip, "another place to see old friends"; Tuscan bean soup, panini, pasta and pizza are "better for lunch than dinner", making for a power-players' midday choice, while the stylish bar is always hopping during happy hour.

### Ping Pang Pong ●　　– │ – │ – │ M │
*Gold Coast Hotel & Casino, 4000 W. Flamingo Rd. (bet. Valley View Blvd. & Wynn Rd.), 702-367-7111; www.goldcoastcasino.com*
Only a smattering of Sinophiles have bounced over to Kevin Wu's "rock-solid" Mandarin west of the Strip, a casual, round room punctuated by Chinese lanterns that offers innovative fusion takes on Asian, but those who have are hit with a "wonderful" meal featuring "fabulous" seafood specialties plucked fresh from the tank at this "gem" located in a recent addition to the Gold Coast Hotel.

### Pink Taco　　20 │ 19 │ 18 │ $23 │
*Hard Rock Hotel & Casino, 4455 Paradise Rd. (bet. Flamingo Rd. & Harmon Ave.), 702-693-5525; www.hardrockhotel.com*
■ "Fresh and tasty" describes the plates and the patrons at the "perfect place to hang before a concert", this "contemporary Mexican" east of the Strip where Tacho Kneeland whips up "kick-ass" "spicy food for hot young things"; in a "party place" pulsing with "loud" music, "a bit of an attitude is expected and delivered" by "stripper-quality waitresses" and "hunky" waiters, along with a "dizzying array of tequilas to wash down the fiery" salsa; the no-rez policy means you have "to wait" to sizzle your taste buds.

## Pinot Brasserie
22 | 21 | 20 | $46

*Venetian Hotel, 3355 Las Vegas Blvd. S. (bet. Flamingo & Spring Mountain Rds.), 702-414-8888; www.patinagroup.com*

☑ "A taste of Paris in a big casino", Joachim Splichal's "charming French" eatery is a "never-pretentious" place for three "elegant" meals on the Strip; the "romantic" dining room is "straight out of *Moulin Rouge*", while the mallside patio is a "vibrant" yet "relaxing" spot to savor "classics" including "fabulous" frites and "to-die-for" spit-roasted chicken; neverthless, snobs sniff "not sure what all the fuss is about" for "good, standard bistro food."

## Planet Hollywood
11 | 19 | 13 | $24

*Forum Shops at Caesars Palace, 3500 Las Vegas Blvd. S. (Flamingo Rd.), 702-791-7827; www.planethollywood.com*

☑ "It's all about" "movie props galore" at this theme chain American in the Forum Shops where "tourists" "who need a place that won't care how noisy their children are" "ogle film memorabilia"; "if you can concentrate when sitting next to the creepy clown from *Poltergeist*, you'll enjoy the tall drinks", but as for the eats, "mom always said 'if you can't say anything nice . . .'"; N.B. the empire expands when the franchise takes over the Aladdin Hotel in the near future.

## Polonez
– | – | – | M

*1243 E. Sahara Ave. (Maryland Pkwy.), 702-369-1556*

For "exposure to Polish and other Eastern European fare", brave the dicey Commercial Center east of the Strip and "try the cabbage rolls" and other "good" grub, including pierogi, bigos and kielbasa, at this "friendly place" for a "decent" hearty meal; "authentic?" – let's just say you should "pray you get an English-speaking server."

## POSTRIO
24 | 23 | 23 | $51

*Venetian Hotel, 3355 Las Vegas Blvd. S. (bet. Flamingo & Spring Mountain Rds.), 702-796-1110; www.wolfgangpuck.com*

■ "The stars shine bright in St. Mark's Square" where stellar chef Wolfgang "Puck scores again" at his "inventive" New American-Mediterranean "jewel" in the Venetian, delivering "delightful" dishes to both "locals" and "Hollywood's A-list"; players say fare "better than at the San Francisco branch" is "served with humor" by a staff that "has its act together" amid a "lovely" "scene"; the "noisy" patio offers a "lighter, simpler" experience compared to the "swanky" dining room, but both options are "very thumbs-up."

## PRIME
27 | 27 | 26 | $72

*Bellagio Hotel, 3600 Las Vegas Blvd. S. (Flamingo Rd.), 702-693-7111; www.bellagio.com*

■ A prime example of "what all steakhouses hope they grow up to be" is the Bellagio's "classic, classy" chophouse, a "carnivore's delight" courtesy of owner Jean-Georges

Vongerichten's "signature panache"; where "rich, rich, rich" refers to the "sumptuous" decor and the "brilliant" beef, "perfectly prepared" following "fabulous appetizers", paired with "unforgettable" sides and settled with "great martinis"; "beautiful fountain views" and "knowledgeable", "gracious service" are themselves "worth the hefty prices."

**Pullman Grille** 23 22 21 $40

*Main Street Station Hotel, 200 N. Main St. (Ogden Ave.), 702-387-1896; www.boydgaming.com*

■ Trainspotters on board for "excellent steaks" "off the beaten track" will find this Downtown cattle car "relaxing", with a "great ambiance" in a dining room "beautifully decorated" with "massive wood accents" and "priceless antiques", plus "Louisa May Alcott's railroad" cabin serving as an "interesting" cigar lounge; "excellent everything" includes "reliable" Black Angus beef, seafood and poultry portered by "superb service."

**Quark's** 16 24 18 $23

*Las Vegas Hilton Hotel, 3000 Paradise Rd. (bet. Desert Inn Rd. & Karen Ave.), 702-697-8725; www.startrekexp.com*

■ "Transport yourself to the 24th century" at this "geeky" "outer space" themed diner in the Star Trek Experience east of the Strip, a "great place" for American "munchies" bearing "weird" names; "you have to try to ask for the Holy Rings of Betazed with a straight face", but you can explore this strange new world with the help of a "Warp Core Breach cocktail" that "will have you in orbit quickly"; sure, the food in this galaxy is "mediocre", but Trekkies hope it lives long and prospers 'cause it's a "fun" "visit for great decor."

**Raffles Cafe** ● 18 16 17 $23

*Mandalay Bay Hotel, 3950 Las Vegas Blvd. S. (Hacienda Ave.), 702-632-7406; www.mandalaybay.com*

◪ For a "peaceful respite from the clanging", go for some "great late-night scarfing" at Mandalay Bay's "dependable" "coffee shop", serving "solid" Traditional American portions that are "enough for two"; pshaw, pout penny-pinchers, it's "pricey" for "diner food" slunk along by "sloooow service."

**Rainforest Cafe** 14 23 16 $24

*MGM Grand Hotel, 3799 Las Vegas Blvd. S. (Tropicana Ave.), 702-891-8580; www.rainforestcafe.com*

◪ "Watch monkeys in trees", thrill to "thunderstorms", chew on "generic" American grub while an "elephant's flailing trunk interrupts your meal" at the MGM's "kid-friendly" "zoo" where the decor "deliver tackiness with panache"; it's "good if you're towing tykes", but service is a bungle in the "jungle" for civilized diners "waiting for the little things – like the waiter, the food, the check", and too bad the "yelling children" aren't "animatronic" like the rest of the "wildlife", as then you could turn the tiny "savages" off.

## Range Steakhouse
23 | 23 | 22 | $49

*Harrah's Las Vegas, 3475 Las Vegas Blvd. S. (Flamingo Rd.),*
*702-369-5000; www.harrahs.com*

■ "With the view, how could the food be bad?" – in fact, the
surf 'n' turf stands up to the "spectacular vista of the Strip"
at Harrah's beef joint where "creative takes on the normal
steakhouse fare", like a "filet on a Gorgonzola-onion
croustade", are "awesome without making you feel broke";
"elegant" servers help you "feel like you are eating in your
own home" on the range.

## Red, White and Blue
– | – | – | E

(fka Bleu Blanc Rouge)

*Mandalay Bay Hotel, 3950 Las Vegas Blvd. S. (Hacienda Ave.),*
*702-632-7405; www.mandalaybay.com*

In a fit of flag-waving, Mandalay Bay's formerly French
eatery has gone stateside, morphing into a Traditional
American serving NY strip steaks and roasted Atlantic
salmon in the bistro, Yankee Doodle burgers in the deli and
marble raspberry cheesecake at the dessert bar; it's lucky
that Betsy Ross' handiwork shares a color scheme with
the *tricolour* – they didn't have to change the decor a lick.

## Redwood Bar & Grill
21 | 17 | 23 | $36

*California Hotel, 12 E. Ogden Ave. (Main St.), 702-385-1222;*
*www.thecal.com*

■ "You can't beat" the "quality for the price" at Downtown's
"favorite" "low-key steakhouse", a "gem" almost "no one
knows about" serving "very good food" at a "great value",
particularly if you "ask for the off-menu" "porterhouse
special"; while it may be a "small room" for this town, it's
"very big in every other way", grilling "properly prepared"
surf 'n' turf served nightly to the strains of "live piano",
which lends the joint that "old Vegas feel."

## RENOIR ⊠
28 | 28 | 28 | $93

*Mirage Hotel, 3400 Las Vegas Blvd. S. (Spring Mountain Rd.),*
*702-791-7353; www.themirage.com*

■ "Having dinner with a Renoir poised over your partner's
head is an experience you'll not soon forget", particularly
as it's accompanied by the "flawless" New French fare of
chef Alessandro Stratta who plates "masterpieces among
masterpieces" to "convert the most Neanderthal diner" in
a "quiet" room that "belies the chaos just outside the door"
at the Mirage; an "exceptional" staff that "guides you
through unfamiliar territory" with "genuine interest" garners
this *Survey*'s Top Service rating; N.B. no smoking.

## Rincon de Buenos Aires
– | – | – | M

*5300 Spring Mountain Rd. (bet. Decatur Blvd. & Lindell Rd.),*
*702-257-3331*

"Like down-home week in Argentina", this casual West
Side storefront "run by locals" grills "terrific steaks" "in

an unpretentious atmosphere" that doubles as a deli and bakery; gauchos of the grape pair the "unusual flavors" with 10 South American wines, all available by the glass.

### Ristorante Zeffirino ◗    21 | 23 | 19 | $54

*Venetian Hotel, 3355 Las Vegas Blvd. S. (bet. Flamingo & Spring Mountain Rds.), 702-414-3500;*
*www.zeffirinolasvegas.com*

◪ You'll "swear" you're "in Italy overlooking the Grand Canal" on the "lovely" patio at this Venetian "slice of *la dolce vita*" where "wonderful" Northern Italian specialties hearken back to the chef's papa's place in Genoa, 1939; a "strolling" "guitar player adds to the romance", but penny-pinching pasta pliers pout "mamma mia – this is expensive" for "not memorable" plates, while the "lackadaisical" "service improves" only if you "chat with the waiters."

### Roadrunner ◗    17 | 16 | 15 | $16

*6910 E. Lake Mead Blvd. (Hollywood Blvd.), 702-459-1889*
*921 N. Buffalo Dr. (Washington Ave.), 702-242-2822*
*9820 W. Flamingo Rd. (Rochelle Ave.), 702-243-5329* ⊠
*2430 E. Pebble St. (Myrtle Beach Dr.), Henderson, 702-948-8282*
*Albertson's Shopping Ctr., 754 S. Boulder Hwy. (Major Ave.), Henderson, 702-566-9999*
*www.roadrunnergaming.com*

◪ Coyotes catch "some of the best-looking waiters in town" at this "friendly" chain of "cute cowboy" roadhouses "right around the corner" from just about everyone, drawing a "good local crowd" with a "fun atmosphere" and "great daily specials" on everything Southwestern from "Dr. Pepper–marinated" rib-eye tacos to spinach dip; foodies might squash "unspectacular" grub, but the Sandhill, Pebble, and Flamingo locations boast outdoor firepits, so "who could ask more for a casual night out?"

### Romano's Macaroni Grill    19 | 17 | 18 | $23

*2001 N. Rainbow Blvd. (Lake Mead Blvd.), 702-648-6688*
*2400 W. Sahara Ave. (Rancho Dr.), 702-248-9500*
*573 N. Stephanie St. (bet. Sunset & Warm Springs Rds.), Henderson, 702-433-2788*
*www.macaronigrill.com*

■ "A rose is a rose" and a Romano's is a Romano's, but if you "just want a simple meal", "there's something to be said for consistency" at these three "rustic", "upbeat" outposts of a "very smart chain" where the pasta is "always" "good" and "fresh"; "there's certainly better Italian" in Vegas, but "a million kids screaming" for the complimentary crayons can't be wrong about this "excellent choice for families."

### ROSEMARY'S    27 | 21 | 25 | $53

*Rio All-Suite Hotel & Casino, 3700 W. Flamingo Rd. (bet. I-15 & Valley View Blvd.), 702-777-2300;*
*www.rosemarysattherio.com*

(continued)
## ROSEMARY'S

*W. Sahara Promenade, 8125 W. Sahara Ave. (bet. Buffalo Dr. & Cimarron Rd.), 702-869-2251; www.rosemarysrestaurant.com*

■ "Locals love" "former Emeril protégé" Michael Jordan and his wife Wendy's "wonderful and creative" West Side New American "with a New Orleans flair"; the couple cooks up "musts" like BBQ shrimp with Maytag blue cheese, as well as "terrific prix fixe" multicourse meals, enticing with "spectacular food in a lovely, unpretentious setting" that's "definitely worth the cab ride" to their "strip mall" location; whether or not the "large" new Rio branch can live "up to the standards of the original", only thyme will tell.

### Rosewood Grille　　　20　17　20　$64

*3339 Las Vegas Blvd. S. (Buccaneer Blvd.), 702-792-6719*

☑ "Dang!" – your lobster might be "the size of a small child", but your "tuxedoed" waiter "can crack it in seconds", and he can also "remember your drink from years ago" at this "old-school" Strip surf 'n' turfer where the "decent" steaks are just "baseball-sized" but the crustaceans are "monstrous"; "grandma would love the '70s menu", and the decor "makes you feel like you're in a mobster movie" – just bring "extra cash" to take out a hit on that "overpriced" clawed shellfish.

### Roxy's Diner ◑　　　14　16　17　$14

*Stratosphere Hotel & Tower, 2000 Las Vegas Blvd. S. (north of Sahara Ave.), 702-383-4834; www.stratlv.com*

☑ "You get a show with your BLT", "cute mini-burgers", "very good shakes" and "other diner fare" from "the good ol' days" when you park it at this "retro" "coffee shop" in the Stratosphere where the "young" "singing and dancing staff" is "very talented"; the joint "always has a strolling waiter or waitress on the microphone crooning classics from the '60s", which means it can be "very noisy" but it also "can be fun", though not 24/7 anymore – now it's only open till midnight.

### Royal Star　　　23　21　22　$41

*Venetian Hotel, 3355 Las Vegas Blvd. S. (bet. Flamingo & Spring Mountain Rds.), 702-414-1888; www.venetian.com*

☑ "For lunch", graze on "outstanding dim sum", and then it's "off to the tables" at the Venetian; at night, "the Peking duck makes you feel like part of the dynasty" at chef Kevin Wu's "lovely", "serene" Chinese, an "intimate" room for a "delicious" "variety of wonderful textures and tastes", some brought forth from a live seafood tank; the food can be "excellent", sigh Sinophiles, but it's "overpriced" for service that can be "clueless."

## ROY'S　　　26　24　25　$47

*620 E. Flamingo Rd. (Palos Verdes St.), 702-691-2053*

(continued)

(continued)
**ROY'S**
*8701 W. Charleston Blvd. (bet. Durango Dr. & Rampart Blvd.),*
*702-838-3620*
*www.roysrestaurant.com*
■ "Chef Roy Yamaguchi is the Wolfgang" Puck of Hawaii,
overseeing one of the "best fusion menus around", featuring
"creative, colorful" Pacific Rim cooking; start with "sticky,
flavorful" ribs and chase the "wonderful" blackened ahi or
another "incredible fish dish" with an "oozing chocolate
soufflé" for a meal "to delight all the senses", and you'll
"exit raving"; "even though it is a chain", these east-of-
Strip and West Side spots offer "fine dining" that'll "send
your taste buds to heaven" with a vibe as "comfortably
unpretentious" as a "honeymoon in Kauai."

**Rubio's Baja Grille**            22 | 13 | 17 | $9 |
*Trails Village Ctr., 1910 Village Center Dr. (Town Center Dr.),*
*702-838-1001*
*7290 W. Lake Mead Blvd. (Tenaya Way), 702-233-0050*
*9310 W. Sahara Ave. (Fort Apache Rd.), 702-804-5860*
*Pebble Mkt., 1500 N. Green Valley Pkwy. (Pebble Rd.),*
*Henderson, 702-270-6097*
*www.rubios.com*
■ "When you need a fish taco fix", this "fresh, quick,
healthy" Mexican "semi–fast food" chain churns out some
of the "best north of Ensenada", but to "experience" them,
"you have to wait while they cook" 'em, along with your
"excellent" lobster or grilled mahi mahi burritos; some say
*las comidas* are "not as good" as that other Baja franchise,
but the "friendly staff" helps make it "a great alternative."

**Ruth's Chris Steak House** ◗            23 | 20 | 22 | $54 |
*Cameron Corner Shopping Ctr., 4561 W. Flamingo Rd.*
*(bet. Arville St. & Decatur Blvd.), 702-248-7011*
*Citibank Park Plaza, 3900 Paradise Rd. (bet. Flamingo Rd. &*
*Twain Ave.), 702-791-7011*
*www.ruthschris.com*
◪ "What more could a carnivore want" besides "red meat
soaked in butter" and "served on a hot cast-iron plate" at
this "well-run" chophouse chain out of New Orleans with
links east and west of the Strip where "huge", "heavenly
sides", "sinful desserts" and a "top-notch" wine list match
"killer steaks" and "fantastic" seafood; critics beef that
it's "overpriced" and "underserviced", sniping "the sizzle
went out a long time ago"; N.B. you can eat a meal to make
your "arteries revolt" until 3 AM nightly on Flamingo Road.

**Sacred Sea Room**            ▽ 23 | 21 | 24 | $61 |
*Luxor Hotel, 3900 Las Vegas Blvd. S. (Tropicana Ave.),*
*702-262-4772; www.luxor.com*
■ For a decade, the Luxor's "great seafooder" has delivered
"very enjoyable" ocean offerings in a "relaxing" ambiance

replete with deep scallop-shaped booths and "beautiful murals" of Egyptian oarsmen; the shrimp appetizers are "dandy", and the "lobster and filet combo" is no slouch either, both sailed to your table by some of the "best service on the Strip."

**Saizen Japanese**　　　　　　　–　–　–　M
**Dining & Sushi Bar** ◐
*San Rémo, 115 E. Tropicana Ave. (Las Vegas Blvd.), 702-739-9000; www.sanremolasvegas.com*
Flying below the radar, this casual dinner-only sushi bar in the San Remo east of the Strip is a small, comfortable spot to enjoy the artful slices and dices of longtime knife-wielder Takafumi Takeda; for those not into eating raw, a menu of Japanese specialties including tempura, tonkatsu and teriyaki is available.

**Samba Brazilian Steakhouse**　21　18　21　$40
*Mirage Hotel, 3400 Las Vegas Blvd. S. (Spring Mountain Rd.), 702-791-7111; www.themirage.com*
◪ "Eat until it hurts" at this "Atkins Dieter's paradise", a "festive" Brazilian rodizio "offering unlimited portions of marinated", "grilled", "flavorful" "meat, meat, meat"; it's a "bust-a-gut" "buffet on a skewer" that "they just keep on bringing" "until you signal them to stop"; beefaholics say "there are better" binges around, and thanks to the "sound of the slots", "you won't forget you are" in the Mirage, but if you're itching to get back to the machines, "you'll have to be rolled out of there" like a pack of nickles.

**Sammy's Woodfired Pizza**　　20　15　18　$19
*Citibank Park Plaza, 3900 Paradise Rd. (bet. Flamingo Rd. & Twain Ave.), 702-836-1999*
*6500 W. Sahara Ave. (Torrey Pines Dr.), 702-227-6000*
*4300 E. Sunset Rd. (Green Valley Pkwy.), Henderson, 702-450-6664*
*www.sammyspizza.com*
■ As the name claims, and this trio of "neighborhood" chainsters do fire up "really nice", "trendy" "gourmet" pies for the "nontraditional" 'zaficionado, as well as "not too shabby" pastas, though herbivores hail the "enormous", "excellent salads" as "the best thing on the menu"; at lunch, "you'll have to wait", and it's "not a place to take a date", but it's still a "good alternative" for a "casual" chow down.

**Samuel's**　　　　　▽　21　6　14　$15
*Green Valley Plaza, 2744 N. Green Valley Pkwy. (Sunset Rd.), Henderson, 702-454-0565*
■ Honorary "good Jewish boy" Tony Scarpa's Green Valley storefront is "one of the better delis in Vegas", foisting "a tray of two types of crispy kosher dills" upon you "as soon as you sit down"; the omelets are "tremendous", the bagels are "good", you'll "love the matzo ball soup", and that "mile-high" pastrami sandwich is the "best west of the

Hudson"; despite dingy decor – or because of it – fans feel it's "as close to NY as you're going to get" in the desert.

**Sam Woo BBQ** 🚭　　　18　8　13　$17
*Chinatown Plaza, 4215 Spring Mountain Rd. (bet. Arville St. & Wynn Rd.), 702-368-7628*
☑ "All crapped out" and still "feeling adventurous"? – "after losing money on the tables", this Chinese west of the Strip "hits the spot"; you can bet on the "real" thing here: "well-prepared, authentic" dishes including "very good noodles and BBQ meat"; "if you don't care about decor" or "nonexistent service", read through the "English subtitles on the menu" to find "interesting" choices at the "noisy" joint "where your Asian friends all eat."

**Seablue**　　　　　–　–　–　E
*MGM Grand Hotel, 3799 Las Vegas Blvd. S. (Tropicana Ave.), 702-891-3486; www.mgmgrand.com*
Chef Michael Mina's new seafooder in the reworked Strip room formerly held by Neyla is already a hot spot for celeb watching, including all those Mr. Limpets in the cylindrical aquarium; stone waterwalls and a central raw bar add to the panache of a place where ocean offerings winged in daily are charred on an open wood-fired grill and finished in a Moroccan clay oven; the tapas-style menu encourages something that's rare in this high-rolling town: sharing.

**Sean Patrick's Irish Pub** ●　　▽　19　22　21　$24
*8255 W. Flamingo Rd. (Cimarron Rd.), 702-227-9793*
☑ "It feels like you're in Ireland", getting comfy amid the "brickstone, brass and antique motif" by the "romantic stone fireplace" and sharing a bit o' the blarney with the "locals" over "a wide range" of "really good comfort food" from Ireland and America at this "little, cozy establishment" on the West Side; "the fish 'n' chips are a must", but suds studs say "go for a beer, eat somewhere else."

**Second Street Grill**　　　24　18　23　$38
*Fremont Hotel & Casino, 200 E. Fremont St. (Casino Center Blvd.), 702-385-6277; www.boydgaming.com*
■ Chef Rachel Breen "has her act together and, boy, is it good" at this Eclectic "jewel" "in the back" of Downtown's "dog-eared" Fremont; "Asian-inspired" with "nouvelle" American flair, the "innovative cuisine will knock your socks off", and though "attentive service" can't completely brighten the "cramped, dark dungeon of a dining room", "taking guests" to this "excellent" "change from the Strip" "makes you seem like a Las Vegas insider."

**Sedona** ●🗷　　　　–　–　–　M
*9580 W. Flamingo Rd. (I-215), 702-320-4700; www.sedonaclub.com*
Launched by Adam Corrigan of the Roadrunner family, this West Side happy-hour spot with a Southwestern modernist exterior featuring a patio with firepit fits right into the larger

Mojave Desert surrounds; the rest of the joint is strictly
Vegas, with slots embedded in the large central bar and a
24/7 menu of American noshes.

### Sergio's Italian Gardens  – | – | – | M

*Napoli Plaza, 1955 E. Tropicana Ave. (bet. Eastern Ave. &
Spencer St.), 702-739-1544; www.sergiosrestaurant.com*
The "gallant" "*signores*" on staff exhibit that "if we have it,
we'll make it" attitude at Sergio and Rosele Oriente's
"accommodating" East Side Italian, an "authentic" upscale
place showcasing a sizable steak and seafood menu; down-
to-earth diners dig at this garden's "pretentiousness", but
weekend piano music helps make it "worth trying."

### Shalimar Fine Indian Cuisine  ∇ | 17 | 15 | 16 | $27

*Citibank Park Plaza, 3900 Paradise Rd. (bet. Flamingo Rd. &
Twain Ave.), 702-796-0302*
☑ "An old standby for Indian food lovers", this "convenient"
east-of-Strip strip maller may be "a little tacky", but the
"better-than-average" offerings keep curry cravers coming
back; a "reliable" lunch buffet lures locals for fare that
some subcontinentals swear is "almost like home-cooked."

### Shanghai Lilly  24 | 24 | 22 | $46

*Mandalay Bay Hotel, 3950 Las Vegas Blvd. S. (Hacienda Ave.),
702-632-7409; www.mandalaybay.com*
■ "Innovative", "exquisitely prepared" Szechuan and
Cantonese, "wonderful", "personable" service and a
"tranquil, modern setting" have some horticulturalists
hailing this "elegant" Mandalay Bay flower as "probably
the best high-end" Asian in town; it may be "the most you'll
ever pay for Chinese", but "great appetizers" and "delicious
Peking duck" served on Limoges china keeps you from
feeling you've been Shanghai'd; plus, the "quiet" room is
"one place you can actually carry on a conversation."

### SHINTARO  26 | 25 | 22 | $59

*Bellagio Hotel, 3600 Las Vegas Blvd. S. (Flamingo Rd.),
702-693-7111; www.bellagio.com*
■ "Whether you're at" the sushi bar backed by a "colorful
jellyfish tank", at "the hibachi tables" or in the "dining room
with a view of the Bellagio water displays, there is always
a feast for your eyes" and "your mouth" at this "superb
Japanese" triple threat; "after a hard day of gambling",
the "luxurious surroundings" are "wonderfully relaxing" for
"unwinding" with plates of "toro like butter" and "tender"
Kobe beef or the chef's "amazing" tasting menu, though
"overpricing" makes it strictly the "rich man's Benihana."

### Simon Kitchen & Bar  ∇ | 23 | 21 | 20 | $50

*Hard Rock Hotel & Casino, 4455 Paradise Rd. (bet. Flamingo Rd. &
Harmon Ave.), 702-693-5000; www.hardrockhotel.com*
■ "With visiting celebs and local über-elite providing the
decoration", "one of the few places that delivers the hype" it

promises is this "noisy", "trendy" New American "'in'-spot" east of the Strip; even "clingers-on" get a "genuinely warm and gracious welcome" from "consummate hosts" Elizabeth Blau and "star-in-his-own-right" chef Kerry Simon; a "sparkling clean" open kitchen puts out "unbelievable" comfort food, and insiders "love the cotton candy" to finish the feast.

### Sir Galahad's Pub & Prime Rib House

21 | 18 | 22 | $35

*Excalibur Hotel, 3850 Las Vegas Blvd. S. (Tropicana Ave.), 702-597-7448; www.excaliburcasino.com*

■ Meat-munching maids and squires say "if you love fine beef" and "personal service", "keep your high-end places and save some money" at the Excalibur's "wonderful" Olde English–styled steakhouse where the Holy Grail is "slow-roasted prime rib", drawn from a "silver domed cart", "cut at your table" and including "all the trimmings"; "truly, it rivals Lawry's, downscaled a bit", but naysaying knights jab "if you aren't eating" the signature, "don't bother."

### SMITH & WOLLENSKY ◕

23 | 19 | 22 | $56

*3767 Las Vegas Blvd. S. (bet. Harmon & Tropicana Aves.), 702-862-4100; www.smithandwollensky.com*

◰ "These guys know beef!" holler "he-men" hoofing it over to this "macho classic steakhouse" on the Strip for "big, honkin' steaks" and "awesome" "crackling pork shank"; it's a "great place for guys" "swaddled in hardwood" and wolfing down "way too much" meat in a "decadent descent into 'the hell with everything healthy' attitude"; demur diners desire a "little less testosterone" and little more "for the money" from the "overpriced" chainster; N.B. the sidewalk cafe serves till 3 AM.

### Sonoma Cellar Steakhouse

▽ 25 | 24 | 24 | $46

*Sunset Station Hotel, 1301 W. Sunset Rd. (Stephanie St.), Henderson, 702-547-7777; www.stationcasinos.com*

■ It just "makes you feel special" to happen upon this "nice little surprise" "tucked into the corner" of a casino in Henderson; "arguably" "the best restaurant" "at any Station", the chophouse delivers "delicious" beef paired with "excellent wines" in a "relaxing", "romantic" room, making for a "very pleasant experience"; best of all, this "winner" is a "good bet if you don't like to wait for a table."

### SPAGO

23 | 20 | 21 | $47

*Forum Shops at Caesars Palace, 3500 Las Vegas Blvd. S. (Flamingo Rd.), 702-369-0360; www.wolfgangpuck.com*

◰ "Wolf is to be praised" "for daring to take on Vegas" with the "restaurant that blazed the trail for all the rest" of the chef's "progeny"; get the "rock star treatment" in the Forum Shops with "satisifying" Californian "signatures", including that "salmon pizza you've been hearing about for years", served "hot with a smile"; "you wanna lick the plate, but it wouldn't look right in this classy" place, say the Puck-struck, even if the "disappointed" deem it "past its prime."

### Spice Market Buffet    23  17  18  $22

*Aladdin Resort & Casino, 3667 Las Vegas Blvd. S. (Harmon Ave.), 702-785-9005; www.aladdincasino.com*

■ "A much-needed breath of fresh spices in a sea of bland buffets", the Aladdin's "tempting and delicious" array incorporates a "mind-blowing selection" of dishes from seemingly all the "different nationalities" "under the sun"; "to keep on trekking, start the day" by grazing through "Italian, American, Chinese, Middle Eastern and Mexican" choices and you're guaranteed "not to get bored" – perhaps the only thing they're missing is "moving sidewalks."

### Spiedini    22  19  20  $39

*J.W. Marriott, 221 N. Rampart Blvd. (Summerlin Pkwy.), 702-869-8500; www.marriott.com*

◪ Maybe "the best of Gustav Mauler's eateries", this "great Italian" at the J.W. Marriott in Summerlin serves "pastas that are homemade and delicious"; "try the gnocchi" and "when possible, eat outside" – "you won't think you're in Vegas"; citing "pushy" servers, "pricey" plates and a "lack of consistency", picky patrons prick it as "passable."

### Stage Deli    20  11  16  $18

*Forum Shops at Caesars Palace, 3500 Las Vegas Blvd. S. (Flamingo Rd.), 702-893-4045*
*MGM Grand Hotel, 3799 Las Vegas Blvd. S. (Tropicana Ave.), 702-597-2899; www.mgmgrand.com*

◪ "Except for the sound of the slots, you'd swear you were in Manhattan" at this "deli-to-die-for" duo on the Strip; the pickles are "crisp and juicy", "the brisket is tender and melting", "the lox is fresh, the latkes are sizzling" and the "matzo ball soup is just like your Jewish grandmother makes"; "the place is a mess, and service is poor, but when you get a sandwich with two pounds of corned beef on rye, who cares?"; still, meshugges kvetch "the real Stage should sue these imposters for pastrami malpractice."

### STEAK HOUSE    26  21  23  $44

*Circus Circus Hotel, 2880 Las Vegas Blvd. S. (Riviera Blvd.), 702-794-3767; www.circuscircus.com*

■ "Cattle prodders" say "fight your way through the sea of parents and sticky, screaming children" in the lobby to get to this "surprisingly good steakhouse" with a fine Sunday brunch in the "most unlikely setting", the "not-so-classy" Circus Circus; as you might expect, there's "a nice bit of theatrics to the meal" that's juggled out of the "open kitchen" into a room "crowded" with "locals" scarfing down "huge" slabs, "brilliantly prepared" at "very reasonable prices" – it's one of the "best deals in Vegas, baby."

### Steakhouse, The    24  21  24  $52
*Treasure Island Hotel, 3300 Las Vegas Blvd. S. (Spring Mountain Rd.), 702-894-7111; www.treasureisland.com*
■ "Bravo!" – "the steak is incredible, and the wine arrives at the perfect temperature" at this cow palace in Treasure Island; "step back in time" when "superlative service, low-key luxury and excellent food" were all the standard, and try to ignore "let down" diners who read it for being "noisy even though it's in a library setting."

### Stefano's    23  21  23  $44
*Golden Nugget Hotel, 129 E. Fremont St. (Main St.), 702-385-7111; www.goldennugget.com*
■ "Take the whole family" to "celebrate a birthday" so granny and sis and junior "don't miss the waiters' rousing version of *Volare* every hour or so during dinner" at this "excellent Italian" veteran Downtown; the decor is as "over the edge" as the entertainment, and so are some diners' nerves: sensitive ears say the "generous portions" are "top-notch", "if the singing servers don't drive you away."

### STERLING BRUNCH    26  20  23  $60
*Bally's Las Vegas Hotel, 3645 Las Vegas Blvd. S. (bet. Flamingo Rd. & Tropicana Ave.), 702-739-4111; www.ballys.com*
■ "A little bit of heaven in Sin City's" AM, Bally's "luxurious" New American brunch lets you "gorge on unlimited" "delicacies such as lobster, caviar, rack of lamb" and "bottomless glasses of fine French champagne", all before 2:30 PM on a Sunday; overseen by "a perfect, old-school" maitre d', it's the "only" spread "where you don't have to fight your way through" "using your fork as a defensive weapon", and the "orgasmic" offerings make it just about the "finest" morning meal "in the United States."

### Summit Restaurant ⊠    ∇ 20  24  23  $32
*2215 Thomas Ryan Blvd. (Lake Mead Blvd.), 702-240-1310*
■ Venture "off the beaten path" and "way up into the hills" of Summerlin for this "lovely" Franco-American "find", a "quiet place for talking" and gawking at the "phenomenal view of the Vegas Valley", particularly "gorgeous at night"; "great steaks", "relaxing lunch and brunch" and "beautiful rustic decor" help make it "worth the drive"

### Sushi Fever    ∇ 24  15  18  $35
*7985 W. Sahara Ave. (Buffalo Dr.), 702-838-2927*
■ "Order the Screaming Orgasm" seared maguro or one of "the best spicy tuna handrolls you've ever had", and your temperature just might rise at this "most original" sushi bar on the West Side, a joint with "no frills" save for the "awesome creations" coming from the ginsu guys; "the waitresses are horrible", but "the chefs are very inventive", so "try the special, and you'll be hooked."

## Swiss Cafe Restaurant ⊠ ▽ 24 21 24 $28
*3175 E. Tropicana Ave. (bet. McLeod & Pecos Rds.), 702-454-2270*

■ Swiss, "German, French and Italian come together" almost as "well" as the members of the European Union at this Continental "favorite" "hidden" in an "unassuming location" on the East Side where "master chef" Wolfgang Haubold and frau Mary "charm" diners with "the highest quality" "fine fish and veal" in a "room jammed with bric-a-brac" or on the "nice patio"; "moderate" prices mean even gamblers down on their luck can "sit, relax and enjoy a romantic dinner."

## Taqueria Canonita 21 22 21 $25
*Venetian Hotel, 3355 Las Vegas Blvd. S. (bet. Flamingo & Spring Mountain Rds.), 702-414-3773; www.venetian.com*

■ "Request a table next to the canal, order a pitcher of sangria" and relish the "singing gondoliers" paddling by at this "tasty Mexican" moored in the Venetian; although the "tacos-and-Italian-love-songs" combination leave cynics sighing "only in Vegas", people-watchers say the prime "location can't be beat."

## Tea Planet ● – – – I
*4355 W. Spring Mountain Rd. (bet. Arville St. & Wynn Rd.), 702-889-9989*

"Page after page of tea variations", including ones with tapioca, fill out the menu of this Taiwanese shop west of the Strip, a "great experience" that's certainly "not like anything else" in town; while the accompanying food is of the snack variety, the preparations are "adventurous" enough and complement the brews nicely.

## Tenaya Creek 20 17 18 $23
## Restaurant & Brewery
*3101 N. Tenaya Way (Cheyenne Ave.), 702-362-7335; www.tenayacreekbrewery.com*

■ The "beers are the draw" at this Northwest microbrewery, although "once you wade through the bar crowd", you'll find "huge portions" of "imaginative" American fare chased by "good" Mississippi mud pie; granted, it may "look cooler from the outside" than it does within, but there's no disputing how "excellent" its "home-brewed root beer" is.

## Terrace Café ● ▽ 18 15 17 $20
*Treasure Island Hotel, 3300 Las Vegas Blvd. S. (Spring Mountain Rd.), 702-894-7372; www.treasureisland.com*

■ "When you need a break from the casino floor" and are "tired of buffets", this "24-hour" Treasure Island coffee shop provides "decent" enough chow, "priced right" and peddled by "super employees"; sure, some dub it merely "average", but if you want "something quick" at 3 AM, you can "sit down and eat like a civilized person" here.

**Terrazza** 🅂 | 22 | 24 | 21 | $45

*Caesars Palace, 3570 Las Vegas Blvd. S. (Flamingo Rd.), 702-731-7731; www.caesars.com*

◪ A "perfect setting" (overlooking the "spectacular pool" at Caesars Palace) and a "supper club atmosphere" make for "romantic" dining at this "expense-account" Northern Italian where fare comes burnished with a "gourmet gloss" straight out of "an exhibition kitchen" with an "authentic, wood-burning brick oven"; those who find it's "not a good value" claim it can be "hit-or-miss", but most agree "in the long run, it still hits."

**Teru Sushi** 🅂 | – | – | – | M

*Las Vegas Hilton Hotel, 3000 Paradise Rd. (bet. Desert Inn Rd. & Karen Ave.), 702-732-5111; www.lvhilton.com*

In 1984, Shuichi Tsukada became Las Vegas' first licensed sushi chef; the pioneer has recently relocated east of the Strip to become a Benihana Villager with this tiny, reservations-required Japanese that some say offers the most authentic raw fin fare in town, sliced and rolled from an enormous school of fish flown in daily from the West Coast.

**TGI Fridays** ◐ | 15 | 14 | 14 | $21

*1800 E. Flamingo Rd. (Spencer St.), 702-732-9905*
*4570 W. Sahara Ave. (bet. Arville St. & Decatur Blvd.), 702-889-1866*
*4330 E. Sunset Rd. (Green Valley Pkwy.), Henderson, 702-990-8443*
*www.fridays.com*

◪ "Reliable" Americana turns up at this trio of links in "ye olde standby" franchise, all "lively", "adequately priced" and "open late"; still, party-poopers citing "tacky" decor, "poor service" and overall "predictability", chant "bland, bland, bland, chain, chain, chain."

**Thai Room** 🅂 | – | – | – | I

*Pecos Plaza, 3355 E. Tropicana Ave. (Pecos Rd.), 702-458-8481*

Signature *tom yam goong* (hot-and-sour shrimp soup) and other dishes are "fantastic" at this small East Side Thai that's "definitely worth the drive or cab ride from your hotel room"; ignore the "hole-in-the-wall" decor because the payoffs are "quality ingredients", "good preparation" and low prices.

**Thai Spice** 🅂 | ▽ 23 | 15 | 23 | $20

*Flamingo & Arville Plaza, 4433 W. Flamingo Rd. (Arville St.), 702-362-5308*

■ An "extensive menu" of "truly authentic", "well-spiced" offerings comes at "modest prices" at this West Side Thai set in a mini-mall that devotees dub "the best" of the genre; insiders claim it's "better for lunch", citing the "plentiful, tasty" options at midday.

### 3950
23 | 24 | 23 | $55

*Mandalay Bay Hotel, 3950 Las Vegas Blvd. S. (Hacienda Ave.), 702-632-7414; www.mandalaybay.com*

◪ "Excellent" bisque and steaks and the "best lobster Thermidor" might be "traditional classics", but they're "finely prepared" with the "creative flair" to match the "colorful", "hi-tech room" at this Continental at Mandalay Bay, and the "attentive service" is just as "snappy" as the "modern" decor; however, you pay by the decibel at the "pricey" place: "trying really hard to be trendy" with music cranked "too loud", it's "crawling with tourists" and a "dressed-to-thrill" "young crowd" who can be "quite noisy."

### Tillerman Restaurant
21 | 23 | 21 | $44

*2245 E. Flamingo Rd. (west of Eastern Ave.), 702-731-4036; www.tillerman.com*

■ Take a "break from the tourist-filled places" at this "relaxing", longtime East Side surf 'n' turfer where the "elegant", "California-style" setup features soaring ceilings and "unique indoor fig trees"; its "older" following applauds the "accommodating service" and "wide variety" of ultra-"fresh fish", and ignores the "pricey" tabs and the fact that there's "always a wait."

### Tinoco's Bistro ⊠
– | – | – | E

*103 E. Charleston Blvd. (Main St.), 702-464-5008*
*310 E. Warm Springs Dr. (Placid St.), 702-263-7880*
*www.tinocosbistro.net*

Chef Enrique Tinoco has doubled his Continental offerings, expanding from south of the Strip to Downtown with a tiny, Manhattan-esque eatery in a hip, semi-industrial space in the Arts Factory where the food is anything but mass-produced; finely crafted dishes include signature Chilean sea bass in curry lobster sauce.

### Tintoretto Bakery & Cafe ◗
22 | 18 | 16 | $15

*Venetian Hotel, 3355 Las Vegas Blvd. S. (bet. Flamingo & Spring Mountain Rds.), 702-414-3400; www.venetian.com*

■ "Bring your sweet tooth" to this "wonderful" Italian bakery in the Venetian, where "real cappuccino" and "to-die-for pastries" make for a requisite "short stop"; if you're hankering for more than a sugary "snack", lasagna, chicken parmigiana and other staples are served in the cafe, while the market offers specialties from The Boot to carry away, all in a "casual" setting that works "any time of day"; indeed, it's so "charming and authentic" that "you almost forget you're in Vegas."

### Todai
19 | 12 | 15 | $29

*Desert Passage at Aladdin, 3663 Las Vegas Blvd. S. (Harmon Ave.), 702-892-0021; www.todai.com*

◪ For an "alternative buffet", check out this Japanese chain link in the Desert Passage where "suckers for sushi" are awed by the "huge" "all-you-can-eat" spread; foes who "feel like horses at a trough" snort at "mainstream" fare prepared "hours ago", but fans who like to "try different things" find it "surprisingly good."

**Togoshi Ramen** ⊄ | - | - | - | I |

*Twain Ctr., 855 E. Twain Ave. (Swenson St.), 702-737-7003*
Folks with a yen for "workingman's Japanese food" recommend this "authentic" ramen house in the Twain Center east of the Strip; you won't find sushi at this modest spot, but you will find a "quick" bowl of traditional noodles accompanied by a nice selection of beer and sake.

**Tokyo Restaurant** | - | - | - | M |

*Commercial Ctr., 953 E. Sahara Ave. (west of Maryland Pkwy.), 702-735-7070*
The "seedy mall" setting might make you "wish it were in another plaza", but once you're inside, this 20-year-old east-of-Strip Japanese "never disappoints" thanks to its "excellent" "traditional" menu and super sushi bar; regulars recommend reserving the "tatami room for large parties."

**Tony Roma's** | 18 | 13 | 16 | $24 |

*620 E. Sahara Ave. (bet. Maryland Pkwy. & Paradise Rd.), 702-733-9914*
*Fremont Hotel & Casino, 200 E. Fremont St. (Casino Center Blvd.), 702-385-6257*
*2040 N. Rainbow St. (Lake Mead Blvd.), 702-638-2100*
*2540 S. Decatur Blvd. (Sahara Ave.), 702-873-0089*
*Stardust, 3000 Las Vegas Blvd. S. (Convention Center Dr.), 702-732-6111*
*555 N. Stephanie St. (Sunset Rd.), Henderson, 702-436-2227*
*www.tonyromas.com*
☑ "Tender, tasty ribs" at "reasonable prices" are the "juicy" justification for this chain BBQ where the "killer onion loaf" gives the babybacks a run for the money; while cynics nix "unremarkable" eats, "lacking" service and "noise", fans stick by it for "dependable" quality; P.S. "don't dress up."

**TOP OF THE WORLD** | 21 | 26 | 22 | $55 |

*Stratosphere Hotel & Tower, 2000 Las Vegas Blvd. S. (north of Sahara Ave.), 702-380-7711; www.stratlv.com*
■ "Every table has a view" at this "revolving" aerie perched high atop the Stratosphere for "stunning", "360-degree" vistas of the Strip that are "great by day" and even "better at night"; the New French–New American menu is "surprisingly good" too (albeit on the "pricey" side), but just "take it easy on those cocktails" if vertigo is a problem.

**TRE** | 20 | 26 | 20 | $46 |

*Boca Park, 1050 S. Rampart Blvd. (north of W. Charleston Blvd.), 702-946-6200*
☑ The Northwest gets a "chic" jolt via this "trendy" new Northern Italian from NY's famed Maccioni restaurant family

(Le Cirque, Circo) that "opened with a bang" but is still trying to "find the right tone"; though the "expensive" food can be "uneven" (ditto the service), the decor and the "pretty" crowd "exceed expectations" so well that many feel it will "turn into a winner eventually."

## Treasure Island Buffet    | – | – | – | I |

*Treasure Island Hotel, 3300 Las Vegas Blvd. S. (Spring Mountain Rd.), 702-894-7355; www.treasureisland.com*
Before or after spying on the pirate show in the lobby at Treasure Island, families on a budget raid this shipshape Eclectic spread for booty from every port of call, including breakfast's new omelette station; it's cheap, it's convenient and it's in endless supply – so what more could a buck-wise buccaneer want?

## Tremezzo ⬤    ▽ | 22 | 21 | 22 | $41 |

*Aladdin Resort & Casino, 3667 Las Vegas Blvd. S. (Harmon Ave.), 702-785-9013; www.aladdincasino.com*
■ "*Viva Italia!*" – one of the "best-kept secrets of the Strip", this eatery in the Aladdin serving the specialties of the Northern part of The Boot has plenty of "zing" thanks to "terrific" tastes like lobster risotto and veal Milanese served in a "simple atmosphere" by "accommodating" servers; ironically, one of the "most notable things about the place is the view" of the competition, i.e. "the Bellagio fountains."

## Triple 7 Brew Pub    | – | – | – | M |

*Main Street Station Hotel, 200 N. Main St. (Ogden Ave.), 702-387-1896; www.mainstreetcasino.com*
Cheer a game on one of twelve big screens while wolfing down wood-fired pizza, ribs, garlic fries and other Eclectic grub at this upscale-casual sports spot in Downtown's Main Street Station; the best thing on the menu, though, just might be the five fresh, workmanlike microbrews to throw back with the locals off-shift in a joint with a raw, industrial vibe.

## Valentino, Piero Selvaggio ⬤    | 24 | 22 | 23 | $66 |

*Venetian Hotel, 3355 Las Vegas Blvd. S. (bet. Flamingo & Spring Mountain Rds.), 702-414-3000; www.welovewine.com*
◪ Scale the heights of the "*alta cucina*" for a "culinary adventure" courtesy of Luciano Pellegrini, an "Italian-born chef with the right attitude", at this "classy" Venetian *cugino* of "maestro" Piero Selvaggio's SaMo original offering "remarkable" Northern dishes and "a wine list envied by Bacchus himself" portered by "smooth service" in a newly enlarged, "elegant" room; still, some stall at lower altitudes, calling cuisine "not up to the standards in CA" "not worth the money"; try a less "pricey" lunch at their adjacent P.S. Grill.

## Venetian Ristorante ⬤    | 19 | 15 | 18 | $31 |

*3713 W. Sahara Ave. (Valley View Blvd.), 702-871-4190*
◪ "Old-school Vegas" is alive and well at this fiftysomething Italian-American west of the Strip "right out of Little Italy"

where "one expects Frank and Dean" to walk in at any minute; but in spite of "huge portions", "reasonable prices" and 24/7 access, foes find it a "shadow of its former self", citing "unpredictable quality" and "spotty service."

### Venni Mac's M & M Soul Food | – | – | – | M |
*4485 S. Jones Blvd. (Harmon Ave.), 702-795-3663*
'Mississippi Mary' McCallum's first foray out of Southern California is a casually elegant Southwest eatery where diners dress up to devour chicken (baked, barbecued, gravy smothered or perfectly fried), short ribs, catfish, steaming hot cornbread and sides such as succotash cabbage, black-eyed peas and the like; they also eat up a hard-to-beat, second-story view of the Strip.

### Ventano ◐ | ▽ 23 | 24 | 22 | $30 |
*191 S. Arroyo Grande Rd. (Horizon Ridge Pkwy.), Henderson, 702-944-4848*
■ "Enjoy a panoramic view of the Vegas Valley" at this "upscale" Henderson Northern Italian where chef Arnauld Briand "visits with every diner and personally thanks you for coming to his restaurant", and a guitar player serenades nightly; the result is a place that "exceeds expectations" with "great food", "happy service" and a "good wine selection" – no wonder it's usually "very busy."

### Verandah | 24 | 24 | 25 | $40 |
*Four Seasons Hotel, 3960 Las Vegas Blvd. S. (Four Seasons Dr.), 702-632-5000; www.fourseasons.com*
■ For an "oasis of tranquility away from the fray", unwind at this "calm", "civilized" spot that's the Four Seasons' "idea of a coffee shop elevated to fine dining"; given the "imaginative" Californian cuisine, "flawless service" and "casual" air, it's "first-class" all the way here; P.S. "everyone should try their high tea at least once in their lives."

### Viaggio | 22 | 23 | 21 | $33 |
*11261 S. Eastern Ave. (just past the Horizon Bridge), Henderson, 702-492-6900; www.viaggio.net*
■ The "million-dollar view" is worth the trek to the nether regions of Henderson's hills for this Italian venue for "excellent appetizers" such as bruschetta and *pasta e fagioli* as well as "generous entree portions" of "wonderful" delectables like signature crab ravioli in "to-die-for sauce" on an "imaginative menu executed with aplomb"; "the flights of wine they offer are fun", though your wings might be "rather cramped for space" in the close room.

### Victorian Room ◐ | 19 | 15 | 17 | $22 |
*Barbary Coast Hotel & Casino, 3595 Las Vegas Blvd. S. (Flamingo Rd.), 702-737-7111; www.barbarycoastcasino.com*
■ "Slide into a pleatherette dinette" and "feel the Rat Pack spirits in a room" where "everyone on staff calls you 'doll'"

and just about "the best hot 'n' sour soup you've ever eaten" chased by "good steak-and-eggs" is "perfect for 3 AM hunger pangs" at this 24/7 Chinese-American diner on the Strip; neither the food, the decor nor the service has any relationship to its name, but "for comic relief", order the "midnight special" and "thank God" "a bit of the old" "weird and wonderful" "Vegas still exists."

### Village Seafood Buffet　　21　14　15　$31
*Rio All-Suite Hotel & Casino, 3700 W. Flamingo Rd. (bet. I-15 & Valley View Blvd.), 702-252-7777; www.playrio.com*
☑ "Anything you can imagine from the sea", "they have it (usually in multiple versions)" at this "paradise" for fin fans west of the Strip where "junkies" find "joy when it's time to pig out" on "tons" of lobster, crab legs and shrimp; critical cats turn their noses up at "food steamed to death" on a not-so-tight ship that has "sunk deeper" "over time."

### Viva Mercado's　　▽　23　15　20　$20
*6182 W. Flamingo Rd. (Jones Blvd.), 702-871-8826; www.vivamercados.com*
■ "With your health in mind", this West Side Mexican "broils, poaches or stir fries in canola oil" only "the leanest meats", using "no animal fat"; with your pleasure sensors in mind, they offer over "10 different salsas" to slather on your "really good" lobster fajitas or chiles rellenos; with your wallet in mind, they keep it all "cheap" for a "must-do" "two miles off the Strip."

### VooDoo　　19　25　20　$38
*Rio All-Suite Hotel & Casino, 3700 W. Flamingo Rd., 50th fl. (bet. I-15 & Valley View Blvd.), 702-247-7800; www.playrio.com*
☑ Put a spell on your date with a "great" meal at this "romantic, dark" duplex on the 50th and 51st floor of the Rio west of the Strip where there's magic in the "excellent views of the city" and the "live music"; the Cajun cuisine is "pretty good", but you'll be hexing yourself if you don't "try the Witch's Brew", a "smoking", "liquor-filled extravaganza served in a fish bowl"; nonbelievers frown upon "irrelevant" food, fussing "they'd have to" cast "voodoo on me to get me to come back."

### Wild Sage Café　　25　20　23　$36
*600 E. Warm Springs Rd. (Amigo St.), Henderson, 702-944-7243*
*8991 W. Sahara Ave. (bet. Durango Dr. & Fort Apache Rd.), 702-304-9453*
■ A "lucky place for non-gambling food-o-philes", Stan Carroll and Laurie Kendrick's "wonderfully anti-Strip" New American "oasis of excellence" in Green Valley now has a "pretty" West Side sibling serving the same "imaginative comfort food" as the "perennial favorite"; wildly sagacious, "low-key" "locals love them" for "grand pork chops",

"delicious chicken" and lunch's "generous, unique sandwiches", not to mention "signature sage biscuits."

### William B's    ▽ 22 | 18 | 25 | $51 |
*Stardust, 3000 Las Vegas Blvd. S. (Convention Center Dr.), 702-732-6205; www.williambs.com*

☑ For 25 years, this "old-school" surf 'n' turfer inside the Stardust has been going "strong, even with competition"; "over-the-top service that makes you feel you matter" exhibits just the "right balance of flair without the schmaltz", and a kitchen that's "trying hard" to keep up has made "recent changes" to the traditional "hollandaise sauce–type menu"; now if only the "shabby" decor could "be upgraded."

### Willy & Jose's Mexican Cantina    ▽ 24 | 21 | 21 | $19 |
*Sam's Town Hotel, 5111 Boulder Hwy. (Flamingo Rd.), 702-456-7777; www.samstownlv.com*

■ "Fajitas overloaded with shrimp" and other "generous portions" – including "42 oz. margaritas" you can "thank God are not overly alcoholic" – make for "outstanding values throughout the menu" at this Mexican joint in Sam's Town on the East Side; "they pack 'em in and hurry you out, but it is delicious" and "fun for a birthday party dinner."

### Wolfgang Puck Cafe    21 | 15 | 18 | $28 |
*MGM Grand Hotel, 3799 Las Vegas Blvd. S. (Tropicana Ave.), 702-895-9653; www.wolfgangpuck.com*

☑ "Good gaudy!" – "the decor is horrific, but the food's terrific" at this "friendly", "gourmet cafe right in the middle of" "the MGM craziness" where "slot addicts" "grab a quick bite" of "Wolfgang's wonderful signature meatloaf", "fantastic artichoke and goat cheese pizza" and other "fabulous" Californian choices; "watch the horse races" "from your table", and don't sweat losing 'cause this is "Puck on a budget", but if you want the real deal, savvy surveyors say "save up and go to Postrio or Chinois instead."

### Yolie's Brazilian Steakhouse    22 | 15 | 20 | $35 |
*Citibank Park Plaza, 3900 Paradise Rd. (bet. Flamingo Rd. & Twain Ave.), 702-794-0700*

■ "Vegetarians beware" of this "carnivore's heaven" east of the Strip where the Brazilian rodizio means "meat, meat and more meat", every "flavorful and juicy" hunk "cut" by "servers who come around" sporting the goods; arrive "with an appetite fit for a king", and if you haven't had enough cholesterol after all that flesh "cooked on a spit", "ask for the fried bananas soaked in caramel and cinnamon" to top off an "eat-till-you-pop" "wonderful experience."

### Zax    22 | 26 | 24 | $37 |
*Golden Nugget Hotel, 129 E. Fremont St. (Main St.), 702-385-7111; www.goldennugget.com*

■ "Finally, a hip place Downtown!" – "a stylish redo of an old California Pizza Kitchen" resulted in this "ultramodern" and "funky" Eclectic that's "actually worth making the trip" to the Golden Nugget; it's a "cool, hip place" "for an after-the-show Caesar salad or quiet dinner"; though there are "many delightful choices on the menu", two words: "lobster tostadas, 'nuff said."

## Z'Tejas Grill

22 | 18 | 19 | $27

*3824 S. Paradise Rd. (Twain Ave.), 702-732-1660*
*9560 W. Sahara Ave. (Fort Apache Rd.), 702-638-0610*
*www.ztejas.com*

■ "Innovative, delicious" "Santa Fe–style" Southwestern will have your "taste buds screaming for more" over the "loud happy-hour" crowd at these spots east of the Strip and in the Northwest, links in a "solid chain that really stands out"; the "Chambord margarita's to die for", but "you don't have to be in a party mood to enjoy" "spicy" savories like the "ancho chile pork" – you just have to be "adventurous."

# Restaurant Indexes

## CUISINES
## LOCATIONS
## SPECIAL FEATURES

# CUISINES

## American (New)
Aureole
Black Mtn. Grill
Bradley Ogden
Café Bellagio
Canyon Ranch
Ice House
Kona Grill
Marc's
Nectar
Postrio
Rosemary's
Simon Kitchen
Sterling Brunch
Top of World
Wild Sage Café

## American (Regional)
Draft House

## American (Traditional)
All American B&G
America
Applebee's
Big Dog's
Big Kit. Buffet
Buffet
Buffet, The
Cafe Lago
Caribe Café
Carson St. Cafe
Center Stage
Cheesecake Fact.
Chicago Brew. Co.
Chili's Grill
Coachman's Inn
Coco's
Country Inn
Egg & I
Fatburger
Feast
Hard Rock Cafe
Harley-Davidson
Hill Top House

Lake Mead Cruises
MGM Grand Buffet
Palace Cafe
Paradise Cafe
Planet Hollywood
Quark's
Raffles Cafe
Rainforest Cafe
Red, White & Blue
Sean Patrick's
Sedona
Summit Rest.
Tenaya Creek
TGI Fridays
Venetian Rist.
Victorian Room

## Argentinean
Rincon/Buenos Aires

## Asian
China Grill
Chinois

## Asian Fusion
Little Buddha
Malibu Chan's
Ping Pang Pong

## Bakeries
Il Fornaio
Rincon/Buenos Aires
Tintoretto Bakery

## Barbecue
Memphis BBQ
Sam Woo BBQ
Tony Roma's

## Brazilian
Samba Brazilian
Yolie's Brazilian

## Cajun
Big Al's Oyster
Commander's Palace

Emeril's
VooDoo

## Californian
Chin Chin
NOBHILL
Spago
Verandah
Wolfgang Puck

## Chinese
(* dim sum specialist)
Amlee Gourmet
Big Kit. Buffet
Cathay House*
Chang of LV*
Chin Chin
Empress Court*
Food Express
Full Ho
Garden of Dragon
Jasmine
Joyful House
Lillie Langtry's
Mayflower Cuis.
Moongate
Noodles*
Noodle Shop
Palace Cafe
Pearl
P.F. Chang's
Ping Pang Pong
Royal Star*
Sam Woo BBQ
Shanghai Lilly
Victorian Room

## Coffee Shops/Diners
Café Bellagio
Caribe Café
Carson St. Cafe
Coco's
Coffee Pub
Grand Lux Cafe
Happy Days
Lindy's

Mr. Lucky's 24/7
Palace Cafe
Paradise Cafe
Raffles Cafe
Roxy's Diner
Terrace Café

## Continental
Buccaneer Bay
Cafe Nicolle
Fresh Market Sq.
Hugo's Cellar
Isis
Michael's
Mirage Buffet
Pahrump Valley
Swiss Cafe Rest.
3950
Tinoco's Bistro

## Creole
Big Al's Oyster
Commander's Palace
Emeril's

## Cuban
Florida Cafe

## Delis
Cafe Heidelberg
Caffe Giorgio
Canter's Deli
Harrie's Bagel.
Montesano's
Rincon/Buenos Aires
Samuel's
Stage Deli

## Dessert
Caffe Giorgio
Cheesecake Fact.
Conrad's
Fiore Steakhse.
Krispy Kreme
MiraLago
Red, White & Blue
Tintoretto Bakery

## Eclectic
Bay Side Buffet
Bellagio Buffet
Carnival World
Courtyard Buffet
Feast Around World
Festival Buffet
Firelight Buffet
French Market
Garden Court
Paradise Buffet
Paradise Garden
Second St. Grill
Spice Mkt. Buffet
Treasure Island
Triple 7 Brew
Zax

## English
Crown & Anchor

## Fondue
Melting Pot

## French
Andre's
Chinois
Crustacean LV
Eiffel Tower
Isis
Le Village
Lutèce
Mayflower Cuis.
Pamplemousse
Summit Rest.

## French (Bistro)
Bonjour
Le Provençal
Marche Bacchus
Mon Ami Gabi
Pinot Brasserie

## French (New)
Alizé
Drai's on Strip
Le Cirque

Les Artistes
Picasso
Renoir
Top of World

## German
Cafe Heidelberg

## Hamburgers
All American B&G
Big Dog's
Fatburger
Hard Rock Cafe
In-N-Out
Monte Carlo Pub
Quark's

## Hawaiian
808
Hawaiian Plantation

## Health Food
Canyon Ranch

## Indian
Gandhi India
Gaylord's
Halal Rest.
India Palace
Shalimar

## Irish
J. C. Wooloughan's
Sean Patrick's

## Italian
(N=Northern; S=Southern)
Al Dente (N)
Andiamo (N)
Anna Bella
Antonio's
Battista's
Bertolini's
Bootlegger Bistro (S)
Caffe Giorgio
Canaletto (N)
Capri Italian (N)
Carluccio's

# Restaurant Cuisine Index

Chicago Joe's
Fasolini's Pizza
Fellini's (N)
Ferraro's
Fiamma Tratt.
Fiore Steakhse. (N)
Francesco's
Gaetano's (N)
Il Fornaio (N)
Jazzed Cafe (N)
Le Provençal
Lombardi's (N)
Lupo, Tratt. del
Mama Jo's (S)
Market City
Metro Pizza
Montesano's
Nora's Cuisine
Onda
Osteria del Circo (N)
Palazzo
Panevino Rist.
Pasta (fa-zool)
Pasta Mia
Pasta Palace
Pasta Shop
Piero's Italian (N)
Piero's Tratt. (N)
Rist. Zeffirino (N)
Romano's
Sergio's Ital.
Spiedini
Stefano's
Terrazza (N)
Tintoretto Bakery
Tre (N)
Tremezzo (N)
Valentino/Piero Selv. (N)
Venetian Rist.
Ventano (N)
Viaggio

## Japanese
(* sushi specialist)
Ah Sin*
Benihana Hibachi

Blue Wave*
Dragon Sushi*
Geisha Steakhse.
Hamada*
Hyakumi*
Makino Rest.*
Mikado*
Nobu*
Osaka Jap.*
Osaka Jap. Cuis.*
Saizen Jap.*
Shintaro*
Sushi Fever*
Teru Sushi*
Todai*
Togoshi Ramen
Tokyo Rest.*

## Kosher
Canter's Deli

## Mediterranean
Andiamo
Cafe Tajine
Grape Street
Medici Cafe
MiraLago
Olives
Paymon's Med.
Picasso
Postrio

## Mexican
Baja Fresh
Bamboleo
Border Grill
Chapala's
Chevys
Chipotle
Doña Maria
Frank & Fina's
Garduño's
Guadalajara
La Barca
La Salsa
Macayo Vegas
MargaritaGrille

Pink Taco
Rubio's Baja
Taq. Canonita
Viva Mercado's
Willy & Jose's

**Middle Eastern**
Paymon's Med.
Spice Mkt. Buffet

**Moroccan**
Marrakech

**Noodle Shops**
Noodles
Noodle Shop
Togoshi Ramen

**Pacific Rim**
Japengo
Malibu Chan's
Roy's

**Pakistani**
Halal Rest.

**Pan-Asian**
Ah Sin
Asia
Dragon Noodle

**Persian**
Habib's Persian

**Peruvian**
Inka Si Señor

**Pizza**
Bootlegger Bistro
California Piz. Kit.
Canaletto
Fasolini's Pizza
Le Provençal
Lupo, Tratt. del
Metro Pizza
Montesano's
Nora's Cuisine
Pasta Palace

Piero's Tratt.
Sammy's

**Polish**
Polonez

**Pub Food**
Chicago Brew. Co.
Crown & Anchor
J. C. Wooloughan's
Monte Carlo Pub
Sean Patrick's
Triple 7 Brew
Venni Mac's

**Sandwiches**
Capriotti's
Harrie's Bagel.
Samuel's
Stage Deli

**Seafood**
Aqua
AquaKnox
Bally's Steakhse.
Bay Side Buffet
Big Al's Oyster
Blue Wave
Broiler
BullShrimp
Burgundy Rm.
Buzio's
Canal St. Grille
Como's Steakhse.
Costa del Sol
Craftsteak
808
Elements
Emeril's
Empress Court
Hilton Steakhse.
Hush Puppy
Joyful House
Kokomo's
La Barca
Luxor Steakhse.

# Restaurant Cuisine Index

Makino Rest.
McCorm. & Schmick's
Morton's
Neros
Palm
Paradise Buffet
Piero's Italian
Ping Pang Pong
Range Steakhse.
Redwood B&G
Rosewood Grille
Ruth's Chris
Sacred Sea Rm.
Seablue
Tillerman Rest.
Village Seafood
William B's

## Soul Food
Venni Mac's

## Southern
Hush Puppy
Kathy's Southern
Venni Mac's

## Southwestern
Chili's Grill
Coyote Cafe/M. Miller's
Garduño's
Roadrunner
Z'Tejas Grill

## Spanish
(* tapas specialist)
Firefly*

## Steakhouses
AJ's Steakhse.
Alan Albert's
Austin's Steakhse.
Bally's Steakhse.
Benihana Hibachi
Billy Bob's
Binion's Ranch
Blackstone's Stk.
Bob Taylor's

Broiler
BullShrimp
Burgundy Rm.
Canal St. Grille
Charlie Palmer
Como's Steakhse.
Conrad's
Craftsteak
Del Frisco's
Delmonico
Elements
Fiore Steakhse.
Fleming's
Gallaghers Steak.
Geisha Steakhse.
Golden Steer
Hilton Steakhse.
Kokomo's
Lawry's Prime Rib
Les Artistes
Lillie Langtry's
Luxor Steakhse.
Mon Ami Gabi
Morton's
Neros
N9ne Steakhse.
Outback Steakhse.
Palazzo
Palm
Prime
Pullman Grille
Range Steakhse.
Redwood B&G
Rosewood Grille
Ruth's Chris
Samba Brazilian
Sir Galahad's
Smith & Wollensky
Sonoma Cellar
Steak House
Steakhouse
Tillerman Rest.
William B's
Yolie's Brazilian

**Taiwanese**
Tea Planet

**Tearooms**
Tea Planet

**Tex-Mex**
Don Miguel's

**Thai**
Bangkok Orchid
Komol Rest.
Lotus of Siam
Thai Room
Thai Spice

**Vietnamese**
Crustacean LV

# LOCATIONS

## Central
Doña Maria
Florida Cafe
Tony Roma's

## Downtown
Andre's
Binion's Ranch
Buffet, The
Burgundy Rm.
Carson St. Cafe
Center Stage
Chicago Joe's
Garden Court
Hugo's Cellar
Ice House
La Salsa
Lillie Langtry's
Paradise Buffet
Pullman Grille
Redwood B&G
Second St. Grill
Stefano's
Tinoco's Bistro
Tony Roma's
Triple 7 Brew
Zax

## East of Strip
AJ's Steakhse.
Andiamo
Battista's
Benihana Hibachi
Buffet
Cafe Heidelberg
Del Frisco's
Firefly
Gandhi India
Garden of Dragon
Halal Rest.
Hard Rock Cafe
Harrie's Bagel.
Hilton Steakhse.
India Palace

Inka Si Señor
Komol Rest.
La Barca
Lawry's Prime Rib
Lotus of Siam
MargaritaGrille
Marrakech
McCorm. & Schmick's
Metro Pizza
Morton's
Mr. Lucky's 24/7
Nobu
Palazzo
Pamplemousse
Paradise Cafe
Paymon's Med.
P.F. Chang's
Piero's Italian
Piero's Tratt.
Pink Taco
Polonez
Quark's
Roy's
Ruth's Chris
Saizen Jap.
Sammy's
Shalimar
Simon Kitchen
Teru Sushi
Togoshi Ramen
Tokyo Rest.
Yolie's Brazilian
Z'Tejas Grill

## East Side
Amlee Gourmet
Anna Bella
Applebee's
Baja Fresh
Big Dog's
Billy Bob's
Broiler
Capriotti's
Carluccio's

# Restaurant Location Index

## West of Strip

Alizé
All American B&G
Antonio's
Bamboleo
Big Al's Oyster
Broiler
Buzio's
Cafe Nicolle
Canal St. Grille
Carnival World
Coffee Pub
Don Miguel's
Dragon Sushi
Egg & I
Feast
Fiore Steakhse.
Food Express
French Market
Garduño's
Gaylord's
Golden Steer
Guadalajara
Habib's Persian
Hamada
In-N-Out
Joyful House
Krispy Kreme
Little Buddha
Macayo Vegas
Mayflower Cuis.
Montesano's
N9ne Steakhse.
Osaka Jap.
Palace Cafe
Pasta Mia
Pasta Palace
Ping Pang Pong
Romano's
Rosemary's
Ruth's Chris
Sam Woo BBQ
Tea Planet
Venetian Rist.
Village Seafood
VooDoo

## West Side

Applebee's
Baja Fresh
Bertolini's
Big Dog's
Capriotti's
Cathay House
Chapala's
Chevys
Chicago Brew. Co.
Chili's Grill
Country Inn
Fasolini's Pizza
Fatburger
Fellini's
Ferraro's
Fleming's
Hush Puppy
In-N-Out
Jazzed Cafe
Krispy Kreme
Macayo Vegas
Makino Rest.
Malibu Chan's
Marche Bacchus
Melting Pot
Metro Pizza
Nora's Cuisine
Outback Steakhse.
Rincon/Buenos Aires
Roadrunner
Rosemary's
Roy's
Rubio's Baja
Sammy's
Sean Patrick's
Sedona
Sushi Fever
TGI Fridays
Thai Spice
Tony Roma's
Viva Mercado's
Wild Sage Café

# SPECIAL FEATURES

(Indexes list the best of many within each category. For multi-location restaurants, the availability of index features may vary by location.)

## Breakfast
(See also Hotel Dining)
Big Dog's
Black Mtn. Grill
Bootlegger Bistro
Chang of LV
Chapala's
Chicago Brew. Co.
Coachman's Inn
Coco's
Coffee Pub
Commander's Palace
Country Inn
Coyote Cafe/M. Miller's
Crown & Anchor
Doña Maria
Draft House
Egg & I
Fatburger
Hamada
Happy Days
Harrie's Bagel.
Ice House
Krispy Kreme
Lake Mead Cruises
Pinot Brasserie
Polonez
Roadrunner
Samuel's
Sam Woo BBQ
Sean Patrick's
Sedona
Stage Deli
Venetian Rist.
Ventano
Verandah

## Brunch
Bellagio Buffet
Black Mtn. Grill
Bootlegger Bistro
Broiler
Buffet, The
Café Bellagio
Cafe Lago
Cafe Tajine
Canyon Ranch
Chang of LV
Cheesecake Fact.
Coffee Pub
Commander's Palace
Courtyard Buffet
Garden Court
Garduño's
Gaylord's
Le Village
Medici Cafe
Mirage Buffet
MiraLago
Rist. Zeffirino
Samuel's
Simon Kitchen
Spice Mkt. Buffet
Stage Deli
Steak House
Sterling Brunch
Treasure Island
Venni Mac's
Verandah
Viva Mercado's
Wild Sage Café
Z'Tejas Grill

## Buffet Served
(Check availability)
Bay Side Buffet
Bellagio Buffet
Big Kit. Buffet
Blue Wave

# Restaurant Special Feature Index

## Catering

Aureole
Blue Wave
BullShrimp
California Piz. Kit.
Canyon Ranch
Capriotti's
Charlie Palmer
Crustacean LV
Del Frisco's
Doña Maria
Fasolini's Pizza
Fellini's
Firefly
Florida Cafe
Grape Street
Habib's Persian
Hamada
Hard Rock Cafe
Inka Si Señor
Japengo
Jazzed Cafe
Kathy's Southern
Lupo, Tratt. del
Lutèce
Macayo Vegas
Malibu Chan's
Marche Bacchus
Marc's
Mayflower Cuis.
Medici Cafe
Memphis BBQ
Metro Pizza
MiraLago
Montesano's
Morton's
Nobu
Nora's Cuisine
Osaka Jap.
Osaka Jap. Cuis.
Panevino Rist.
Pasta Mia
Pasta Shop
Paymon's Med.
Piero's Italian
Postrio
Rosemary's

Royal Star
Roy's
Sammy's
Shalimar
Simon Kitchen
Spago
Spiedini
Tinoco's Bistro
Tintoretto Bakery
Tony Roma's
Venetian Rist.
Ventano
Viaggio
Viva Mercado's
Wild Sage Café
Wolfgang Puck
Z'Tejas Grill

## Child-Friendly

(Besides the normal fast-food places; * children's menu available)

America*
Applebee's*
Bay Side Buffet
Bellagio Buffet
Black Mtn. Grill*
Bootlegger Bistro*
Border Grill*
Cafe Heidelberg*
Cafe Lago*
Cafe Tajine*
California Piz. Kit.*
Capri Italian
Capriotti's*
Caribe Café
Chapala's*
Cheesecake Fact.
Chevys*
Chicago Brew. Co.*
Chili's Grill*
Chipotle*
Coco's*
Coffee Pub
Country Inn*
Doña Maria
Don Miguel's

# Restaurant Special Feature Index

Egg & I*
Fasolini's Pizza
Fatburger
Feast
Festival Buffet
Firelight Buffet*
Florida Cafe
Fresh Market Sq.*
Full Ho
Garden Court
Garduño's*
Geisha Steakhse.
Grape Street
Guadalajara
Halal Rest.
Happy Days*
Hard Rock Cafe*
Harley-Davidson*
Hawaiian Plantation
Hill Top House*
Hush Puppy*
India Palace*
In-N-Out
Kathy's Southern*
Kona Grill*
Lake Mead Cruises*
La Salsa*
Lindy's*
Lombardi's
Lotus of Siam
Macayo Vegas*
Mama Jo's*
Market City
Medici Cafe*
Memphis BBQ*
Metro Pizza*
MGM Grand Buffet
Mirage Buffet
MiraLago*
Montesano's*
Mr. Lucky's 24/7*
Neros
Nora's Cuisine
Outback Steakhse.*
Paradise Garden
Pasta (fa-zool)*
Pasta Mia

Pasta Palace
Pasta Shop*
Paymon's Med.*
Pearl
P.F. Chang's
Picasso
Planet Hollywood*
Polonez*
Quark's*
Raffles Cafe
Rainforest Cafe*
Red, White & Blue*
Rincon/Buenos Aires
Roadrunner*
Romano's*
Roxy's Diner
Royal Star
Roy's*
Rubio's Baja*
Sammy's*
Samuel's*
Second St. Grill
Shalimar
Sir Galahad's*
Stage Deli*
Sushi Fever*
Swiss Cafe Rest.*
Tenaya Creek*
TGI Fridays*
Tony Roma's*
Treasure Island
Venni Mac's
Ventano
Viaggio*
Viva Mercado's*
Wild Sage Café
Wolfgang Puck*
Z'Tejas Grill*

## Cigars Welcome
AJ's Steakhse.
Alan Albert's
Andre's
Bootlegger Bistro
Carluccio's
Charlie Palmer
Chicago Brew. Co.

Chili's Grill
Craftsteak
Crown & Anchor
Delmonico
Fellini's
Ferraro's
Fiore Steakhse.
Harley-Davidson
Hugo's Cellar
Inka Si Señor
J. C. Wooloughan's
Medici Cafe
Memphis BBQ
Monte Carlo Pub
Morton's
Palazzo
Palm
Piero's Italian
Pink Taco
Pinot Brasserie
Pullman Grille
Quark's
Rosemary's
Ruth's Chris
Simon Kitchen
Smith & Wollensky
Sonoma Cellar
Spiedini
Tenaya Creek
Tillerman Rest.
Tony Roma's
Tremezzo
Venetian Rist.
William B's
Willy & Jose's
Yolie's Brazilian
Z'Tejas Grill

Blue Wave
Bootlegger Bistro
California Piz. Kit.
Capriotti's
Chicago Brew. Co.
Chili's Grill
Coffee Pub
Country Inn
Florida Cafe
Food Express
Frank & Fina's
Gandhi India
Harrie's Bagel.
India Palace
Lombardi's
Mama Jo's
Mayflower Cuis.
Memphis BBQ
Metro Pizza
Montesano's
Osaka Jap.
Pasta Mia
Pasta Shop
Piero's Tratt.
Polonez
Rosemary's
Sammy's
Samuel's
Thai Room
Thai Spice
Tinoco's Bistro
Tony Roma's
Tremezzo
Venni Mac's
Ventano
Viva Mercado's
Wild Sage Café

**Critic-Proof**
(Get lots of business
despite so-so food)
Battista's
Rainforest Cafe

**Delivery**
Amlee Gourmet
Bangkok Orchid

**Dining Alone**
(Other than hotels and places
with counter service)
Blue Wave
Coco's
Coffee Pub
Fleming's
Frank & Fina's
Gaetano's

## Restaurant Special Feature Index

Hawaiian Plantation
Inka Si Señor
Lotus of Siam
Malibu Chan's
Mama Jo's
Paymon's Med.
Piero's Tratt.
Polonez
Rosemary's
Shalimar
Stage Deli
Thai Spice
Todai
Wild Sage Café
Z'Tejas Grill

### Entertainment
(Call for days and times of performances)

AJ's Steakhse. (piano)
Antonio's (guitar)
Bootlegger (jazz/karaoke)
Cafe Heidelberg (accordion)
Cafe Lago (piano)
Cafe Nicolle (piano/vocals)
Carluccio's (piano)
Center Stage (piano)
Chapala's (guitar/mariachi)
Charlie Palmer (piano)
China Grill (DJs)
Coachman's Inn (piano/vocals)
Commander's Palace (jazz)
Crown & Anchor (bands)
Crustacean LV (DJs/jazz)
Del Frisco's (piano/vocals)
Delmonico (piano)
Egg & I (dinner theater)
Eiffel Tower (piano)
Fellini's (piano/vocals)
Ferraro's (keyboard/piano)
Habib's Persian (belly dancing)
Hard Rock Cafe (bands)
Harley-Davidson (rock)
Ice House (DJs)
Inka Si Señor (Latin)
Isis (harp/piano)
Jazzed Cafe (jazz)

J. C. Wooloughan's (Irish)
La Barca (mariachi)
Lake Mead Cruises (bands)
Le Provençal (singing servers)
Little Buddha (DJ)
Marrakech (belly dancing)
Medici Cafe (piano)
Monte Carlo Pub (band)
N9ne Steakhse. (DJ)
Nora's Cuisine (swing trio)
Onda (piano)
Osaka Jap. Cuis. (piano)
Outback Steakhse. (magician)
Pahrump Valley (guitar/harp)
Palazzo (piano)
Panevino Rist. (piano)
Piero's Italian (piano)
Piero's Tratt. (jazz)
Range Steakhse. (jazz/piano)
Redwood B&G (piano)
Rist. Zeffirino (guitar/piano)
Roxy's Diner (dance/vocals)
Ruth's Chris (band/jazz)
Sacred Sea Rm. (piano)
Sergio's Ital. (piano)
Stefano's (singing servers)
Tenaya Creek (acoustic guitar)
Terrazza (jazz trio)
Tony Roma's (clown)
Triple 7 Brew (varies)
Venni Mac's (varies)
Ventano (guitar)
Verandah (piano)
Viva Mercado's (guitar/vocals)
VooDoo (jazz)

### Fireplaces
Andre's
Anna Bella
Black Mtn. Grill
Bob Taylor's
Canal St. Grille
Chicago Brew. Co.
Chicago Joe's
Coachman's Inn
Fellini's
Fiamma Tratt.

Fiore Steakhse.
Ice House
J. C. Woolloughan's
Lawry's Prime Rib
McCorm. & Schmick's
Memphis BBQ
Pamplemousse
Panevino Rist.
Pullman Grille
Roadrunner
Ruth's Chris
Sean Patrick's
Sedona
Tillerman Rest.
Z'Tejas Grill

### Hotel Dining

Aladdin Resort & Casino
  Elements
  La Salsa
  P.F. Chang's
  Spice Mkt. Buffet
  Tremezzo
Bally's Las Vegas Hotel
  Al Dente
  Bally's Steakhse.
  Big Kit. Buffet
  Chang of LV
  Sterling Brunch
Barbary Coast Hotel
  Drai's on Strip
  Michael's
  Victorian Room
Bellagio Hotel
  Aqua
  Bellagio Buffet
  Café Bellagio
  Jasmine
  Le Cirque
  Nectar
  Noodles
  Olives
  Osteria del Circo
  Picasso
  Prime
  Shintaro

Binion's Horseshoe Hotel
  Binion's Ranch
Boulder Station Hotel
  Broiler
  Feast
  Guadalajara
Caesars Palace
  Bradley Ogden
  Cafe Lago
  808
  Empress Court
  Hyakumi
  Neros
  Terrazza
California Hotel
  Redwood B&G
Casino Royal Hotel
  Outback Steakhse.
Circus Circus Hotel
  Steak House
Desert Passage at Aladdin
  Commander's Palace
  Crustacean LV
  Lombardi's
  Todai
Excalibur Hotel
  Krispy Kreme
  Sir Galahad's
Fiesta Rancho
  Festival Buffet
  Garduño's
Flamingo Las Vegas
  Conrad's
  Hamada
  Lindy's
  Paradise Garden
Forum Shops at Caesars
  Bertolini's
  Cheesecake Fact.
  Chinois
  La Salsa
  Palm
  Planet Hollywood
  Spago
  Stage Deli

# Restaurant Special Feature Index

## "In" Places

## Late Dining

(Weekday closing hour)

Cafe Lago (24 hrs.)
California Piz. Kit. (varies)
Canter's Deli (12 AM)
Caribe Café (24 hrs.)
Carson St. Cafe (24 hrs.)
Chapala's (varies)
Chicago Brew. Co. (24 hrs.)
Coachman's Inn (24 hrs.)
Crown & Anchor (24 hrs.)
Draft House (24 hrs.)
Fatburger (varies)
Firefly (3 AM)
Food Express (2 AM)
Grand Lux Cafe (24 hrs.)
Hamada (varies)
Hard Rock Cafe (12 AM)
Ice House (24 hrs.)
Il Fornaio (varies)
In-N-Out (1 AM)
Jazzed Cafe (12 AM)
J. C. Wooloughan's (1 AM)
Joyful House (3 AM)
Krispy Kreme (varies)
La Salsa (varies)
Lindy's (24 hrs.)
Malibu Chan's (2 AM)
Metro Pizza (varies)
Monte Carlo Pub (3 AM)
Mr. Lucky's 24/7 (24 hrs.)
N9ne Steakhse. (12 AM)
Noodles (2 AM)
Noodle Shop (3 AM)
Osaka Jap. (varies)
Outback Steakhse. (varies)
Palace Cafe (24 hrs.)
Paradise Cafe (24 hrs.)
Paymon's Med. (1 AM)
P.F. Chang's (varies)
Ping Pang Pong (3 AM)
Raffles Cafe (24 hrs.)
Rist. Zeffirino (12 AM)
Roadrunner (varies)
Roxy's Diner (12 AM)
Ruth's Chris (varies)
Saizen Jap. (12 AM)
Sean Patrick's (12 AM)

Sedona (24 hrs.)
Smith & Wollensky (3 AM)
Tea Planet (2 AM)
Terrace Café (24 hrs.)
TGI Fridays (varies)
Tintoretto Bakery (12:30 AM)
Tremezzo (12 AM)
Valentino/Piero Selv. (12 AM)
Ventano (24 hrs.)
Victorian Room (24 hrs.)

## Noteworthy Newcomers

Ah Sin
AquaKnox
Bradley Ogden
Caffe Giorgio
Canter's Deli
Crustacean LV
Fiamma Tratt.
Firefly
Gaylord's
Kona Grill
Marche Bacchus
Seablue
Teru Sushi
Tinoco's Bistro
Tre

## Offbeat

Crown & Anchor
Florida Cafe
Harley-Davidson
Hawaiian Plantation
Inka Si Señor
Jazzed Cafe
Little Buddha
Marrakech
Melting Pot
Paymon's Med.
Pink Taco
Polonez
Quark's
Rincon/Buenos Aires
Tinoco's Bistro
Todai
Venni Mac's
Yolie's Brazilian

# Restaurant Special Feature Index

## Outdoor Dining
(G=garden; P=patio;
S=sidewalk; T=terrace;
W=waterside)
Ah Sin (P)
Andre's (G, P, T)
Bertolini's (P)
Black Mtn. Grill (P)
Bootlegger Bistro (P)
Border Grill (P)
Café Bellagio (P)
Cafe Lago (P)
Cafe Nicolle (G, P)
Cafe Tajine (P)
Cheesecake Fact. (P)
Chicago Brew. Co. (P)
Coffee Pub (P)
Egg & I (P)
Fellini's (P)
Fiore Steakhse. (T)
Firefly (P)
Frank & Fina's (P)
Garduño's (P)
Grape Street (P)
Habib's Persian (P, T)
Ice House (P, T)
Il Fornaio (P)
India Palace (W)
In-N-Out (P)
Japengo (P, W)
Jazzed Cafe (P)
J. C. Wooloughan's (P, S)
Kona Grill (P)
Le Provençal (P)
Little Buddha (P)
Lupo, Tratt. del (P)
Lutèce (P)
Mama Jo's (P)
Marche Bacchus (T, W)
Marc's (P)
Mayflower Cuis. (P)
McCorm. & Schmick's (P)
Medici Cafe (P)
MiraLago (P)
Mon Ami Gabi (P, S)

Monte Carlo Pub (T)
Nobu (P, W)
Olives (P, W)
Pahrump Valley (G, P, S, T)
Palazzo (P)
Palm (P)
Pasta Mia (P)
Paymon's Med. (P, S)
P.F. Chang's (P, W)
Picasso (P)
Pink Taco (P, S)
Rincon/Buenos Aires (P)
Roadrunner (P)
Roy's (P)
Sammy's (P)
Samuel's (P)
Sedona (P)
Shintaro (P)
Simon Kitchen (P, T, W)
Smith & Wollensky (P, S)
Spiedini (P)
Summit Rest. (T)
Swiss Cafe Rest. (P)
Tenaya Creek (P)
Terrazza (P, T, W)
Tinoco's Bistro (P)
Tintoretto Bakery (P)
Tony Roma's (G, P, S)
Tremezzo (P, T)
Ventano (P)
Verandah (P)
VooDoo (T)
Wild Sage Café (P)
Yolie's Brazilian (P)
Z'Tejas Grill (P)

## People-Watching
AJ's Steakhse.
Aqua
Aureole
Bertolini's
Bootlegger Bistro
Charlie Palmer
Cheesecake Fact.
Chinois
Commander's Palace

Craftsteak
Delmonico
Drai's on Strip
808
Fiamma Tratt.
Inka Si Señor
Kona Grill
Le Cirque
Little Buddha
Lupo, Tratt. del
Michael's
Mon Ami Gabi
Mr. Lucky's 24/7
N9ne Steakhse.
Nobu
Olives
Osteria del Circo
Palm
Pearl
Picasso
Piero's Italian
Piero's Tratt.
Pink Taco
Postrio
Renoir
Ruth's Chris
Seablue
Simon Kitchen
Spago
Spiedini
Stage Deli
Taq. Canonita
Tillerman Rest.
Tintoretto Bakery
Valentino/Piero Selv.
VooDoo
Wild Sage Café
Wolfgang Puck
Zax
Z'Tejas Grill

## Power Scenes
Andre's
Aqua
AquaKnox
Aureole

Bradley Ogden
BullShrimp
Charlie Palmer
Chinois
Coffee Pub
Commander's Palace
Craftsteak
Drai's on Strip
Eiffel Tower
Fellini's
Le Cirque
Lupo, Tratt. del
Nobu
Olives
Osteria del Circo
Palm
Pearl
Picasso
Piero's Italian
Piero's Tratt.
Postrio
Prime
Renoir
Rosemary's
Ruth's Chris
Spago
Spiedini
Tillerman Rest.
Valentino/Piero Selv.
Wild Sage Café

## Pre-Theater Menus
(Call for prices and times)
Lupo, Tratt. del
Nectar
Shintaro

## Private Rooms
(Restaurants charge less at
off times; call for capacity)
Andiamo
Andre's
AquaKnox
Aureole
Bootlegger Bistro
Buccaneer Bay

BullShrimp
Cafe Nicolle
Canaletto
Carluccio's
Cathay House
Chang of LV
Charlie Palmer
China Grill
Chinois
Commander's Palace
Como's Steakhse.
Conrad's
Courtyard Buffet
Coyote Cafe/M. Miller's
Craftsteak
Crustacean LV
Del Frisco's
Delmonico
Dragon Noodle
Drai's on Strip
Eiffel Tower
Elements
Emeril's
Ferraro's
Fiamma Tratt.
Fleming's
Francesco's
Gallaghers Steak.
Garduño's
Gaylord's
Golden Steer
Habib's Persian
Hilton Steakhse.
Ice House
Japengo
Jasmine
J. C. Wooloughan's
Lawry's Prime Rib
Les Artistes
Marche Bacchus
Marc's
McCorm. & Schmick's
MiraLago
Mon Ami Gabi
Monte Carlo Pub
Morton's

N9ne Steakhse.
Nobu
Osaka Jap.
Osteria del Circo
Pahrump Valley
Palm
Pamplemousse
Panevino Rist.
Pearl
Piero's Italian
Piero's Tratt.
Pinot Brasserie
Postrio
Pullman Grille
Rist. Zeffirino
Rosemary's
Royal Star
Roy's
Ruth's Chris
Seablue
Sergio's Ital.
Shanghai Lilly
Shintaro
Simon Kitchen
Smith & Wollensky
Sonoma Cellar
Spago
Steakhouse
Tenaya Creek
Tillerman Rest.
Tremezzo
Valentino/Piero Selv.
Venetian Rist.
Ventano
Viaggio
Wild Sage Café
William B's
Z'Tejas Grill

## Prix Fixe Menus
(Call for prices and times)
Aqua
Bonjour
Chang of LV
Coffee Pub
Courtyard Buffet

Eiffel Tower
Emeril's
Ferraro's
Full Ho
Geisha Steakhse.
India Palace
Japengo
Jazzed Cafe
Le Cirque
Lutèce
Makino Rest.
Marrakech
Nobu
Olives
Osaka Jap.
Osaka Jap. Cuis.
Palm
Picasso
Pinot Brasserie
Renoir
Rist. Zeffirino
Rosemary's
Roy's
Sacred Sea Rm.
Shintaro
Sir Galahad's
Steakhouse
Sterling Brunch
Top of World
Valentino/Piero Selv.
Verandah
Viaggio
Yolie's Brazilian

**Quiet Conversation**
Alizé
Bonjour
BullShrimp
Coco's
Craftsteak
Firefly
Gaetano's
Golden Steer
Hawaiian Plantation
Hill Top House
Lutèce

Marche Bacchus
Marc's
Palazzo
Pasta (fa-zool)
Pearl
Prime
Second St. Grill
Terrazza
Tinoco's Bistro
Venni Mac's
Verandah
Viaggio
William B's

**Reserve Ahead**
Anna Bella
Antonio's
Aqua
AquaKnox
Aureole
Bally's Steakhse.
Benihana Hibachi
Binion's Ranch
Blackstone's Stk.
Border Grill
Bradley Ogden
Broiler
Buccaneer Bay
Canaletto
Conrad's
Craftsteak
Delmonico
808
Emeril's
Empress Court
Fellini's
Ferraro's
Fiamma Tratt.
Gallaghers Steak.
Golden Steer
Il Fornaio
Jasmine
Kokomo's
Lake Mead Cruises
Le Cirque
Lillie Langtry's

Michael's
Mikado
N9ne Steakhse.
Nobu
Osteria del Circo
Pahrump Valley
Pamplemousse
Picasso
Polonez
Postrio
Prime
Range Steakhse.
Samba Brazilian
Seablue
Spiedini
Steak House
Stefano's
Sterling Brunch
Sushi Fever
Tea Planet
Tenaya Creek
Teru Sushi
3950
Tillerman Rest.
Tokyo Rest.
Top of World
Tremezzo
Valentino/Piero Selv.
VooDoo
Wild Sage Café
William B's

## Romantic Places
Alizé
Andre's
Aureole
Charlie Palmer
Chicago Joe's
Eiffel Tower
Fiamma Tratt.
Hugo's Cellar
Le Cirque
Marche Bacchus
Marc's
Michael's
NOBHILL

Pamplemousse
Pearl
Picasso
Prime
Renoir
Rist. Zeffirino
Royal Star
3950
Top of World
Valentino/Piero Selv.
Viaggio

## Senior Appeal
Benihana Hibachi
Blue Wave
Bootlegger Bistro
Center Stage
Cheesecake Fact.
Coco's
Coffee Pub
Country Inn
Egg & I
Fleming's
Florida Cafe
Garden Court
Hawaiian Plantation
Hill Top House
Hugo's Cellar
Hush Puppy
Mama Jo's
Palazzo
Pasta (fa-zool)
Pasta Palace
Pasta Shop
Piero's Tratt.
Polonez
Redwood B&G
Summit Rest.
Swiss Cafe Rest.
Taq. Canonita
Terrace Café
Thai Room
Tintoretto Bakery
Todai
Tony Roma's
Treasure Island

Verandah
Victorian Room
Village Seafood
Viva Mercado's
Wild Sage Café
Willy & Jose's
Wolfgang Puck

### Singles Scenes
AJ's Steakhse.
Benihana Hibachi
Cheesecake Fact.
Drai's on Strip
808
Fleming's
Gaetano's
Hamada
Harley-Davidson
Hawaiian Plantation
Ice House
Inka Si Señor
J. C. Woolboughan's
Kona Grill
Little Buddha
Lupo, Tratt. del
Mama Jo's
Marrakech
Nectar
N9ne Steakhse.
Nobu
Panevino Rist.
Paymon's Med.
Pearl
P.F. Chang's
Piero's Tratt.
Pink Taco
Roadrunner
Roy's
Sean Patrick's
Sedona
Simon Kitchen
Smith & Wollensky
Spago
Taq. Canonita
TGI Fridays
Todai

Triple 7 Brew
Viaggio
Village Seafood
Viva Mercado's
VooDoo
Wild Sage Café
Zax
Z'Tejas Grill

### Sleepers
(Good to excellent food,
but little known)
AJ's Steakhse.
Andiamo
Anna Bella
Burgundy Rm.
Cafe Heidelberg
Capri Italian
Carluccio's
Conrad's
Don Miguel's
Elements
Fasolini's Pizza
Florida Cafe
Gandhi India
Golden Steer
Hush Puppy
Inka Si Señor
In-N-Out
Japengo
Jazzed Cafe
Joyful House
Kathy's Southern
Lombardi's
Makino Rest.
Medici Cafe
Montesano's
N9ne Steakhse.
Nora's Cuisine
Pahrump Valley
Panevino Rist.
Pasta Mia
Pasta Palace
Paymon's Med.
Pearl
Piero's Tratt.

Sacred Sea Rm.
Samuel's
Simon Kitchen
Sonoma Cellar
Summit Rest.
Sushi Fever
Swiss Cafe Rest.
Thai Spice
Tremezzo
Ventano
Viva Mercado's
William B's
Willy & Jose's

## Teen Appeal
Bangkok Orchid
Benihana Hibachi
Blue Wave
Buccaneer Bay
Center Stage
Cheesecake Fact.
Chevys
Coco's
Florida Cafe
Grand Lux Cafe
Happy Days
Hard Rock Cafe
Harley-Davidson
Hawaiian Plantation
Inka Si Señor
In-N-Out
La Salsa
Mama Jo's
Melting Pot
Paradise Garden
Planet Hollywood
Quark's
Rainforest Cafe
Roxy's Diner
Taq. Canonita
Thai Room
Tintoretto Bakery
Todai
Top of World
Victorian Room
Village Seafood

Viva Mercado's
Wild Sage Café
Wolfgang Puck

## Views
Alizé
Aqua
Buccaneer Bay
Café Bellagio
Cafe Tajine
Center Stage
Eiffel Tower
Garden of Dragon
Japengo
Lake Mead Cruises
Marche Bacchus
Medici Cafe
Olives
Osteria del Circo
Panevino Rist.
Picasso
Range Steakhse.
Terrazza
Top of World
Venni Mac's
Ventano
Viaggio
VooDoo

## Visitors on Expense Account
Alan Albert's
Aqua
Aureole
BullShrimp
Charlie Palmer
Commander's Palace
Craftsteak
Delmonico
Eiffel Tower
808
Fiore Steakhse.
Hilton Steakhse.
Hugo's Cellar
Le Cirque
Lutèce

Morton's
Neros
N9ne Steakhse.
Nobu
Osteria del Circo
Palm
Piero's Italian
Prime
Rosemary's
Rosewood Grille
Royal Star
Roy's
Ruth's Chris
Shintaro
Smith & Wollensky
Steakhouse
Sterling Brunch
Terrazza
3950
Tillerman Rest.
Top of World
Tremezzo
Venetian Rist.
Yolie's Brazilian

## Winning Wine Lists

Alan Albert's
Alizé
Andre's
Aureole
Charlie Palmer
Craftsteak
Drai's on Strip
Fiore Steakhse.
Grape Street
Jazzed Cafe
Le Cirque
Marche Bacchus
Osteria del Circo
Picasso
Piero's Italian
Postrio
Renoir
Spago
Terrazza
Valentino/Piero Selv.
Viaggio
VooDoo

# Nightlife

# Most Popular

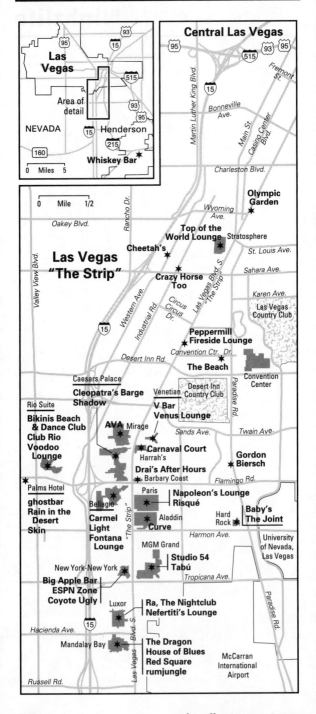

**Las Vegas**

Area of detail

NEVADA

Henderson

**Whiskey Bar**

0 Miles 5

**Central Las Vegas**

Fremont St.

Martin Luther King Blvd.

Bonneville Ave.

Main St.

Casino Center Blvd.

Charleston Blvd.

0 Mile 1/2

Rancho Dr.

**Olympic Garden**

Wyoming Ave.

Oakey Blvd.

**Top of the World Lounge**

Stratosphere

St. Louis Ave.

**Cheetah's**

**Las Vegas "The Strip"**

Sahara Ave.

**Crazy Horse Too**

Karen Ave.

Valley View Blvd.

Western Ave.

Industrial Rd.

Circus Circus Dr.

Las Vegas Blvd. S. "The Strip"

Las Vegas Country Club

**Peppermill Fireside Lounge**

Convention Ctr. Dr.

Desert Inn Rd.

**The Beach**

Paradise Rd.

Convention Center

Caesars Palace

**Cleopatra's Barge Shadow**

Venetian

Desert Inn Country Club

Rio Suite

**Bikinis Beach & Dance Club**
**Club Rio**
**Voodoo Lounge**

**AVA**

Mirage

**V Bar**
**Venus Lounge**

Sands Ave.

Twain Ave.

**Carnaval Court**

Harrah's

**Gordon Biersch**

**Drai's After Hours**

Barbary Coast

Flamingo Rd.

Palms Hotel

**ghostbar**
**Rain in the Desert**
**Skin**

Bellagio

Paris

**Napoleon's Lounge**
**Risqué**

**Baby's**
**The Joint**

Hard Rock

**Carmel**
**Light**
**Fontana Lounge**

Aladdin

**Curve**

Harmon Ave.

University of Nevada, Las Vegas

MGM Grand

**Studio 54**
**Tabú**

New York-New York

**Big Apple Bar**
**ESPN Zone**
**Coyote Ugly**

Tropicana Ave.

Luxor

**Ra, The Nightclub**
**Nefertiti's Lounge**

Paradise Rd.

Hacienda Ave.

Las Vegas Blvd. S.

Mandalay Bay

**The Dragon**
**House of Blues**
**Red Square**
**rumjungle**

McCarran International Airport

Russell Rd.

# Most Popular

1. rumjungle
2. House of Blues
3. Light
4. ghostbar
5. Red Square
6. Studio 54
7. Drai's After Hours
8. Coyote Ugly
9. Rain in the Desert
10. Ra, The Nightclub
11. ESPN Zone
12. V Bar
13. Baby's
14. Olympic Garden
15. VooDoo Lounge
16. Fontana Lounge
17. Cleopatra's Barge
18. Caramel
19. Big Apple Bar
20. Carnaval Court
21. Top of the World*
22. Venus Lounge
23. Whiskey Bar
24. Club Rio
25. Shadow
26. Bikinis Beach
27. Crazy Horse Too
28. Beach, The
29. Peppermill Fireside
30. Cheetah's
31. Joint, The
32. Tabú*
33. Curve
34. Risqué
35. Dragon, The
36. AVA
37. Napoleon's Lounge*
38. Nefertiti's Lounge*
39. Gordon Biersch
40. Skin

Budget-conscious night-crawlers can find a list of the top Best Buys on page 132.

---

* Indicates a tie with place above

# Top Rated Nightlife Spots

Top lists exclude places with low voting.

## Top Appeal

26 ghostbar
VooDoo Lounge
Fontana Lounge

25 Light
Red Square
Olympic Garden

## Top Decor

26 ghostbar
Whiskey Bar
25 Fontana Lounge
Red Square
rumjungle

## Top Service

22 Skin
Olympic Garden
21 Red Square
Peppermill Fireside
Risqué

## By Category
Listed in order of Appeal rating

**After-Hours Dance Clubs**
25 Light
Rain in the Desert
24 Drai's After Hours
22 rumjungle
Venus Lounge

**Music Clubs**
24 Joint, The
23 House of Blues
21 AVA
Oasis Lounge
17 Beach, The

**Happy Hour**
23 V Bar
Napoleon's Lounge
19 Gordon Biersch
Bahama Breeze
17 Coyote Ugly

**Strip Clubs**
25 Olympic Garden
24 Cheetah's
Crazy Horse Too
22 Club Paradise
12 Girls of Glitter Gulch

**Lounges**
26 ghostbar
VooDoo Lounge
Fontana Lounge
25 Light
Skin

**Views**
26 ghostbar
VooDoo Lounge
Fontana Lounge
24 Top of the World
22 Club Rio

## Best Buys

1. Skin
2. Peppermill Fireside
3. Carnaval Court
4. VooDoo Lounge
5. ghostbar
6. Kahunaville
7. Rain in the Desert
8. Fontana Lounge
9. ESPN Zone
10. Venus Lounge

subscribe to zagat.com

# Ratings & Symbols

**Name, Address, Phone Number & Web Site**

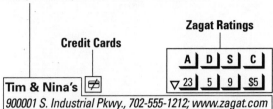

**Zagat Ratings**

**Credit Cards**

| A | D | S | C |
|---|---|---|---|
| ▽ 23 | 5 | 9 | $5 |

**Tim & Nina's** 🚫

*900001 S. Industrial Pkwy., 702-555-1212; www.zagat.com*

☑ "Take a whirl on the poles" used by the strippers in *Showgirls* or "order a *Leaving Las Vegas* cocktail" at this "unique" bar southwest of the Strip that's devoted to Sin City cinema; while some insist that "the Hard Rock has nothing to worry about" and that "Elvis was nowhere to be found in the building", more shout "viva Las Vegas!" and "are you in?"

**Review, with surveyors' comments in quotes**

Nightspots with the highest overall ratings and greatest popularity and importance are printed in CAPITAL LETTERS.

Before each review a symbol indicates whether responses were uniform ■ or mixed ☑.

**Credit Cards:** 🚫 no credit cards accepted

**Ratings:** Appeal, Decor and Service are rated on a scale of **0** to **30**. The Cost (C) column reflects surveyors' estimated price of a typical single drink.

| A | Appeal | D | Decor | S | Service | C | Cost |
|---|--------|---|-------|---|---------|---|------|
| 23 | | 5 | | 9 | | $5 | |

| | |
|---|---|
| **0–9** poor to fair | **20–25** very good to excellent |
| **10–15** fair to good | **26–30** extraordinary to perfection |
| **16–19** good to very good | ▽ low response/less reliable |

For places listed without ratings or a numerical cost estimate, such as an important newcomer or a popular write-in, the price range is indicated by the following symbols.

| | | | |
|---|---|---|---|
| **I** | below $5 | **E** | $9 to $11 |
| **M** | $5 to $8 | **VE** | more than $11 |

# Nightlife Directory

### Alesium After Hours at Seven ▽ 20 20 16 $13
*3724 Las Vegas Blvd. S. (Harmon Ave.), 702-739-7744;*
*www.sevenlasvegas.com*
■ "Some of the world's best DJs" do the cooking late night
at this "fab" hot spot in the heart of the Strip where a buffet
of beautiful beaus and belles boogeys to "a mix of house,
hip-hop, trance and drum 'n' bass"; "the place to go for
after hours in Las Vegas" may not "get going till around 3
AM", but by then, the young holdouts are ready to party
until "well after the sun comes up" over the patio.

### Armadillo, The – – – E
*Texas Station Hotel, 2101 Texas Star Ln. (bet. Lake Mead Blvd. &*
*Rancho Dr.), North Las Vegas, 702-631-1000;*
*www.texasstation.com*
Spend your "21st birthday" doing all 16 dances to Loveshack,
an '80s cover band rocking with impersonations of everyone
from the B-52s to Blondie at this no-frills club in North Las
Vegas' Texas Station; other nights, swingers go even more
retro jitterbugging to the big band sounds of the '30s and
'40s; you "could do worse" than to "have a blast" "without
being too pretentious."

### Ava 21 22 20 $11
*Mirage Hotel, 3400 Las Vegas Blvd. S. (Spring Mountain Rd.),*
*702-791-7111; www.themirage.com*
■ 'Ava fruity cocktail and unwind at this "contemporary
tiki bar (if there is such a thing) serving specialty drinks in
a tropical environment"; the new Polynesian lounge in The
Mirage on the Strip offers live entertainment in the form of
several waterfalls as well as bands cranking out original
rock 'n' roll, funk and covers every night of the week.

### BABY'S 22 19 16 $10
*Hard Rock Hotel & Casino, 4455 Paradise Rd. (bet. Flamingo Rd. &*
*Harmon Ave.), 702-693-5000; www.babyslasvegas.com*
■ "Hip crowds" "get crazy" just east of the Strip in this
"subterranean" "sweatbox" that "kicks ass" deep down
"under the glare of the raucous Hard Rock Hotel"; though
the "bumpin'" was "better in its heyday, it's still pretty fun",
so for a "sleazy/sophisticated" "blast", "weasel your way
into" the "fantastic VIP areas" or "shake your thang" on
the dance floor to "great hip-hop" with "beautiful bunnies
and Baldwins" who "know how to paarrtay!"

### Bahama Breeze 19 20 19 $10
*375 Hughes Center Dr. (bet. Flamingo & Paradise Rds.),*
*702-731-3252; www.bahamabreeze.com*
◪ "Office happy-hour" hordes and "tourists" get in sync
with island time over "tasty margaritas" and other "fun
summertime drinks" at this "tropical-themed" spot east of
the Strip; go for a "group gathering", but "at prime times,
be prepared to wait to get into" the "cheesy" joint where

the "loud" "hit-or-miss entertainment on the patio" "has little appeal for that intimate night on the town."

### Bar at Times Square
– | – | – | M

*New York-New York Hotel & Casino, 3790 Las Vegas Blvd. S. (Tropicana Ave.), 702-740-6969; www.nynyhotelcasino.com*
Renovated, just like its namesake Manhattan locale, for the onslaught of masses en route to the new multimillion-dollar Zumanity Theatre, this watering hole inside New York-New York is the closest stop to Cirque du Soleil's highbrow, adult-themed show; after sitting through 90 minutes of simulated sexual activity, you may need a drink, as well as the comic distraction of The Dueling Pianos.

### Beach, The
17 | 16 | 16 | $8

*365 Convention Center Dr. (Paradise Rd.), 702-731-1925; www.beachlv.com*
■ "You'll forget that you're in the desert" when you ride the surf into this "*Girls Gone Wild*"–esque "meat market" east of the Strip, where it's "spring break" year-round with "young", "gorgeous, bikini-clad babes and studs" doing "cheap" "body shots" and "beer tubes" to "rock 'n' roll" "into the wee hours"; it's "the place" to "relive" your "juvenile" fantasies 'cause "if you can't hook up here, you can't hook up anywhere."

### Big Apple Bar
20 | 20 | 17 | $9

*New York-New York Hotel & Casino, 3790 Las Vegas Blvd. S. (Tropicana Ave.), 702-740-6969; www.nynyhotelcasino.com*
■ "Wanna feel like you're at a bar in midtown Manhattan?"; follow "homesick" "NYers" to this "casual" "pub" chock-full of "reminders" of Gotham on the Strip; resident acts like the R&B outfit Soul Desire and the band American Pop help make the place as "wildly energetic" as "the real Big Apple", only more "manageable" and "cheaper."

### Bikinis Beach & Dance Club
19 | 19 | 18 | $9

*Rio All-Suite Hotel & Casino, 3700 W. Flamingo Rd. (bet. I-15 & Valley View Blvd.), 702-777-6582; www.playrio.com*
☑ "Those in search of eye candy" may feel like they've "died and gone to heaven" 'cause the atmosphere is "hot, hot, hot" as hell at this "awesome club" at the Rio west of the Strip where "bikini-clad bartenders" and "thonged cocktail servers" tend to a "young crowd"; despite "babe"-alicious peformers who get all wet "in the shower" at the indoor "beach" on this "tropical island", the natives are restless, calling it "swanky and fun" some nights and "half-empty" and "blah" on others.

### Bootlegger Bistro
– | – | – | E

*7700 Las Vegas Blvd. S. (Robindale Rd., opp. Belz Factory Outlet World), 702-736-4939; www.bootleggerlasvegas.com*
"Local legends" like Buddy Greco and Sonny King (the singer/comedian who introduced Dean Martin to Jerry

Lewis) hang out, suck down moonshine and take to the stage at this thirtysomething "slice of old Las Vegas", a 24/7 Italian bistro south of the Strip; "lots of celebs" "get dragged into the act" during "Monday night karaoke", and you might even catch a torch song from the joint's proprietor, lounge singer/Nevada Lt. Gov. Lorraine Hunt.

### Breeze Bar
▽ 21 | 21 | 18 | $10 |

*Treasure Island Hotel, 3300 Las Vegas Blvd. S. (Spring Mountain Rd.), 702-894-7111; www.treasureisland.com*

◧ Kick back and enjoy a Churchill in this casual, cigar-friendly, 24-hour bar on the Strip inside Treasure Island (or the TI, as the resort's image-conscious spin doctors now prefer to call it); though it's a bit of a "loser's lounge", it's an "ok" place to "play the slots", shoot the breeze and wait for the doors to open for the long-running Cirque du Soleil production, *Mystere.*

### Cafe Nicolle
– | – | – | E |

*Sahara Pavilion, 4760 W. Sahara Ave. (Decatur Blvd.), 702-870-7675; www.cafenicolle.com*

Live music six nights a week, usually jazz, but some Top 40, provides a pleasing atmosphere in the piano lounge of this popular, classy restaurant on the West Side; the steaks are so tender you can cut them like butter and the music so sweet you always come back for more, between breaths of fresh air in the garden.

### Capozzoli's Ristorante
– | – | – | M |

*3353 S. Maryland Pkwy. (bet. Desert Inn Rd. & Sierra Vista Dr.), 702-731-5311; www.capozzolis-restaurant.com*

The man with the mojo just can't get enough of the mike, so "if you're lucky", after he tears it up for the Strip's panty-throwing ladies, "Tom Jones" will "treat you to an impromptu performance"; "or maybe Joe Pesci will come in and get an order of pasta", and you can ask him to autograph your manicotti in between open mike, big band and pop sets in the lounge at this revered East Side Italian where local celebs make cameos.

### CARAMEL
21 | 23 | 19 | $12 |

*Bellagio Hotel, 3600 Las Vegas Blvd. S. (Flamingo Rd.), 702-693-7111; www.bellagio.com*

■ The high-rolling Bellagio's newest watering hole is "smooth, silky and sophisticated", "sweet as caramel, very chic, very hip" – "a New York bar in Vegas" that serves what some Adams and Eves call the "best apple martini around" in a "relaxed atmosphere" to patrons "dressed to impress" and "chilling out" on "comfy couches"; it's "a nice, small lounge to warm yourself up for the night" with a "pricey drink" and a peek at the "beautiful women none of us can afford."

## Carnaval Court

22 | 19 | 19 | $8

*Harrah's Las Vegas, 3475 Las Vegas Blvd. S. (Flamingo Rd.),
702-369-5000; www.harrahs.com*

■ "Flair bartending is at its finest" at this "fun outdoor
bar" in Harrah's where the "champion" "theatrics" of the
"entertaining" mixologists stoke the "infectious" "party"
vibe; order a "yard of margarita", boogey down on the
"large dance" floor, take in a "band in the back" and
definitely don't miss the medallion-laden legendary king
of kitschy entertainment, "Cook E. Jarr performing some
nights" and keeping alive the Las Vegas lounge tradition.

## Casbar Lounge

▽ 19 | 18 | 18 | $12

*Sahara Hotel & Casino, 2535 Las Vegas Blvd. S. (Sahara Blvd.),
702-737-2111; www.saharavegas.com*

◪ If the walls could talk at the Sahara's "very old-school"
lounge, they'd tell tales about such legendary entertainers
as Louis Prima, Don Rickles and Mel Tormé who rocked
the Casbar early in their careers while the likes of Elvis
Presley and Frank Sinatra sat in the audience; fifty years
later, it's still "a fine place to hang out for the evening
enjoying drinks, conversation" and a rotating roster of
R&B, soul and jazz groups.

## Celebration Lounge

– | – | – | I

*Tropicana Hotel, 3801 Las Vegas Blvd. S. (Tropicana Ave.),
702-739-2222; www.tropicanalv.com*

"If you're at the hotel, why not" throw a celebration at this
lounge after attending the legendary topless to-do, *Folies
Bergere*?; its location next door to the glamorous show's
Tiffany Theater at the Tropicana, along with its nightly live
music, makes it a "fun spot for everyone" but particularly
appealing to voyeurs who might catch a glimpse of a
showgirl unwinding *with* her shirt on.

## Cellar Lounge, The

– | – | – | E

*3601 W. Sahara Ave. (Valley View Blvd.), 702-362-6268*

"There's something about going down into a cellar" that
makes this dark, intimate bar on the West Side "kind of cool"
to locals – maybe it's because the atmosphere hearkens
back to the era of speakeasies and bathtub gin; or maybe
it's the jazz and blues blown by some of the Strip's most
stellar musicians who drop by Thursdays through Sundays
to jam till the sun comes up.

## CHEETAH'S

24 | 14 | 19 | $10

*2112 Western Ave. (bet. Sahara & Wyoming Aves.),
702-384-0074; www.girlsofcheetahs.com*

■ "Woo-hoo!" – with "friendly" females "ranging from
school-girl-next-door types to Pam Anderson copycats",
there's "plenty of debauchery" for "bachelor party"-goers
at this "wild" nudie nest west of the Strip where Paul
Verhoeven shot his kitsch classic, *Showgirls*; the digs might

be "shabby", but if you want "classy decadence", the "compact" club offers some of the "best lap dances in Vegas"; just keep in mind, "service depends on the thickness of your . . . wallet."

### Cleopatra's Barge    18 | 19 | 18 | $9

*Caesars Palace, 3570 Las Vegas Blvd. S. (Flamingo Rd.), 702-731-7110; www.caesars.com*

☑ "If *Rain Man* can pick up a girl here, you can do the same", particularly when it's reportedly "chock-full of hookers after midnight"; "insomniac chicks", "out-of-town guests" and "cranky servers" ferrying "strong drinks" help give this (literally) "rockin'" bar(ge) afloat in the middle of Caesars Palace "campy" "people-watching" potential; it's "hopelessly tasteless, but that's part of the charm", so "hop on" board – that is, if you don't suffer from "sea sickness."

### Club Madrid    – | – | – | M

*Sunset Station Hotel, 1301 W. Sunset Rd. (Las Vegas Blvd.), Henderson, 702-547-7777; www.sunsetstation.com*

Get outta town, at least just by a few miles, for "great cheap concerts" at Henderson's answer to neighboring Las Vegas' nightlife, located in the Sunset Station Hotel; this versatile club offers a roster of mostly weekend events, from comedy to dancing and, from time-to-time, the legendary Richard Cheese and his Rage Against the Lounge band.

### Club Monaco    – | – | – | E

*1487 E. Flamingo Rd. (bet. Escondido & Tamarus Sts.), 702-737-6212*

If you like your clubbing "nice and dark", one of the East Side's venerable locals' bars is a "good place to hang out, have a drink, play the machines and chill" to Sinatra-style singers Tuesdays–Saturdays; "the bands aren't that great", but there's a dance floor if you're inspired to try and hustle to their sounds, and if the joint and its service "need a face-lift", the food is decent enough for soaking up the sauce.

### Club Paradise    22 | 20 | 17 | $10

*4416 Paradise Rd. (bet. Flamingo Rd. & Harmon Ave.), 702-734-7990*

■ What a "pleasant surprise" blubber boob lovers – "these ladies can actually dance" to the "excellent music" grinding out of the speakers at this "classy topless lounge" east of the Strip where "tasty appetizers" and "courteous service" are both literal and figurative terms; all this and "women are welcome too"? – "what more can you want?"

### Club Rio    22 | 20 | 18 | $10

*Rio All-Suite Hotel & Casino, 3700 W. Flamingo Rd. (bet. I-15 & Valley View Blvd.), 702-252-7727; www.playrio.com*

☑ "Everyone's a VIP" within this "cavernous" club on the West Side where "girls, girls, girls" shaking to "loud" rock and hip-hop means "the dance floor never fails to get the heart racing"; still, "if you're looking for the hottest spot in Vegas not named ghostbar", this might not be it – "once the mecca for hardcore clubbers", it's "cooled down" recently.

### Club Tequila
– – – M

*Fiesta Rancho, 2400 N. Rancho Dr. (Lake Mead Blvd.), 702-638-3771; www.fiestacasino.com*

Who would've thought the Fiesta Rancho in the Northwest would uncork a club as potent as its namesake?; there are sports on the jumbo screen, and a variety of acts pour on the entertainment: follow Yellow Brick Road through classic rock covers, try Full Metal Jacket on for hair-band tributes or bang it up two-step–style with Derek Sholl and the Shooters.

### Como's Steakhouse, Jazz Lounge at
– – – E

*Lake Las Vegas Resort MonteLago Village, 10 Via Brianza (Lake Mead Dr.), Henderson, 702-567-9950; www.lakelasvegas.com*

Go for a gondola ride in the nearby man-made lake on the far east side of Henderson; stroll down the narrow streets of a faux Italian village at the Casino MonteLago on the shore; dine at the exquisitely designed and decorated restaurant and then relax with a cocktail mixed from among an impressive selection of vodkas in the upstairs lounge while listening to live jazz and blues a few nights a week.

### Coral Reef
– – – M

*Mandalay Bay Hotel, 3950 Las Vegas Blvd. S. (Hacienda Ave.), 877-632-7800; www.mandalaybay.com*

Location, location, location may be the keys to the success of this tropical lounge in the casino at Mandalay Bay, but some pretty good dance bands don't hurt, either; swim up to the sushi bar for a nibble or go fishing among the crowd before cruising neighboring reefs, Red Square and rumjungle.

### COYOTE UGLY
17 16 15 $9

*New York-New York Hotel & Casino, 3790 Las Vegas Blvd. S. (Tropicana Ave.), 702-740-6050; www.nynyhotelcasino.com*

◪ "Yippee!" – "this place was built to be a party"; "dancing on the bar isn't only allowed but encouraged", so get up to "get down 'n' dirty", but "be careful of the fire-breathing", "scantily clad" "hot chicks" pouring the drinks at New York-New York's "wild and wacky" imitation of Manhattan's "legendary bar"; "it's a great place to let loose", if you want to make "like a sardine" with a "packed" "roomful of single guys" and "cheesy" "tourists" "acting like fools."

### Crazy Armadillo
– – – M

*Stratosphere Hotel & Tower, 2000 Las Vegas Blvd. S. (north of Sahara Ave.), 702-383-5230; www.stratospherehotel.com*

Flair bartenders, karaoke, live music, a decent dance floor and drink specials lure the young and young-at-heart boozers for an "atmosphere of a college town on Friday night" at this lounge/oyster bar in the Stratosphere; sober hotel guests deem it "too open and noisy for its location near the elevators", and even the "enthusiastic hosts" might agree that the south-of-the-border eats are "mediocre."

## CRAZY HORSE TOO GENTLEMEN'S CLUB

24 | 15 | 17 | $10

*2476 Industrial Rd. (bet. Northbridge St. & Sahara Ave.), 702-382-8003; www.crazyhorsetoo.com*

☑ "Service with a smile (and a pair of tatas)" is the key to the "finest strip club off the Strip"; "the girls are really beautiful, really friendly" and really good at "wrangling the money from the pockets" of "drooling men" who pony up a steep cover, don blinders to ignore the "past-its-prime" decor and giddy up for "high-contact lap dances"; in other words, "the expensive drinks are the cheapest part of the night" at this West Side "sleaze"-fest.

## Curve

20 | 21 | 17 | $11

*Aladdin Resort & Casino, 3667 Las Vegas Blvd. S. (Harmon Ave.), 702-785-5555; www.curvelasvegas.com*

☑ It's "so chic, you'll be shocked it's in the un-fabulous Aladdin"; "claustrophobic" "beautiful people" consider it "very cool" that this "upscale lounge" tucked into the London Club is "not as well-known as some other spots", as it's "usually easy to get into" and it's always "laid-back"; "hook up" on "scattered couches" in "hidden" corners in a space "set up like a billionaire's living room", and try not to mind that the scene here can be "dead, dead, dead."

## Double Down Saloon ⇔

– | – | – | M

*4640 Paradise Rd. (Naples Dr.), 702-791-5775; www.doubledownsaloon.com*

"Like moths to a light", "slumming" surveyors are "drawn in" to swarm among the "punks, rockabilly" rollers, bikers, artists, "cool chicks", witness protection program enrollees and businessmen on the downlow at one of the "favorite places in Vegas to hide", a dive with "cheap beer" and loud bands that will have you gasping "I can't believe I love this place"; it's open 24/7, but the "best part [of the day] is when the strippers get off work and come in."

## Dragon, The

20 | 21 | 16 | $13

(aka China Grill)

*Mandalay Bay Hotel, 3950 Las Vegas Blvd. S. (Hacienda Ave.), 702-632-7404; www.mandalaybay.com*

■ Such a "cool layout" should never lie fallow, so after the diners have nibbled their last, the "must-see decor" at Mandalay Bay's China Grill is still at work on Wednesdays for this "chic" after-hours club; a "beautiful, low-key crowd" "drinks and dances the night away" to "fantastic" techno and hip-hop beneath a laser-lit ceiling in a space featuring luminescent unisex restroom pods; suffer the "long lines" and "expensive" cover 'cause this scene can be "amazing."

### DRAI'S AFTER HOURS

24 | 20 | 17 | $11

*Barbary Coast Hotel & Casino, 3595 Las Vegas Blvd. S. (Flamingo Rd.), 702-737-0555; www.draislasvegas.com*
■ "Holy hot chicks", Batman! – "you pre-partied, you partied and now it's time to post-party", that is if "you want to dance with a Las Vegas showgirl" in the Barbary Coast's Batcave-like after-hours "dungeon"; "its subterranean location gives it the feeling of a speakeasy from back in the day", but all those "beautiful", "wild" "people coming down from their club buzzes" and "chillin'" to "techno" amid "candles and leopard-skin furniture" are up-to-the-minute, "off-the-hook", "early-morn" "naughty."

### Ellis Island Lounge

‒ | ‒ | ‒ | I

*Ellis Island Casino & Brewery, 4178 Koval Ln. (Flamingo Rd.), 702-733-8901; www.ellisislandcasino.com*
With so many wanna-be Wayne Newtons migrating to Vegas' oldest karaoke scene, this East Side lounge can be "very busy", and you'll have to "prepare to wait" for your "gambling break" from the casino's many "1¢ and 5¢ machines"; there are "pretty good payouts" from the slots, however, so even when you're nickle-and-diming it, you might win enough to afford the "cheap beer."

### ESPN ZONE

19 | 19 | 16 | $9

*New York-New York Hotel & Casino, 3790 Las Vegas Blvd. S. (Tropicana Ave.), 702-933-3776; www.espnzone.com*
◪ "Tons of TVs", "big leather seats" and "heaps" of "beers and burgers" – "what more can a guy ask for in front of his wife?"; "if you don't want to watch a game in a sportsbook", this "couch potato's paradise" on the Strip is "the next best" place to root for your "favorite team in a relaxing setting" where you "don't have to worry about the spread"; still, it's a good bet that snobby "jocks" think it's a "tourist trap."

### Fadó Irish Pub

‒ | ‒ | ‒ | I

*Green Valley Ranch Station Hotel, 2300 Paseo Verde Pkwy. (Green Valley Pkwy.), Henderson, 702-407-8691; www.fadoirishpub.com*
The Emerald Isle meets Henderson at this link in a chain of Gaelic pubs; plant your gambled-out bones on a bar stool imported, along with the rest of the furnishings and decor, from Ireland and tap your toes to genuine Celtic sounds while you work your way through a Guinness on tap and that Irish version of the potato pancake, the boxty.

### Fitzgeralds Events Center

‒ | ‒ | ‒ | M

*Fitzgeralds Casino & Hotel, 301 Fremont St. (3rd St.), 702-388-2400; www.fitzgeralds.com*
"For the cost of a drink", the entertainment is "actually quite good" at this theater/lounge in Downtown's Fitzgeralds

Casino far afield of the Vegas Strip; "you can see either a convincing Elvis impersonator, a magic or comedy act" or the long-legged songstresses of Diva-licious for a "cheap and easy", if none too cushiony, "start to the night" – the "seats could be more comfortable, but shows only last an hour anyway."

### FONTANA LOUNGE   26   25   21   $11
*Bellagio Hotel, 3600 Las Vegas Blvd. S. (Flamingo Rd.), 702-693-7111; www.bellagio.com*
■ "Couples" aged "30+" "hang out all night to listen to Jimmy Hooper" and other singers, "watch the fountains and drink Bellinis" "on the patio" at this "sophsticated", "romantic lounge" in the Bellagio ; the "superb" "old-school cocktails" are "pricey" and, due to the "spectacular view", it's "hard to find a seat on almost any night", but if you've got the payout and the patience, you can "relax" in the lap of "luxe" for a "quintessentially Vegas experience."

### GHOSTBAR   26   26   19   $11
*Palms Casino Hotel, 4321 W. Flamingo Rd., 55th fl. (Arville St.), 702-942-7777; www.n9negroup.com*
■ No wonder "those guys on *The Real World Las Vegas*" made this their "regular haunt": altitude matches Appeal score at the top-rated club in town, an "indoor/outdoor" "super-chic joint" 55 stories up at the Palms west of the Strip; unless you're "acrophobic", it's a "nice place to see stars of both varieties" amid "ultrahip surroundings" ranking No. 1 for nightlife Decor; "snobby bouncers" and a "high cover keep out the riff-raff", who you can stare down upon through the "vertigo-inducing" "Plexiglas" "hole in the floor" on the heavenly patio.

### Gilley's Dance Hall & Saloon   ▽ 18   18   17   $9
*Frontier Hotel, 3120 Las Vegas Blvd. S. (bet. Desert Inn & Fashion Show Rds.), 702-794-8200; www.frontierlv.com*
■ Sure, the whole city goes a little bit country during the National Finals Rodeo in December, but Gilley's gives honky-tonk year-round in the Frontier in the Northwest; this "hillbilly heaven" is highlighted by "bikini bull riding", "very good live music" and "hot" "cowboys" "doin' the two-step" with their "casual pickups" after branding their gullets with a few too many Texas Red Hots (Bloody Mary shots with jalapeños).

### Gipsy   _   _   _   E
*4605 Paradise Rd. (Naples Dr.), 702-731-1919*
"The city's center boîte for gay life" is "the nicest bar" in the area affectionately known as the Fruit Loop on the East Side of town; this "true survivor" is more settled in than its name implies – it's "had a longer life than many of its patrons" who "it keeps in full motion" with cabaret shows, go-go boys, free shots, drag performances and Latin nights.

### Girls of Glitter Gulch
12 | 10 | 11 | $11

*20 Fremont St. (Main St.), 702-385-4774*

◪ You might be in for an "unforgettable lap dance when you open your wallet" in this Downtown bazonga den, but as "Lou Reed sang", it's "a hustle here and a hustle there", so "look out for guys saying 'no cover' then getting you for a two-drink minimum that can cost you $30" in a "skanky joint" where neither the "over-inflated" "talent" nor the "scary clientele" are "up to Vegas' high standards for decadence"; in other words, "ugh."

### Golden Gate Casino Shrimp Bar & Deli ☉
▽ 21 | 16 | 20 | $6

*Golden Gate Hotel & Casino, 1 Fremont St. (Main St.), 702-385-1906; www.goldengatecasino.net*

■ With 99 cents to spare on crustaceans, "this Downtown landmark is the perfect spot to chow down on a shrimp cocktail" chased by beer or wine 24/7 while "a pianist pounds out the classics on a baby grand" in an Old San Francisco setting; "come for a cheap fix, but wipe the ketchup off the tables" before you set your elbows down.

### Gordon Biersch
19 | 17 | 20 | $9

*3987 Paradise Rd. (bet. Flamingo Rd. & Sands Ave.), 702-312-5249; www.gordonbiersch.com*

■ "If you're looking to pick up a lawyer or banker", "Friday happy hour is the professional's meat market" for both "long-term and one-night" dates at this "fun brewpub" chainster east of the Strip; "they host a mean Oktoberfest", but any time of year, it's a "great place to get away from the techno beats and enjoy a nice beer", "good food" and "yuppyish" "people-watching."

### Hookah Lounge
– | – | – | I

*Paymon's Mediterranean Café, 4147 S. Maryland Pkwy. (Flamingo Rd.), 702-731-6030; www.hookahlounge.com*

You will feel like a sultan, or a sultana, puffing on a water pipe and savoring any of 20 flavors of tobacco at a low-slung round table in this cozy little East Side oasis amid Middle Eastern decor; gaze into your Genies' Navel, a cocktail mixed with peach liqueur, or order a potent Red Bull-and-Absolut Mandarin Flying Carpet Ride and take off into specialty drink heaven.

### Houlihan's
▽ 12 | 11 | 14 | $10

*1951 N. Rainbow Blvd. (bet. Lake Mead Blvd. & Vegas Dr.), 702-648-0300; www.houlihans.com*

■ "Chain – that's all I need to say" you might say if you're a tourist; but if you're a Las Vegas local, you could come here anyway to meet up with your cronies after work, throw back two cocktails for the price of one and chomp on cut-rate appetizers while the Dolphins dive at the ball on the tube and the video games ping and buzz.

## HOUSE OF BLUES
23 | 21 | 18 | $10

*Mandalay Bay Hotel, 3950 Las Vegas Blvd. S. (Hacienda Ave.), 702-632-7600; www.hob.com*

■ "The hippest bands in the desert" and "top-notch" touring acts alike "pack 'em in" for a "rockin'" "thrill ride" at this "flashy", "funky" franchise in Mandalay Bay on the Strip; despite a rep that's more "middle of the road" than crossroads, the joint "maintains broad appeal" with "down-home hospitality", "spectacular" "folk art", a "spacious dance floor" and a "not-to-be-missed gospel brunch"; for a "way cooler" experience, "sneak up" to the "exclusive" Foundation Room and hobnob with the "pretty people."

### Ibiza USA
18 | 15 | 17 | $11

*Desert Passage at Aladdin, 3663 Las Vegas Blvd. S. (Harmon Ave.), 702-836-0830; www.ibizausa.com*

◩ "A place to dance the night (and the next day) away" is on the "huge floor" on weekends at this club adjacent to the Aladdin on the Strip; "if you've been to Ibiza", "you sure won't mistake this place" for the real one, "but it's an honest Vegas-style effort" to "cash in on the coolness" of the international rave scene's favorite island; "it could be up-and-coming", warn wallet-watchers, "but $10 [or more] for a drink in a plastic cup is kinda crappy."

### Ice
– | – | – | E

*200 E. Harmon Ave. (Koval Ln.), 702-699-9888; www.icelasvegas.com*

Ice, ice, baby – it's all in the name at this new mega-circus east of the Strip where the state-of-the-art liquid nitrogen air conditioning system keeps the temperature beneath the vaulted, leather-and-stud ceiling as cool as the goings-on courtesy of globally renowned DJs like Boy George, plus a plethora of go-go dancing, flying, miming and contorting performers; warm up by shaking it on the sprawling dance floor or by retreating to the pelt-lined Fur Room.

### Jack's Irish Pub
– | – | – | M

*Palace Station Hotel, 2411 W. Sahara Ave. (Rancho Dr.), 702-364-5225; www.jacksirishpub.com*

"Every expat from the Old Sod drinks" at this bar west of the Strip – after all, "who else in Vegas serves Black Bush?"; despite an eclectic array of potables that includes "tequila shots", the "great" "traditional" bands, "jig contests" and rugby on the tellies make it one "shockingly authentic Irish pub", a "good choice" for "serious" swilling "as long as you hide enough cab fare to get yourself home", or to your hotel.

### Jaguar's
– | – | – | E

*3355 S. Procyon St. (bet. Desert Inn & Spring Mountain Rds.), 702-732-1116; www.jaguarslv.cc*

With lavish adult productions on stage at so many of the major casinos now (*X* at the Aladdin, *La Femme* at MGM,

*Skintight* at Harrah's, to name a few), one would think business at local bosom bars would be sagging, but it's pert as ever; this sin den entices randy cats west of the Strip to elegant, marble-dressed surroundings, including an elite VIP room appointed with chandeliers, a fireplace and, of course, some of the best-looking ladies in town.

### Jazzed Cafe & Vinoteca    – | – | – | E

*8615 W. Sahara Ave. (Durango Dr.), 702-233-2859;*
*www.jazzedcafe.com*
"What more could you ask for" but "phat drinks" and "fab jazz" in a "nice atmosphere" at this "quirky, out-of-the-way place" on the West Side?; how about "groovy" Italian eats and "wonderful service for the price" at one place for "a perfect rendezvous for lovers"?

### Jillian's    17 | 18 | 16 | $10

*Neonopolis Entertainment Complex, 450 Fremont St.*
*(Las Vegas Blvd.), 702-759-0450; www.jillians.com*
☑ "Eat, drink and bowl – what a combination" at this sprawling indoor amusement park Downtown; "watch a game, shoot some pool", have a drink, pig out, shake your booty to a variety of tunes and lose all sense of proportion on any number of video challenges for a "fun and friendly" fiesta "for the family" or "friends"; best of all, since plenty of partiers peg it as "tired", "you have the place to yourself."

### Joint, The    24 | 21 | 18 | $10

*Hard Rock Hotel & Casino, 4455 Paradise Rd. (bet. Flamingo Rd. &*
*Harmon Ave.), 702-693-5000; www.hardrockhotel.com*
■ "When this Joint gets to jumpin', look out": "it's standing only, literally – there are no chairs" on the main floor of the Hard Rock's "small" club east of the Strip where the world's "hottest acts" do "scaled-down shows" for a "hip" audience that includes "lots and lots of men" on the make for "the most ridiculous collection of women this side of Los Angeles"; hug the stage to get "intimate" with The Rolling Stones and other rockers, or plant your butt on a stool in the VIP area.

### Kahunaville    17 | 17 | 18 | $8

*Treasure Island Hotel, 3300 Las Vegas Blvd. S.*
*(Spring Mountain Rd.), 702-894-7390;*
*www.kahunaville.com*
☑ "Throwing bottles, twirling glasses and making a show of pouring your drink", "the bartenders whip themselves into a frenzy" and so will you, as "you have to wave your finger and scream a little to get their attention when it's busy" at this tropical-themed chainster "buried in the back" of Treasure Island; suck down enough "good, fruity", "smoking" potions on the patio "out at the pool", and you might get soused enough to mistake the "cheesy" "hangout" for "Key West."

---

**La Playa Lounge**　　　　　　▽ 21 | 18 | 18 | $6
*Harrah's Las Vegas, 3475 Las Vegas Blvd. S. (Flamingo Rd.),
702-369-5000; www.harrahs.com*

◪ "Dueling pianists", "mainstream" bands "playing a variety
of musical mixes including Latin, rhythm, jazz, pop and
Brazilian" and other "top-notch entertainment" create a
"great atmosphere" in this "nice little hideaway" on the
Strip; sure, you might "classify it as a dive", but the acts
"get people who are passing by dancing", and the "tropical
drinks" help you forget your surroundings.

**LIGHT**　　　　　　　　　　　25 | 24 | 19 | $12
*Bellagio Hotel, 3600 Las Vegas Blvd. S. (Flamingo Rd.),
702-693-8300; www.lightlv.com*

◪ "Bold, brash, noisy and crowded" as "an NYC subway at
rush hour", the Bellagio's Gotham import is "a recommended
spot" to "dance till you drop" to "outstanding [DJ] mixes"
with "the Strip's prettiest people", particularly "on Sundays
during industry night"; its name belies the "dark" "cave"-
like interior, the "infamous", ponderous velvet rope and
the heavy prices that "lighten wallets faster than a slot
machine"; "if you can float it", make like "a Rockefeller"
and "reserve a booth" for bottle service and a floorside
view of the "booty shakers."

**Mist**　　　　　　　　　　　▽ 21 | 23 | 20 | $12
(fka Hideaway Lounge)
*Treasure Island Hotel, 3300 Las Vegas Blvd. S.
(Spring Mountain Rd.), 702-894-7111; www.mistbar.com*

◼ "You wouldn't think to find this" newcomer in what you
might consider to be "a kids' hotel", "but once there",
you'll discover it's "very comfortable and different from the
attached" Treasure Island; in other words, the elegant
surroundings, weekly karaoke, live music, dancing and
"darn good drinks" attract enough age-appropriate partiers
to make it "one of the coolest little spots on the Strip" in
which to "take time out when you're losing at the tables."

**Moose McGillycuddy's**　　　－ | － | － | I
*4770 S. Maryland Pkwy. (Lorilyn Ave.), 702-798-8337*

A "Hawaiian transplant that translates well to the high
desert clime", this East Side neighborhood bar is "great
for eyeing cuties" from the nearby University of Nevada
Las Vegas; join the "college crowd" for cheap drinks, and
dance the night away to the DJ's tunes while studying
members of the opposite sex to see if they make the grade –
if they flunk, you can always grab a cue and invest some of
your textbook funds in a game of pool.

**Murphy's Pub**　　　　　　　－ | － | － | I
*3985 E. Sunset Rd. (Annie Oakley Dr.), 702-458-5516*

"It's nice to know you can find a good Irish pub in any
town", including Henderson where there's this "great, out-

of-the-way place for a bachelor party or [just] hanging", shooting pool and listening to live sounds, from Monday's big bands to Wednesday's jazz and weekend rock; come in on Thursday for karaoke, and if you polish up enough, you can audition on Tuesday for your own gig.

### Napoleon's Lounge                23   23   20   $12

*Paris Las Vegas, 3655 Las Vegas Blvd. S. (bet. Flamingo Rd. & Harmon Ave.), 702-946-7000; www.paris-lv.com*
■ It's "just good times with [live] jazz and a Cohiba" at this "elegant", "low-key" "bubbly" specialist, a "great place to take a date after dinner but before clubbing" at the Paris on the Strip; ignore the club kids who snicker that there are "more exciting bars than this", order "a flight of champagne" or a "single malt" and "relax" in a "comfy chair" amid the "cigar-smoking, sport jacket–wearing" clientele sighing "fabulous, dahhling."

### Naughty Ladies Saloon                −   −   −   I

*Arizona Charlie's Hotel Casino, 740 S. Decatur Blvd. (bet. Alta Dr. & Charleston Blvd.), 702-258-5200; www.azcharlies.com*
Las Vegas legends Sweet Louie and Sonny Charles of the soul duo The Checkmates have been capturing crowds for more than 40 years, and they frequently bring their "good music" to this "dark" "lounge" on the West Side where their legions of fans get naughty on the "nice dance floor" trying to avoid each other's toes after a few "cheap drinks"; on other nights, a variety of acts perform, including a Friday happy-hour big band.

### Nefertiti's Lounge                19   20   16   $9

*Luxor Hotel, 3900 Las Vegas Blvd. S. (Tropicana Ave.), 702-262-4400; www.luxor.com*
■ "You can't go wrong with the old Egyptian theme", and though you might not feel like a pharaoh at this "kitschy", "little" bar in the Luxor, the "nice surroundings" are "cool, relaxed and comfortable" enough for taking in "some pretty good Vegas lounge singers" and "people-watching" everyone from partiers "not lucky enough to get into Rain" to "working girls" off shift.

### Nine Fine Irishmen                −   −   −   M

*New York-New York Hotel & Casino, 3790 Las Vegas Blvd. S. (Tropicana Ave.), 702-740-6969; www.ninefineirishmen.com*
A half-dozen bars built in Ireland and reassembled here in recent years, including this one at New York-New York, prove Vegas' Celtic chops; the joint's name was inspired by the Young Irelanders who struggled for their country's independence in the mid-19th century, but the only fight here will be over a stool to sit on and savor some fine Gaelic grub washed down with a Murphy's Irish Red while enjoying storytelling, singing and dancing.

## Oasis Lounge　　　　　　21　20　18　$11

*Golden Nugget Hotel, 129 E. Fremont St. (1st St.), 702-385-7111; www.goldennugget.com*

☒ "So Vegas it's scary", this long-lived Downtown watering hole inside the Golden Nugget (a casino Frank Sinatra once was pitchman for) can be a "great time" when one of the many rockin' bands on the weekly lineup kicks up a tune, but it might not be worth the trek unless you're jonesing for a joint that "reeks of suntan oil with mullets aplenty."

## OLYMPIC GARDEN　　　　25　15　22　$11

*1531 Las Vegas Blvd. S. (Wyoming Ave.), 702-385-8987; www.ogvegas.com*

☒ What's 'service' mean in Vegas? – put it this way: the No. 1 Service in the nightlife Survey is "very hands-on" and lands right in your "lap" at this "oldie but goodie", "equal opportunity" gazonga garden on the Strip; downstairs, "guys sit and stare" at a "gyrating", topless "smorgasbord of women of all sizes, shapes and ethnicities", while upstairs, "bachelorette parties galore" gag over "Calvin Klein–type models mixed in with Fabios"; get "hot", "mingle if desired" and "leave juiced up" – "woo-hoo!"

## Omaha Lounge ⌀　　　　–　–　–　I

*Plaza Hotel & Casino, 1 S. Main St. (Fremont St.), 702-386-2110; www.plazahotelcasino.com*

Fans "can't believe the Sunspots from Manila are still playing together" in this lounge at the Plaza in Downtown Las Vegas; they teamed up more than 40 years ago, plied the U.S. military base circuit throughout Asia until the mid-'60s and then came to Vegas where they work their kitschy pop mojos at this joint that's so downscale, it "looks like a Keno area."

## OPM　　　　　　　　　　–　–　–　E

*Forum Shops at Caesars Palace, 3500 Las Vegas Blvd. S. (Cleopatra Rd.), 702-369-4998; www.o-pm.com*

When über-chef Wolfgang Puck hungered for more than a simple restaurant at Caesars Palace on the Strip, he installed this "very chic", "pulsing" new lounge atop Chinois where clubbers get "comfy" "pretending to be" emperor, "looking out over the commoners" browsing the Forum Shops below; "friendly doormen, quick bar service, good music" by "sexy DJs" and the maestro's "cuisine at three in the morning" make for an "inviting place to crash" or dance.

## Palapa Lounge　　　　　　–　–　–　M

*Palms Casino Hotel, 4321 W. Flamingo Rd. (Arville St.), 702-942-7777; www.palms.com*

The Palms, west of the Strip, is the hottest spot in Las Vegas, luring in celebrities, celebrity-watchers, the young, the rich and the beautiful with such clubs as Rain and ghostbar; largely unheralded is this comfortable lounge just off the casino floor, which features a list of acts that perform for free, including all-girl Groove Kitty and Acoustic Asylum's evolving host of unplugged players.

### Palomino Club                      ▽ | 19 | 10 | 16 | $11 |

*1848 Las Vegas Blvd. N. (bet. Oakley Blvd. & St. Louis Ave.), North Las Vegas, 702-642-2984; www.palomino-club.com*
◪ "If you want a full Monty and a full beer, this is your place"; "the only totally nude spot in town with a liquor license" was once "the crown jewel of strip clubs", but in recent years, the North Vegas bare den "has been sliding downhill" while the "median age of its dancers" has been creeping up, leading lascivious loungers to label it the "stripper retirement home."

### Peppermill Fireside Lounge      | 19 | 19 | 21 | $8 |

*2985 Las Vegas Blvd. S. (bet. Convention Center Dr. & Riviera Blvd.), 702-735-7635*
■ "Get your [early] '70s on", "baby!" at the "Rat Pack–era" "watering hole" "that time forgot", a "Vegas kitsch" landmark behind a 24/7 restaurant on the Strip where "leggy waitresses" in "long, black" "slit skirts" "sit down to take your order" and "characters from the casinos" meet for a "virtually unnoticed rendezvous" in a "huge, cushy booth" beneath the "lights" in the plastic "trees" beside the "gigantic floating fire pit"; sip your "enormous" "retro" cocktail, "unwind and remember when."

### Pogo's Tavern  ⊘             | – | – | – | I |

*2103 N. Decatur Blvd. (bet. Sawyer & Stacey Aves.), 702-646-9375*
The "Friday night jazz is excellent", so suffer the long drive to this neighborhood bar on the West Side where Irv Kruger, the 85-year-old drumming veteran of Artie Shaw's Gramercy Five and other bygone big-name outfits, leads a combo of oldsters who jam with anyone who shows up to blow; it's "not the best food", the "decor is divey", "the service is slow and the beer on tap tastes stale", but "the music is classic", so "you'll keep coming back."

### Prana Lounge                     | – | – | – | M |

*Aladdin Resort & Casino, 3663 Las Vegas Blvd. S. (Harmon Ave.), 702-650-0507; www.pranalasvegas.com*
Recline on antique Vietnamese opium beds beneath the massive red-and-blue-lit chandelier in this lounge inside the delicious Beverly Hills import Crustacean on the Strip, in the Desert Passage shops; the decor is inspired by French Indochina, while Saturday night's dance crowd finds inspiration in the DJs spinning into the wee hours.

### Railhead, The                    | – | – | – | I |

*Boulder Station Hotel, 4111 Boulder Hwy. (Lamb Blvd.), 702-432-7777; www.stationcasinos.com*
Local blues lovers swarm this "excellent place to see concerts" inside Boulder Station on the East Side for free

Thursday night sessions by some of the country's best artists, like harmonica player Norton Buffalo and Guitar Shorty; other evenings the club is reserved for paying customers to scope out such Vegas performers as Ray Price, the DeCastro Sisters and Hal Ketchum.

### RAIN IN THE DESERT
**25 23 19 $10**

*Palms Casino Hotel, 4321 W. Flamingo Rd. (Arville St.), 702-942-7777; www.n9negroup.com*

◪ "Throbbing, pulsing, pounding" Rain makes the desert bloom with "lots of stars", "go-go dancers" and "more beautiful girls per square foot than anywhere else in the world" for "a pretty happening place" at the Palms west of the Strip; as "flames burst above the dance floor, water flows beneath" and VIPs chill in "private cabanas" and sky boxes, "young and crazy club kids rev it up" in a "wall-to-wall sea of sweating" bodies – if they can get in: ya gotta "wait for hours" to gorge on what snobs call a "cheesefest."

### RA, THE NIGHTCLUB
**21 20 17 $11**

*Luxor Hotel, 3900 Las Vegas Blvd. S. (Tropicana Ave.), 702-262-4000; www.rathenightclub.com*

◪ Join the "freak show" with the "fire-breathing bartenders, scantily clad go-go girls", "trapeze artists", "cage dancers" and clientele "dressed in drag, bubble wrap, you name it" at this "raging" party palace "oozing with sex", "a New York–style hip spot set in Ancient Egypt" inside the Luxor; beneath an "amazing light show", "world-renowned DJs" "energize" a "sweaty, rave-y techno" scene, even though hard-core clubbers dis it as "hit-or-miss."

### RED SQUARE
**25 25 21 $11**

*Mandalay Bay Hotel, 3950 Las Vegas Blvd. S. (Hacienda Ave.), 702-632-7407; www.mandalaybay.com*

■ "The drinks are strong, the vodka menu is long" and the scene – punctuated by "a bar made of a block of ice" – is "chill" at this "opulent" *perestroika* "paradise" in Mandalay Bay on the Strip where "serious" sippers can choose from nearly 100 varieties of "Mother Russia's" national drink to toast the "decapitated Lenin statue"; if their post-dose "blurry memories" serve them correctly, "Socialists scrounging" for the rubles for a "dangerously delicious martini" and caviar swear the "VIP back room" filled with icy bottles is "interesting to visit."

### Risqué
**20 19 21 $11**

*Paris Las Vegas, 3655 Las Vegas Blvd. S. (bet. Flamingo Rd. & Harmon Ave.), 702-946-4589; www.risquelasvegas.com*

◪ One of the latest entries in the race for sexiest "later-in-the-evening hot spot" is this provocatively named "classy club" in the Paris on the Strip; there's "great fun" to be had, particularly on Sundays during the Vamp Girlie Review burlesque show, which "gets me excited!" pant partiers;

on other nights, the "cool, little" joint is "hidden" enough to be downright "slow."

**RUMJUNGLE**    22 | 25 | 18 | $10

*Mandalay Bay Hotel, 3950 Las Vegas Blvd. S. (Hacienda Ave.), 702-632-7408; www.mandalaybay.com*

☑ "Play *Sex and the City*" with the "beautiful people" beneath "acrobats" "swinging from trapezes" who somehow avoid the "volcanic mountain of rum", "fire walls and waterfalls" at the Most Popular club in this *Survey* in Mandalay Bay; "eat a late dinner" "to avoid the cover", "spring for a coveted bottle table" or make like a "survivor" and "fend for yourself" in the "wilds" of this "manufactured" "jungle" amid a "meat market" mob "swimming in liquor" to "Caribbean and African beats with techno thrown in."

**Sand Dollar Lounge** ⌑    – | – | – | I

*3355 W. Spring Mountain Rd. (Polaris Ave.), 702-871-6651; www.sanddollarblues.com*

White-collar, blue-collar and no-collar crowds get a "great time for a cheap price", downing "pretty mean drinks", shooting stick and "dancing" to "excellent live" blues at this diamond in the rough of the West Side; it's "not very pretty to look at", but the music – particularly during zero-dollars-down Monday jam sessions – sure sounds sweet.

**Sapphire**    22 | 21 | 19 | $10

*3025 S. Industrial Rd. (Desert Inn Rd.), 702-796-6000; www.sapphirelasvegas.com*

☑ "Huge" refers more to the space than the wares at the "biggest gentlemen's club in Las Vegas" (and at 74,000 sq. ft., maybe the world) "employing a wide variety" of talent and sporting – "ooohh, baby" – "sky boxes" for "big rollers" on the West Side; paltry pockets pout that the "great women" are "snapped up by the greedy dudes who shell out major cash", while "the rest of the girls are average."

**Shadow**    21 | 20 | 19 | $10

*Caesars Palace, 3570 Las Vegas Blvd. S. (Flamingo Rd.), 702-731-7110; www.caesars.com*

☑ "Silhouettes of near-naked women, and sometimes men", "dancing behind a screen" keep "singles and couples" "slack-jawed", but "great drinks" from "out-of-this-world flair bartenders" are as "strangely erotic" as the "shadow" "T&A" at this "mellow lounge"; "not family-friendly but still tastefully enticing", "Caesars' answer" to making Sin City "more adult" is "difficult to leave", even if hard-core hedonists huff "you're in Vegas – go see the real thing."

**SKIN**    25 | 20 | 22 | $9

*Palms Casino Hotel, 4321 W. Flamingo Rd. (Arville St.), 702-942-7777; www.n9negroup.com*

■ Check out all the "lovely, young hardbodies" relaxing on "lounge chairs", but keep one eye on the water's edge so as "not to fall into the pool after a few too many drinks" at this relatively "mellow getaway from Rain" outside at the Palms west of the Strip; with a "mix of intelligent locals for good conversation", it "feels like your own private backyard party" – that is, if your lawn features "mermaids and dancers", "swings and private cabanas."

### Spearmint Rhino
　　　　　　– | – | – | E
*3344 Highland Dr. (Spring Mountain Rd.), 702-796-3600; www.spearmintrhino.com*
Why settle for your run-of-the-mill lap dance when you can have a $100 VIP set of dances or even a $200 VIP champagne dance at this topless franchise west of the Strip?; the club may not be as large as some of the others, but the dancers here can stack up against any in the city, and there are plans in the works for an expansion.

### STUDIO 54
　　　　　　22 | 22 | 18 | $11
*MGM Grand Hotel, 3799 Las Vegas Blvd. S. (Tropicana Ave.), 702-891-1111; www.studio54lv.com*
☑ With "buff, sexy dancers" "in cages", "on swings" and "even on bungees" "bouncing and spinning" "titillatingly" above the "huge" "post-apocalyptic" space, the MGM Grand's "revamp" of the "'70s favorite" "does its best to encourage legendary memories every night"; indeed, when the "bumpin'" music "constantly changes" "from Top 40 to hip-hop to techno and disco", "it's hard to get bored", but this "tourist trap" is still "not as fun as the NY one in its heyday", even if the "wait in line" is just as long.

### Tabú
　　　　　　24 | 23 | 20 | $13
*MGM Grand Hotel, 3799 Las Vegas Blvd. S. (Tropicana Ave.), 702-891-7183; www.mgmgrand.com*
☑ "Ya, baby, ya!" – "slick, sleek, sexy, sassy" and "über-chic", this "small", new lounge at the MGM Grand "cost millions to build and was worth every penny"; "knockout waitresses" "cater to the beautiful and trendy" who "see and are seen" around "digital tabletops" while "great music" plays; still, discerning scenesters say "it's nibbling at ghostbar's heels, but it won't catch up", as "the only thing ultra about it is the entry fee."

### Tilted Kilt
　　　　　　– | – | – | M
*Rio All-Suite Hotel & Casino, 3700 W. Flamingo Rd. (bet. I-15 & Valley View Blvd.), 702-777-2463; www.playrio.com*
Only in Las Vegas is an Irish/Scottish pub staffed by "sexy mini-skirted tartan-clad waitresses" who dish out "great service" (kilt tilting not included); this "cheap and cheerful" chuggery at the Rio west of the Strip serves up 24 "good, interesting" beers on tap, including $1 domestics at happy hour, plus live music, karaoke, darts, pinball, pool and hearty grub for an easy 'n' "light night destination" when the casinos have tuckered you out.

## Tommy Rocker's Cantina & Grill   ⏤ | ⏤ | ⏤ | I

*4275 S. Industrial Rd. (bet. Flamingo Rd. & Tropicana Ave.), 702-261-6688; www.tommyrocker.com*

"Try to catch" "the Jimmy Buffett of Las Vegas" with his band, Conched Out, and get loaded "with all the other Parrotheads in the area" who "sing along" to "old favorites", joining Tommy and the guys onstage at his eponymous "laid-back bar with a cool vibe" west of the Strip; a "fun, casual atmosphere", Mexican-American noshes and, of course, "good margaritas" make it one of the "best party places" in town for a "mostly local" crowd.

## TOP OF THE WORLD LOUNGE   24 | 20 | 19 | $11

*Stratosphere Hotel & Tower, 2000 Las Vegas Blvd. S. (north of Sahara Ave.), 702-380-7777; www.stratospherehotel.com*

■ "Watch the world spin" – not on account of a "few" "great drinks", but because you're sitting in this "rotating lounge" on the 107th floor of the "highest tower in the western U.S.", where the view is accordingly "fantastic"; "enjoy the sunset and later look out over the glittering neon of the entire Strip", but don't neglect the scenery close up because the "tasteful", "peaceful" place for "an evening cocktail" to the strains of a "good jazz band" is "a must for closing a deal with your date."

## V BAR   23 | 23 | 20 | $12

*Venetian Hotel, 3355 Las Vegas Blvd. S. (bet. Flamingo & Spring Mountain Rds.), 702-414-1000; www.arkvegas.com*

■ "Breaking up the Venetian theme", or at least extending it à la Marco Polo, this "swanky little lounge" has been feng shui'd for a "dark and mysterious" "Asian feel" – "NYC style", that is; in other words, "pretty people" perch on "big, flat sofas" of leather with "cool cocktails" for "audible conversation" over "low-key house" music in a "modern", "minimalist" space on the Strip; "once the toast of the town", it's "cooled off a little", so you can "relax" here if "you just wanna" "drink with your crew."

## Venus Lounge   22 | 23 | 20 | $10

*Venetian Hotel, 3377 Las Vegas Blvd. S. (bet. Flamingo & Spring Mountain Rds.), 702-414-1000; www.arkvegas.com*

◪ "It may be a little loud and glitzy, but" this ultra-lounge inside the Venetian on the Strip "is a real kick": "an intimate, sexy, playful", "Shag-influenced bar" whose "retro" vibe "with a 'tude" is stoked by "overstuffed velvet leopard couches", "lots of egg chairs" and "plenty of room to dance" to "great Sinatra-type music"; the crowded adjacent "throwback" space is "tiki-fied all the way down to the glasses, straws and napkins", which can "wear thin after a couple of drinks."

## VOODOO LOUNGE
26 | 24 | 19 | $10

*Rio All-Suite Hotel & Casino, 3700 W. Flamingo Rd. (bet. I-15 & Valley View Blvd.), 702-247-7923; www.playrio.com*

☑ "Get the Witch Doctor" cocktail to lift the curse of the casinos' "hustle" and "escape to the patio" "where the Strip is laid out before you" at this "psychedelically appealing", "funky" lounge 51 stories up atop the Rio just to the west; "with more space and less of the attitude of others", it "caters to everyone from 21 to 101" who has the wardrobe for the "stuffy dress code", and all comers "get a lot of drink for the money, and music and dancing and conversation", but perhaps "not exactly a jet-set crowd."

## WHISKEY BAR
24 | 26 | 20 | $11

*Green Valley Ranch Station Hotel, 2300 Paseo Verde Pkwy. (Green Valley Pkwy.), Henderson, 702-617-7777; www.midnightoilbars.com*

■ "You don't have to be right on the Strip to have an amazing nightclub experience"; "hip" lounge impresario Rande Gerber "has done it again" at this "Vegas-gone-Hollywood" "hot" spot that might be "a looong way from the action" but is "always jumping" nevertheless inside Green Valley Ranch Station in Henderson; "beautiful people working" as well as "making out" on "lots of cushy sofas and beds" "poolside" or "dancing" and "holding a conversation" inside amid "groovy", "ultramodern" decor "give new meaning to the word 'cool'."

## Zuri
– | – | – | E

*MGM Grand Hotel, 3799 Las Vegas Blvd. S. (Tropicana Ave.), 702-891-1111; www.mgmgrand.com*

Get liquid 24/7 at this "hip" libation station serving "one hell of a martini" and "good people-watching" in the lobby of the MGM Grand; if you pair that fine Cohiba from the humidor with one too many "stiff", fruit-infused cocktails while the occasional ivories are tickled by night, rest assured that the hair of the dog that bit you comes in all sorts of breeds in the AM when you can lap up brandy-, tequila- and vodka-laced rescue remedies to quiet your barking brow.

# Nightlife
# Indexes

## LOCATIONS
## SPECIAL APPEALS

# LOCATIONS

# Nightlife Location Index

Crazy Horse Too
ghostbar
Jack's Irish Pub
Jaguar's
Palapa Lounge
Rain in the Desert
Sand Dollar
Sapphire
Skin
Spearmint Rhino

Tilted Kilt
VooDoo Lounge

## West Side
Cafe Nicolle
Cellar Lounge
Houlihan's
Jazzed Cafe
Naughty Ladies

# SPECIAL APPEALS

Indexes list the best of many within each category.

For some categories, schedules may vary; call ahead or check Web sites for the most up-to-date information.

## After Work
Bahama Breeze
Bar at Times Square
Cafe Nicolle
Capozzoli's
Cleopatra's Barge
Club Monaco
ESPN Zone
Fadó Irish Pub
Gordon Biersch
Houlihan's
Kahunaville
Nine Fine Irishmen
Pogo's Tavern
Red Square

## Bachelorette Parties
Armadillo
Baby's
Olympic Garden

## Bachelor Parties
Baby's
Cheetah's
Club Paradise
Crazy Horse Too
Girls of Glitter Gulch
Jaguar's
Murphy's Pub
Olympic Garden
Shadow
Spearmint Rhino

## Beautiful People
Baby's
Bahama Breeze
Beach, The
Coyote Ugly
Curve
Drai's After Hours
ghostbar
Gordon Biersch
Ice
Joint

Light
Prana Lounge
Rain in the Desert
Ra, The Nightclub
Red Square
rumjungle
Studio 54
V Bar
VooDoo Lounge

## Biker Bars
Double Down
Sand Dollar

## Blues
Como's Steakhouse
House of Blues
Railhead
Sand Dollar

## Cabaret
House of Blues

## Dancing
Armadillo
Baby's
Beach, The
Celebration Lounge
Cleopatra's Barge
Club Madrid
Club Monaco
Club Tequila
Crazy Armadillo
Curve
Dragon
Drai's After Hours
Fontana Lounge
Gilley's
Gipsy
Ibiza USA
Joint
Kahunaville
La Playa Lounge
Light

Mist
Moose McGillycuddy's
Napoleon's Lounge
Naughty Ladies
Nefertiti's Lounge
OPM
Railhead
Rain in the Desert
Ra, The Nightclub
Risqué
rumjungle
Sand Dollar
Shadow
Studio 54
Tilted Kilt
Tommy Rocker's
V Bar
Venus Lounge

### Dives
Double Down
Omaha Lounge

### DJs
(Call ahead to check nights and times)
Alesium After Hours
Baby's
Beach, The
Bikinis Beach
Cheetah's
Cleopatra's Barge
Club Paradise
Club Rio
Club Tequila
Crazy Armadillo
Crazy Horse Too
Curve
Dragon
Drai's After Hours
ghostbar
Gilley's
Gipsy
Girls of Glitter Gulch
Ibiza USA
Ice
Jaguar's
Kahunaville
Light
Mist
Moose McGillycuddy's
Olympic Garden

OPM
Palomino Club
Prana Lounge
Rain in the Desert
Ra, The Nightclub
Risqué
rumjungle
Sapphire
Shadow
Skin
Studio 54
Tabú
V Bar
Venus Lounge

### Drink Specialists
#### Beer
Jack's Irish Pub

#### Cocktails
Cafe Nicolle
Coyote Ugly
Fontana Lounge
Hookah Lounge
Nefertiti's Lounge
Red Square

#### Euro
Baby's
Beach, The
Club Rio
Curve

### Frat House
Beach, The
Double Down
ESPN Zone
House of Blues
Moose McGillycuddy's

### Gay
Gipsy

### Group-Friendly
Bar at Times Square
Bootlegger Bistro
Fadó Irish Pub
Hookah Lounge
House of Blues
Moose McGillycuddy's
Nine Fine Irishmen
Palapa Lounge

## Grown-Ups
Capozzoli's
Jaguar's
Naughty Ladies
Omaha Lounge
Palapa Lounge
Spearmint Rhino

## Happy Hour
Bahama Breeze
Bootlegger Bistro
Cellar Lounge
Club Monaco
Club Tequila
Como's Steakhouse
Coyote Ugly
Crazy Armadillo
Double Down
Fadó Irish Pub
Gipsy
Gordon Biersch
Houlihan's
Jack's Irish Pub
Jazzed Cafe
Mist
Moose McGillycuddy's
Napoleon's Lounge
Sand Dollar
Tilted Kilt
Tommy Rocker's
V Bar

## Hotel Bars
Aladdin Resort & Casino
　Curve
　Prana Lounge
Arizona Charlie's Hotel Casino
　Naughty Ladies
Barbary Coast Hotel & Casino
　Drai's After Hours
Bellagio Hotel
　Caramel
　Fontana Lounge
　Light
Boulder Station Hotel
　Railhead
Caesars Palace
　Cleopatra's Barge
　Shadow

Desert Passage at Aladdin
　Ibiza USA
Fiesta Rancho
　Club Tequila
Fitzgeralds Casino & Hotel
　Fitzgeralds
Forum Shops at Caesars
　OPM
Frontier Hotel
　Gilley's
Golden Gate Hotel & Casino
　Golden Gate
Golden Nugget Hotel
　Oasis Lounge
Green Valley Ranch Station
　Fadó Irish Pub
　Whiskey Bar
Hard Rock Hotel & Casino
　Baby's
　Joint
Harrah's Las Vegas
　Carnaval Court
　La Playa Lounge
Lake Las Vegas Resort
　Como's Steakhouse
Luxor Hotel
　Nefertiti's Lounge
　Ra, The Nightclub
Mandalay Bay Hotel
　Coral Reef
　Dragon
　House of Blues
　Red Square
　rumjungle
MGM Grand Hotel
　Studio 54
　Tabú
　Zuri
Mirage Hotel
　AVA
New York-New York Hotel
　Bar at Times Square
　Big Apple Bar
　Coyote Ugly
　ESPN Zone
　Nine Fine Irishmen
Palace Station Hotel
　Jack's Irish Pub

Palms Casino Hotel
  ghostbar
  Palapa Lounge
  Rain in the Desert
  Skin
Paris Las Vegas
  Napoleon's Lounge
  Risqué
Plaza Hotel & Casino
  Omaha Lounge
Rio All-Suite Hotel & Casino
  Bikinis Beach
  Club Rio
  Tilted Kilt
  VooDoo Lounge
Sahara Hotel & Casino
  Casbar Lounge
Stratosphere Hotel & Tower
  Crazy Armadillo
  Top of the World
Sunset Station Hotel
  Club Madrid
Texas Station Hotel
  Armadillo
Treasure Island Hotel
  Breeze Bar
  Kahunaville
  Mist
Tropicana Hotel
  Celebration Lounge
Venetian Hotel
  V Bar
  Venus Lounge

## Irish
Jack's Irish Pub
Murphy's Pub
Tilted Kilt

## Live Entertainment
(Call to check nights, times
and covers; see also Blues,
Cabaret, Strip Clubs)
Armadillo (big band/80s)
AVA (varies)
Bahama Breeze (reggae)
Bar at Times Square (piano)
Beach, The (varies)
Big Apple Bar (varies)
Bootlegger Bistro (jazz/piano)
Cafe Nicolle (piano/vocals)
Capozzoli's (jazz)
Carnaval Court (varies)
Casbar Lounge (R&B/soul)
Celebration Lounge (varies)
Cellar Lounge (jazz)
Cleopatra's Barge (bands)
Club Madrid (varies)
Club Monaco (piano)
Club Tequila (varies)
Coral Reef (bands)
Coyote Ugly (bartendresses)
Crazy Armadillo (line dancing)
Ellis Island (karaoke)
Fadó Irish Pub (bands)
Fitzgeralds (varies)
Fontana Lounge (jazz/top 40)
Gilley's (country)
Gipsy (drag/go-go)
Golden Gate (piano)
House of Blues (varies)
Jack's Irish Pub (varies)
Jazzed Cafe (jazz)
Joint (rock)
Kahunaville (reggae)
Light (varies)
Mist (varies)
Moose McGillycuddy's (varies)
Murphy's Pub (varies)
Napoleon's Lounge (jazz)
Nefertiti's Lounge (varies)
Nine Fine Irishmen (Irish)
Oasis Lounge (top 40)
Palapa Lounge (acoustic)
Pogo's Tavern (jazz)
Prana Lounge (jazz)
rumjungle (varies)
Skin (varies)
Tilted Kilt (rock)
Tommy Rocker's (rock)
Venus Lounge (varies)
VooDoo Lounge (jazz)

## Meat Markets
Baby's
Bahama Breeze
Beach, The
Club Monaco
Coyote Ugly
Curve
Double Down
Dragon
Drai's After Hours

ghostbar
Gipsy
Gordon Biersch
Joint
Light
Rain in the Desert
Ra, The Nightclub
rumjungle
Shadow
Studio 54
V Bar
VooDoo Lounge

## Neighborhood Scenes
Armadillo
Bootlegger Bistro
Cafe Nicolle
Capozzoli's
Cellar Lounge
Club Monaco
Crazy Horse Too
Double Down
Ellis Island
Gipsy
Gordon Biersch
Houlihan's
Jack's Irish Pub
Jazzed Cafe
Naughty Ladies
Oasis Lounge
Peppermill Fireside
Pogo's Tavern
Railhead
Sand Dollar

## Old Las Vegas
(Year opened; * building)
1900  Girls of Glitter Gulch*
1906  Golden Gate*
1946  Oasis Lounge

## Open 24 Hours
Bar at Times Square
Big Apple Bar
Bootlegger Bistro
Breeze Bar
Celebration Lounge
Cellar Lounge
Cheetah's
Club Monaco
Crazy Horse Too
Double Down

Ellis Island
Golden Gate
Jaguar's
Naughty Ladies
Nefertiti's Lounge
Oasis Lounge
Olympic Garden
Peppermill Fireside
Sand Dollar
Sapphire
Spearmint Rhino
Tommy Rocker's
Zuri

## Outdoor Spaces
Alesium After Hours
Bahama Breeze
Beach, The
Bootlegger Bistro
Cafe Nicolle
Carnaval Court
Como's Steakhouse
Fontana Lounge
Gordon Biersch
Jack's Irish Pub
Jazzed Cafe
Kahunaville
Moose McGillycuddy's
Skin
Tommy Rocker's
VooDoo Lounge

## People-Watching
Baby's
Bar at Times Square
Beach, The
Bootlegger Bistro
Carnaval Court
Celebration Lounge
Cleopatra's Barge
Coyote Ugly
Curve
Double Down
Dragon
Gipsy
House of Blues
Jack's Irish Pub
Joint
Kahunaville
Nine Fine Irishmen
Peppermill Fireside
Red Square

Studio 54
VooDoo Lounge

## Quiet Conversation
Cafe Nicolle
Golden Gate
La Playa Lounge
Napoleon's Lounge
Nefertiti's Lounge

## Romantic
Jazzed Cafe
Top of the World
VooDoo Lounge

## Sports Bars
ESPN Zone

## Strip Clubs
Cheetah's
Club Paradise
Crazy Horse Too
Girls of Glitter Gulch
Jaguar's
Olympic Garden
Palomino Club
Spearmint Rhino

## Swanky
Cafe Nicolle
Ice
Jazzed Cafe
Joint
Light
Rain in the Desert
Ra, The Nightclub
rumjungle
Studio 54

## Tourist Favorites
Baby's
Bahama Breeze
Carnaval Court
Celebration Lounge
Cleopatra's Barge
Club Paradise
Coyote Ugly
Crazy Horse Too
Curve
Dragon
Drai's After Hours
ESPN Zone
Fontana Lounge
Golden Gate

Kahunaville
Napoleon's Lounge
Nefertiti's Lounge
Nine Fine Irishmen
Oasis Lounge
Peppermill Fireside
Rain in the Desert
Ra, The Nightclub
rumjungle
Top of the World

## Transporting Experiences
Bahama Breeze
Rain in the Desert
Red Square
rumjungle
Venus Lounge

## Trendy
Baby's
Bahama Breeze
Beach, The
Coyote Ugly
Curve
Dragon
Drai's After Hours
ghostbar
Ice
Kahunaville
Light
Prana Lounge
Rain in the Desert
Ra, The Nightclub
rumjungle
Shadow
Studio 54
V Bar

## Velvet Rope
Baby's
Curve
ghostbar
Joint
Studio 54

## Views
Club Rio
Como's Steakhouse
Fontana Lounge
ghostbar
Top of the World
VooDoo Lounge

# Noteworthy Hotels with Casinos

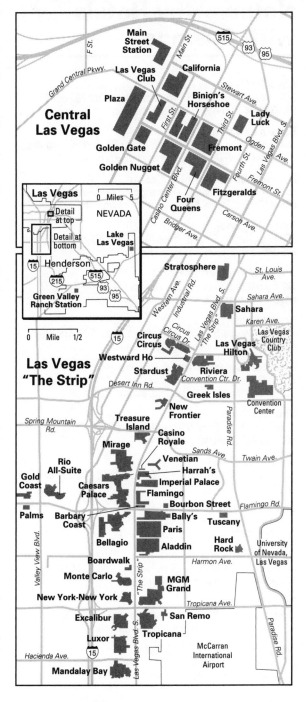

# Noteworthy Hotels with Casinos

**Aladdin Resort & Casino**
*3667 Las Vegas Blvd. S. (Harmon Ave.), 702-785-5555;*
*877-333-9474; www.aladdincasino.com*

**Bally's Las Vegas Hotel**
*3645 Las Vegas Blvd. S. (bet. Flamingo Rd. & Tropicana Ave.),*
*702-967-4111; 800-721-5597; www.ballyslv.com*

**Barbary Coast Hotel & Casino**
*3595 Las Vegas Blvd. S. (Flamingo Rd.), 702-737-7111;*
*888-227-2279; www.barbarycoastcasino.com*

**Bellagio Hotel**
*3600 Las Vegas Blvd. S. (Flamingo Rd.), 702-693-7111;*
*888-987-6667; www.bellagiolasvegas.com*

**Binion's Horseshoe Hotel**
*128 E. Fremont St. (Main St.), 702-382-1600; 800-937-6537;*
*www.binions.com*

**Boardwalk**
*3750 Las Vegas Blvd. S. (E. Harmon Ave.), 702-735-2400;*
*800-635-4581; www.hiboardwalk.com*

**Bourbon Street Hotel & Casino**
*120 E. Flamingo Rd. (Las Vegas Blvd.), 702-737-7200;*
*800-634-6956; www.bourbonstreethotel.com*

**Caesars Palace**
*3570 Las Vegas Blvd. S. (Flamingo Rd.), 702-731-7110;*
*800-634-6661; www.caesars.com*

**California Hotel**
*12 E. Ogden Ave. (Main St.), 702-385-1222; 800-634-6255;*
*www.thecal.com*

**Casino Royale & Hotel**
*3411 Las Vegas Blvd. S. (Flamingo Rd.), 702-737-3500;*
*800-854-7666; www.casinoroyalehotel.com*

**Circus Circus Hotel**
*2880 Las Vegas Blvd. S. (Riviera Blvd.), 702-734-0410;*
*877-224-7287; www.circuscircus.com*

**Excalibur Hotel**
*3850 Las Vegas Blvd. S. (Tropicana Ave.), 702-597-7777;*
*877-750-5464; www.excaliburlasvegas.com*

**Fitzgeralds Casino & Hotel**
*301 Fremont St. (3rd St.), 702-388-2400; 800-274-5825;*
*www.fitzgeraldslasvegas.com*

**Flamingo Las Vegas**
*3555 Las Vegas Blvd. S. (Flamingo Rd.), 702-733-3111;
888-308-8899; www.flamingolasvegas.com*

**Four Queens Casino Hotel**
*202 Fremont St. (Casino Center Blvd.), 702-385-4011;
800-634-6045; www.fourqueens.com*

**Fremont Hotel & Casino**
*200 E. Fremont St. (Casino Center Blvd.), 702-385-3232;
800-634-6182; www.fremontcasino.com*

**Gold Coast Hotel & Casino**
*4000 W. Flamingo Rd. (bet. Valley View Blvd. & Wynn Rd.),
702-367-7111; 888-402-6278; www.goldcoastcasino.com*

**Golden Gate Hotel & Casino**
*1 Fremont St. (Main St.), 702-385-1906; 800-426-1906;
www.goldengatecasino.net*

**Golden Nugget Hotel**
*129 E. Fremont St. (1st St.), 702-385-7111; 800-846-5336;
www.goldennugget.com*

**Greek Isles Hotel & Casino**
*305 Convention Center Dr. (Paradise Rd.), 702-734-0711;
800-633-1777; www.greekislesvegas.com*

**Green Valley Ranch Station Hotel**
*2300 Paseo Verde Pkwy. (Green Valley Pkwy.), Henderson,
702-617-7777; 866-782-9487;
www.greenvalleyranchresort.com*

**Hard Rock Hotel & Casino**
*4455 Paradise Rd. (bet. Flamingo Rd. & Harmon Ave.),
702-693-5000; 800-473-7625; www.hardrockhotel.com*

**Harrah's Las Vegas**
*3475 Las Vegas Blvd. S. (Flamingo Rd.), 702-369-5000;
800-427-7247; www.harrahs.com*

**Imperial Palace**
*3535 Las Vegas Blvd. S. (Flamingo Rd.), 702-731-3311;
800-634-6441; www.imperialpalace.com*

**Lady Luck Casino Hotel**
*206 N. Third St. (Ogden Ave.), 702-477-3000; 800-523-9582;
www.ladylucklv.com*

**Lake Las Vegas Resort**
*1600 Lake Las Vegas Pkwy. (5 mi. east of Boulder Hwy.),
Henderson, 702-564-1600; 800-564-1603;
www.lakelasvegas.com*

**Las Vegas Club**
*18 E. Fremont St. (Main St.), 702-385-1664; 800-634-6532;
www.vegasclubcasino.net*

### Las Vegas Hilton Hotel
*3000 Paradise Rd. (bet. Desert Inn Rd. & Karen Ave.),*
*702-732-5111; 888-732-7117; www.lv-hilton.com*

### Luxor Hotel
*3900 Las Vegas Blvd. S. (Tropicana Ave.), 702-262-4000;*
*888-777-0188; www.luxor.com*

### Main Street Station Hotel
*200 N. Main St. (Ogden Ave.), 702-387-1896; 800-465-0711;*
*www.mainstreetcasino.com*

### Mandalay Bay Hotel
*3950 Las Vegas Blvd. S. (Hacienda Ave.), 702-632-7777;*
*877-632-7000; www.mandalaybay.com*

### MGM Grand Hotel
*3799 Las Vegas Blvd. S. (Tropicana Ave.), 702-891-7777;*
*800-929-1111; www.mgmgrand.com*

### Mirage Hotel
*3400 Las Vegas Blvd. S. (Spring Mountain Rd.), 702-791-7111;*
*800-627-6667; www.mirage.com*

### Monte Carlo Resort & Casino
*3770 Las Vegas Blvd. S. (bet. Harmon & Tropicana Aves.),*
*702-730-7777; 888-529-4828; www.monte-carlo.com*

### New Frontier Hotel & Casino
*3120 Las Vegas Blvd. S. (Cathedral Way), 702-794-8200;*
*800-634-6966; www.frontierlv.com*

### New York-New York Hotel & Casino
*3790 Las Vegas Blvd. S. (Tropicana Ave.), 702-740-6969;*
*888-696-9887; www.nynyhotelcasino.com*

### Palms Casino Hotel
*4321 W. Flamingo Rd. (Arville St.), 702-942-7777;*
*866-942-7777; www.palms.com*

### Paris Las Vegas
*3655 Las Vegas Blvd. S. (bet. Flamingo Rd. & Harmon Ave.),*
*702-946-7000; 888-266-5687; www.parislasvegas.com*

### Plaza Hotel & Casino, The
*1 S. Main St. (Fremont St.), 702-386-2110; 800-634-6575;*
*www.plazahotelcasino.com*

### Rio All-Suite Hotel & Casino
*3700 W. Flamingo Rd. (bet. I-15 & Valley View Blvd.),*
*702-777-7777; 888-746-7482; www.playrio.com*

### Riviera, The
*2901 Las Vegas Blvd. S. (Convention Center Dr.), 702-734-5110;*
*800-634-3420; www.theriviera.com*

**Sahara Hotel & Casino**
*2535 Las Vegas Blvd. S. (Sahara Blvd.), 702-737-2111;*
*888-696-2121; www.saharavegas.com*

**San Rémo**
*115 E. Tropicana Ave. (Las Vegas Blvd.), 702-739-9000;*
*800-522-7366; www.sanremolasvegas.com*

**Stardust**
*3000 Las Vegas Blvd. S. (Convention Center Dr.), 702-732-6111;*
*800-824-6033; www.stardustlv.com*

**Stratosphere Hotel & Tower**
*2000 Las Vegas Blvd. S. (north of Sahara Ave.), 702-380-7777;*
*800-998-6937; www.stratospherehotel.com*

**Treasure Island Hotel**
*3300 Las Vegas Blvd. S. (Spring Mountain Rd.), 702-894-7111;*
*800-288-7206; www.treasureisland.com*

**Tropicana Hotel**
*3801 Las Vegas Blvd. S. (Tropicana Ave.), 702-739-2222;*
*800-468-9494; www.tropicanalv.com*

**Tuscany Hotel & Casino**
*255 E. Flamingo Rd. (Koval Ln.), 702-893-8933; 877-887-2261;*
*www.tuscanylasvegas.com*

**Venetian Hotel**
*3355 Las Vegas Blvd. S. (bet. Flamingo & Spring Mountain Rds.),*
*702-414-1000; 877-283-6423; www.venetian.com*

**Westward Ho**
*2900 Las Vegas Blvd. S. (Stardust Rd.), 702-731-2900;*
*800-634-6803; www.westwardho.com*

# Wine Vintage Chart

This chart is designed to help you select wine to go with your meal. It is based on the same 0 to 30 scale used throughout this *Survey*. The ratings (prepared by our friend **Howard Stravitz,** a law professor at the University of South Carolina) reflect both the quality of the vintage and the wine's readiness for present consumption. Thus, if a wine is not fully mature or is over the hill, its rating has been reduced. We do not include 1987, 1991–1993 vintages because they are not especially recommended for most areas. A dash indicates that a wine is either past its peak or too young to rate.

| | '85 | '86 | '88 | '89 | '90 | '94 | '95 | '96 | '97 | '98 | '99 | '00 | '01 | '02 |
|---|---|---|---|---|---|---|---|---|---|---|---|---|---|---|
| **WHITES** | | | | | | | | | | | | | | |
| **French:** | | | | | | | | | | | | | | |
| Alsace | 24 | 18 | 22 | 28 | 28 | 26 | 25 | 24 | 24 | 26 | 24 | 26 | 27 | – |
| Burgundy | 26 | 25 | – | 24 | 22 | – | 29 | 28 | 24 | 23 | 25 | 24 | 21 | – |
| Loire Valley | – | – | – | – | 24 | – | 20 | 23 | 22 | – | 24 | 25 | 23 | – |
| Champagne | 28 | 25 | 24 | 26 | 29 | – | 26 | 27 | 24 | 24 | 25 | 25 | 26 | – |
| Sauternes | 21 | 28 | 29 | 25 | 27 | – | 21 | 23 | 26 | 24 | 24 | 24 | 28 | – |
| **California (Napa, Sonoma, Mendocino):** | | | | | | | | | | | | | | |
| Chardonnay | – | – | – | – | – | – | 25 | 21 | 25 | 24 | 24 | 22 | 26 | – |
| Sauvignon Blanc/Semillon | – | – | – | – | – | – | – | – | – | 25 | 25 | 23 | 27 | – |
| **REDS** | | | | | | | | | | | | | | |
| **French:** | | | | | | | | | | | | | | |
| Bordeaux | 24 | 25 | 24 | 26 | 29 | 22 | 26 | 25 | 23 | 25 | 24 | 27 | 24 | – |
| Burgundy | 23 | – | 21 | 24 | 27 | – | 26 | 28 | 25 | 22 | 28 | 22 | 20 | 24 |
| Rhône | 25 | 19 | 27 | 29 | 29 | 24 | 25 | 23 | 24 | 28 | 27 | 26 | 25 | – |
| Beaujolais | – | – | – | – | – | – | – | – | 22 | 21 | 24 | 25 | 18 | 20 |
| **California (Napa, Sonoma, Mendocino):** | | | | | | | | | | | | | | |
| Cab./Merlot | 26 | 26 | – | 21 | 28 | 29 | 27 | 25 | 28 | 23 | 26 | 23 | 26 | – |
| Pinot Noir | – | – | – | – | – | 26 | 23 | 23 | 25 | 24 | 26 | 25 | 27 | – |
| Zinfandel | – | – | – | – | – | 25 | 22 | 23 | 21 | 22 | 24 | – | 25 | – |
| **Italian:** | | | | | | | | | | | | | | |
| Tuscany | 26 | – | 24 | – | 26 | 22 | 25 | 20 | 29 | 24 | 28 | 26 | 25 | – |
| Piedmont | 26 | – | 26 | 28 | 29 | – | 23 | 27 | 27 | 25 | 25 | 26 | 23 | – |